ON F.R. SCOTT: ESSAYS ON HIS CONTRIBUTIONS TO LAW, LITERATURE, AND POLITICS

Edited by Sandra Djwa and R. St J. Macdonald

For over five decades, F.R. Scott has been a leading figure in law, literature, and politics in Canada. He was engaged by the nationalist movement in art and literature in the twenties, by politics and constitutional law in the thirties, by internationalism in the forties, and by the struggle for human rights and fundamental freedoms in the fifties and sixties. As well, as a resident of Quebec and an active participant in its culture and politics, he has been a spokesman for both anglophones and francophones. Any summary of Scott's achievements is an index to twentieth-century Canadian culture and society.

Included in this book are personal recollections of F.R. Scott by Thérèse Casgrain, Leon Edel, and J. King Gordon; examinations of Scott's poetry by Louis Dudek, D.G. Jones, and F.W. Watt; discussions of Scott's involvement in the League for Social Reconstruction, the Co-operative Commonwealth Federation, and the Canadian political tradition by Michiel Horn, David Lewis, and Kenneth McNaught; essays on Scott's contribution to legal education, constitutional law, and social and civil legislation by Gerald Le Dain, William R. Lederman, Douglas Sanders, and Walter Tarnopolsky; essays on Scott and the Quebec Civil Code, and on Scott as a translator and a Quebecer by Paul-A. Crépeau, D.G. Jones, and Michael Oliver; and an essay by Thomas Berger on Scott and the idea of Canada. These fifteen essays, arising out of a conference at Simon Fraser University in 1981, reflect the wide range of F.R. Scott's interests and achievements.

SANDRA DJWA is a professor of English at Simon Fraser University. She is currently preparing a biography of F.R. Scott. R. ST J. MACDONALD is a professor of international law at Dalhousie University and a judge of the European Court of Human Rights in Strasbourg, France.

On F.R.SCOTT

Essays on His Contributions to Law, Literature, and Politics

Edited by
Sandra Djwa and R. St J. Macdonald

McGill-Queen's University Press
Kingston and Montreal

© McGill-Queen's University Press 1983
ISBN 0-7735-0397-8 (cloth)
ISBN 0-7735-0398-6 (paper)
Legal deposit 3rd quarter 1983
Bibliothèque nationale du Québec

Printed in Canada

Canadian Cataloguing in Publication Data

Main entry under title:
On F.R. Scott : essays on his contributions to law, literature,
and politics

Papers presented at a conference held at Simon Fraser
University, Feb. 20-21, 1981.
Includes index.
ISBN 0-7735-0397-8 (bound). – ISBN 0-7735-0398-6 (pbk.)

1. Scott, F.R. (Francis Reginald), 1899-   –
Congresses. 2. Law teachers – Canada – Biography.
3. Writers – Canada – Biography. I. Djwa, Sandra,
1939-   II. Macdonald, R. St. J. (Ronald St. John),
1928-

FC601.s4605   971.06'092'4   c83-098102-0
F1034.3.s4605

This book has been published with the help of a grant from the
Canadian Federation for the Humanities, using funds provided by the
Social Sciences and Humanities Research Council of Canada.
Publication has also been assisted by the Canada Council under its
block grant program.

Cover photograph by Lois Lord

CONTENTS

Contents

ACKNOWLEDGMENTS

The editors express their thanks to Simon Fraser University faculty and administration and the Social Sciences and Humanities Research Council of Canada, who brought into being the F.R. Scott Conference in Vancouver in February 1981, and as a direct consequence, this book of essays. Particular thanks are extended to the members of the conference planning committee: Peter Buitenhuis, Beatrice Donald, Gene Homel, Jack Little, and Kathy Mezei of SFU, Douglas Sanders of the University of British Columbia and Grace MacInnis and Mr Justice Thomas Berger of Vancouver, as well as to the Director of the Centre for Canadian Studies, Parzival Copes, the Dean of Arts, R.C. Brown, and the SFU Vice-President, Academic, J.M. Munro. Final preparation of the essays was assisted by George Curtis, former dean of law at UBC, and Richard Yates of the British Columbia Institute of Technology. We are greatly indebted to Marilyn G. Flitton for her able editorial assistance and preparation of the index. The editing of these essays was assisted by the Killam Family Foundation, the Dean of Arts Contingency Fund at Simon Fraser University, and by the Samuel and Saidye Bronfman Family Foundation.

We are grateful to the following for permission to quote from material in copyright. F.R. Scott for excerpts from his poetry and essays. The Canadian Publishers, McClelland and Stewart Limited, Toronto, for lines from *The Collected Poems of F.R. Scott*. University of Toronto Press for excerpts from *Essays on the Constitution: Aspects of Canadian Law and Politics* by Frank R. Scott. Mrs Laura Huxley, Chatto and Windus Ltd, and Harper and Row, Publishers, Inc for lines from 'Fifth Philosopher's Song' from *The Collected Poetry of Aldous Huxley*, edited by Donald Watt. Copyright 1920 by Aldous Huxley. Al Purdy for lines from 'The Country of the Young' from *North of Summer*. Graham Spry for an excerpt from a letter to J. King Gordon. H.B. Neatby, Literary Executor of F.H. Underhill, for an excerpt from a letter written by F.H. Underhill.

INTRODUCTION ✓

ANY SUMMARY of F.R. Scott's achievements reads as an index to Canadian culture and society over five decades. He was largely engaged by the nationalist movement in art and poetry in the twenties, by politics and constitutional law in the thirties, by internationalism in the forties, and by the struggle for human rights and fundamental freedoms in the fifties and sixties. His greatest contribution to poetry was also made in the fifties and sixties when he published six books of poetry. A rare Canadian, his life's work spans the three disciplines of law, literature, and politics, and the two cultures of Quebec and English Canada.

The following essays are largely the revised proceedings of a conference, 'The Achievement of F.R. Scott,' organized by the Centre for Canadian Studies at Simon Fraser University, 20 and 21 February 1981. Part One is a personal introduction to the man as seen by his friends, beginning with the late Senator Thérèse Casgrain, through the decades from 1920 to 1940. A pioneer in the field of women's rights in Quebec and a former president of the Quebec CCF, Madame Casgrain pays affectionate tribute to a brave man, a fellow Quebecer, and 'a great Canadian.' Subsequent essays, in Parts Two to Six, are grouped by topic to provide ease of access to the specialist.

I

Francis Reginald Scott was born on 1 August 1899 in Quebec City, an anglophone in predominantly French Quebec. From his family background he inherited a tradition of public service and a strong sense of social justice. His grandfather, Dr William Edward Scott, professor of anatomy at McGill, was known for his courage in attending victims of the cholera and typhus epidemics that ravaged Montreal in the mid-nineteenth century. His father, Canon Frederick George Scott, the 'Poet of the Laurentians' and the beloved padre of the Great War, was ordered to leave Winnipeg in 1919 because of his support of the General Strike. Again in 1923, Canon Scott, along with J.S. Woodsworth, took up the cause of the striking Cape Breton steel workers against the giant British Empire Steel Corporation.

Educated in Quebec City and at Bishop's College, Lennoxville, F.R. Scott won a Rhodes scholarship to Oxford in 1919. There he studied history, receiving a BA in 1922 and a B.Litt. in 1923. In his first year at Oxford he took part in two Student Christian Movement study groups, one on 'Christianity and Industrial Problems,' based on the Report of the Anglican Bishops to the Lambeth Conference (1920), and the other on R.H. Tawney's *The Acquisitive Society*; both directed him towards Fabian socialism.

His return to Canada in October 1923 was a great disappointment. Montreal, with its foot-high curbs, its false facades, and its lack of indigenous culture, seemed barren and ugly when compared with the art and architecture of the great European capitals. After a year as schoolmaster at Lower Canada College in Montreal, Scott enrolled, in the fall of 1924, in the Faculty of Law at McGill University. There he came under the influence of H.A. Smith, one of the first academic lawyers in Canada to point out that the British Privy Council's interpretations of the Canadian constitution were opposed to the intentions of the Fathers of Confederation. Scott graduated with a BCL in 1927, and became a full-time member of the Montreal firm of Lafleur, Mac-Dougall, Macfarlane and Barclay. In February the following year he married Marian Dale, a young Montreal painter. A month later, in March 1928, he accepted Dean Percy Corbett's invitation to join the Faculty of Law at McGill, where he began his long and influential career as a teacher and scholar of federal and constitutional law.

His successive careers in law, literature, and politics are united by the fact that each took root in the fertile nationalist soil of the Canadian twenties and each is permeated by a basically religious belief in 'the spirit of man.' Socialism, in effect, was the new faith of the thirties. When his friend the Reverend J. King Gordon, son of the crusading Presbyterian 'Ralph Connor,' was considering nomination as a CCF candidate in the general election of 1935, Scott wired his encouragement: 'POLITICS IS THE ONLY ROAD TO HEAVEN NOW.' Scott, who had entered the twenties as a conventional young Victorian, an anglophile, and an aesthete, had become by 1927 a modern, a nationalist, and a socialist. It was the concept of a Canadian nation – and then a Canadian poetry and a Canadian constitution to express the cultural, political, and legal aspects of this nationality – that fired his imagination.

The process of transformation began in 1924 with a circle of young Montrealers who were drawn to nationalism and federalism. 'The Group,' as they called themselves, included Brooke Claxton, John Farthing, G.R. McCall, T.W.L. MacDermot, Raleigh Parkin, Arthur Terroux, and V.C. Wansborough. Many were war veterans, most had been to Oxford, and all were concerned with Canada's future. They discussed the development of Canadian autonomy, the possibility of an independent foreign policy for Canada, Canadian immigration, the problems of the Jews in Montreal, D.H. Lawrence, Fabianism, the Group of Seven, and Canada's position in the Empire.

In addition to these discussions, the land itself was a shaping component in Scott's nationalism. Because it was open, unexplored, unpeopled, the vast stretch of the Pre-Cambrian shield presented itself as a fresh canvas for the artist's impression. The aeons of geological time were, for Scott, transmuted into a substitution for a historical past. He was soon composing a poetry in which nationalism and landscape united. 'Child of the North,' he wrote,

> Here is a new soil and a sharp sun
>
> Turn from the past,
> Walk with me among these indigent firs,
> Climb these rough crags[1]

It was in this natural landscape that Canada's new identity, literary as well as political, must be found.

II

With fellow McGill students, A.J.M. Smith, the late poet and critic, and Leon Edel, now the distinguished Henry James scholar, Scott became a member of the editorial board of *The McGill Fortnightly Review* (1925-7), the little magazine that helped spark the modern movement in English-Canadian poetry. Smith, as Scott recalls, was the catalyst which jogged him from the Victorian into the modern. Fellow members of the *Fortnightly* and subsequent scholars have believed that Smith discovered the anthology *The New Poetry* (1917), and with it W.B. Yeats and T.S. Eliot, in the Westmount Public Library. In fact, Smith had accompanied his family to England during the war and learned of the Georgians at Harold Munro's bookshop in London.[2] After his return to Canada and McGill, he came under the influence of Lancelot Hogben, an assistant professor in McGill's Department of Zoology. It was Hogben who gave Smith a slim, brown paper-covered copy of T.S. Eliot's *Prufrock* of 1917, and Smith in turn brought the book – and with it the modern movement – to Scott and Edel.

The new techniques and startling images of *The Waste Land* were to fuel Scott's parody of the faded romanticism of the then contemporary Canadian verse in his poem 'The Canadian Authors Meet' (1927). With Louis Schwartz, later the founder of the American Abelard Press, and the poet Leo Kennedy, Scott edited the avant-garde little magazine *The Canadian Mercury* (1927-9), which advertised itself as 'fearless,' 'bold,' and 'original': its colophon was a stout, naked Mercury thumbing his nose, presumably at the good citizens of Montreal. In 1928 Barker Fairley persuaded Scott to join the editorial board of *The Canadian Forum* which, in addition to its role as a journal of left-wing politics, became almost a poetry 'little mag' during the depression. It was here that Scott published his two-part manifesto for modern poetry, 'New Poems for Old' in 1931, and his first social poetry, 'An Up-to-date Anthology of Canadian Poetry' in 1932 and 'Social Notes' in 1935.

In 1936 he successfully held together a group of conservative and progressive poets to bring into print *New Provinces*, the first anthology of modern Canadian verse, a book which he co-edited with Smith. In addition to their own work it contained poems by Robert Finch, Leo Kennedy, A.M. Klein, and E.J. Pratt. Scott was also the moving force which brought together the *Preview* (1942-5) group of poets: Patrick Anderson, A.M. Klein, P.K. Page, and Neufville Shaw. In 1945, he presided at *Preview*'s amalgamation with the rival poets Louis Dudek, Irving Layton, and John Sutherland of *First Statement* (1942-5) to form *Northern Review* (1945-56). In 1955 he was instrumental in organizing the influential Canadian Writers' Conference at Queen's University, which brought a new sense of community to Canadian poets; a further result of this conference was Malcolm Ross's decision to develop a New Canadian Library series which, by reprinting essential texts in popular editions, provided a basis for the academic study of Canadian literature. In 1964 with the late John Glassco, writer and translator, Scott helped to organize the Foster Poetry Conference for poets in Quebec.

Scott's books of poetry range from the mid-forties to the eighties: *Overture* (1945), *Events and Signals* (1954), *The Eye of the Needle* (1957), *Signature* (1964), *Selected Poems* (1966), *Trouvailles: Poems from Prose* (1967), *The Dance Is One* (1973), and *The Collected Poems of F.R. Scott*, which received the Governor General's Award for 1981. Scott is also a distinguished translator of poetry from the French: *St-Denys Garneau & Anne Hébert: Translations/Traductions* was published in 1962 and his correspondence with Anne Hébert on the art of translation, with a preface by Northrop Frye, was published in 1970 under the title *Dialogue sur la traduction à propos du 'Tombeau des rois.'* A collection of his translations, *Poems of French Canada* (1977), was awarded the Canada Council Award for Translation. Scott's influence on younger Canadian poets has been profound: aspects of his poetic voice and distinctive evolutionary landscape are reflected in poets as diverse in tone as Al Purdy and Margaret Atwood. With E.J. Pratt and Earle Birney, he takes his place as one of the major twentieth-century Canadian poets.

Scott first wanted to be a poet; 'nothing else matters' he wrote to his brother in 1928.[3] It is appropriate, therefore, that the first extended essay of this book, Leon Edel's 'The Young Warrior in the Twenties,' introduces Scott the poet – 'the tall, angular young man ... with uncommon use of words and a brilliant and often searching gleam in his eye' – within the context of a semi-military McGill University presided over by General Sir Arthur Currie. In Part Two some aspects of Scott's poetic vision and his relationship to the Canadian tradition are examined. Each of the literary studies emphasizes a fundamental duality in Scott's poetic vision. In 'Polar Opposites in F.R. Scott's Poetry,' Louis Dudek, a close friend since the early thirties, comments on Scott's characteristic secularization of religious myth and then, taking up his long-standing battle with modernism, emphasizes that it is precisely Scott's preoccupation with the 'unpoetic' and the 'ephemeral' which stamps his poetry as modern. Dudek finds that the split between Scott the humanist on the one hand and Scott the social scientist on the other engenders a division in the poetry: in its more blatant manifestation, the lyric voice of true feeling alternates with a more intrusive, didactic voice.

D.G. Jones in 'Private Space and Public Space,' a consideration of Scott the public and the private poet, stresses the continuity between Scott's public poems and the late eighteenth- and nineteenth-century Canadian tradition. Jones views Scott as an essentially eighteenth-century man whose very diversity of interests accommodates balance and reason, characteristics which unify all of his poetry, including his translations from the French. F.W. Watt in 'The Poetry of Social Protest' offers a moving introduction to the full range of Scott's poetry. Intrigued by the division in Scott's poetic vision, which he characterizes as the Laurentian and the socialist visions, Watt finds a paradoxical unity in the fact that 'the poet who is drawn or driven to the empty, inhuman, everlasting immensities of the northern wilderness is also the poet which is nourished by group experience.'

III

F.R. Scott's world changed drastically with the Great Crash of 1929. In Montreal, then Canada's financial heartland, the consequences of excessive laissez-faire were particularly apparent; mass unemployment, long lines of hungry men, workers' demonstrations, and families in desperate need of food, shelter, and medical care were everywhere in evidence. Suffering was commonplace in Montreal. More than in any other Canadian city, perhaps with the exception of Winnipeg in 1919, there was great reliance on force by the authorities in order to break up demonstrations by the unemployed, especially if the unfortunates happened to be immigrants and thus liable for automatic dismissal as 'Bolsheviks' or 'red' troublemakers. For Scott, a poetry and a politics that did not address the social issues of the times could no longer be contemplated. His letter of February 1931 to the Montreal *Gazette*, protesting police suppression of meetings of the unemployed, became a turning point in his career. The discouraged aesthete now turned to reform of the legal and social order.

In August 1931, after meeting the University of Toronto history professor Frank Underhill at a conference in Williamstown, Massachusetts, Scott agreed to organize a research group on Fabian lines in Montreal while Underhill did the same in Toronto. Such groups would develop a thorough analysis of the capitalist system in Canada. Scott recalls Underhill as an attractive man, 'rather shy in his manner' but with 'a sharp mind.' Both men recognized that the depression would very likely result in the formation of a new Canadian progressive party and that a theoretical basis for a new program of political action would be required. The new group took the name of the League for Social Reconstruction and J.S. Woodsworth became honorary president with a national executive of Underhill, J.F. Parkinson, and E.A. Havelock from Toronto, and Scott and J. King Gordon from Montreal. Eugene Forsey, though not a member of the executive, was one of the group. In the LSR Manifesto (1931), members described themselves in Tawneyesque terms as an association 'working for the establishment in Canada of a social order in which the basic principle regulating production, distribution and service will be the common good rather than private profit.'

A year later, in August 1932, the anticipated progressive party emerged when the Co-operative Commonwealth Federation was founded in Calgary and J.S. Woodsworth was elected as president. Members of the LSR were invited to assist with drafting a party program for the first convention of the CCF in Regina in 1933. Scott, a delegate to this convention, contributed substantially to the drafting of the Regina Manifesto by demonstrating that the aims of the CCF could be accomplished within the existing provisions of the British North America Act, Canada's constitution. Subsequently, through the CCF, which acted as a pressure group of the successive governments of prime ministers R.B. Bennett and William Lyon Mackenzie King, much of the theoretical socialism of the LSR found its way into official statutes. Many of these principles, such as the establishment of a central bank, economic planning, medicare, and the recurrent issue of repatriation of the constitution, strongly influenced the character of Canada today.

Scott's deep commitment to the socialist cause was inspired not only by his humanism – 'the spirit of man, this light of faith and conscience and decency on which all civilization depends,' as he defined it in his address to the 1950 National Convention of the CCF – but also by his nationalism, the concept of a new Canadian society, north of the 49th parallel, a society as just and egalitarian as it was possible to make it. As Scott wrote to Gordon in the thirties, 'We have to express through the C.C.F. the idea that our people came to North America to build a fair city ... and that we have obviously fallen down lamentably on the job.' His vision of a fair city, the ideal Canada, implied a society free of colonial restrictions, of the more crippling aspects of capitalism, and of those legislative restrictions which impeded freedom of speech and assembly. As a member of the LSR Committee and closely associated with the CCF in the thirties, Scott urged these views in a number of publications, including *Canada and Socialism* (1934) with V.C. Wansborough, *Social Reconstruction and the BNA Act* (1934), and *Social Planning for Canada* (1935), which he co-signed with Eugene Forsey, J. King Gordon, Leonard Marsh, J.F. Parkinson, Graham Spry, and Frank Underhill. The LSR's brief to the Rowell-Sirois Commission on Dominion-Provincial Relations, written by Scott, was published as *Canada One or Nine?: The Purpose of Confederation* (1938). At the request of the Canadian Institute of International Affairs, he wrote the principal Canadian paper for the Second British Commonwealth Relations Conference held in Sydney, Australia, in 1938. A revised version, *Canada Today: A Study of Her National Interests and National Policy*, was published in 1939. In the forties, Scott co-edited with David Lewis, later national chairman of the CCF, the influential handbook *Make This Your Canada* (1943). From 1942 to 1950 Scott was national chairman of the CCF.

J. King Gordon introduces the social and political career in 'The Politics of Poetry.' Gordon, who came to Montreal in 1931 as professor of Christian ethics, reminds us of the 'spirit' which animated socialism and of the warm friendships among a group of young intellectuals, excited by the possibilities of a new era. 'The old orthodoxies were unravelling. The sacred cows were out of their pasture and cluttering the highways.' In Part Three, a survey of some aspects of Scott's political career, Michiel Horn, in 'F.R. Scott, the Great Depression, and the League for Social Reconstruction,' reviews the political context of the early thirties, including Scott's battles for freedom of speech, and describes the founding and significance of the LSR.

'F.R. Scott's Contribution to the CCF,' an essay by the late David Lewis, is a personal review of three decades of socialist politics which gives a sense of their personal friendship as well as of Scott's substantial contributions to the CCF. Lewis, when speaking of his father's premature death and the memorial service at which Scott captured the ethical principles which had guided his father's life, could not have known that his good friend would perform the same service for him a few months later. Kenneth McNaught's 'Socialism and the Canadian Political Tradition' questions traditional responses to Canadian socialism, which he characterizes as having been ground between the millstones of self-serving historiography from both the left and right, and offers a spirited defence of the significant role that socialism has played in Canada. Both Gordon and McNaught emphasize the vision of unlimited human potential, a basically religious spirit, which characterized the thinking of LSR and CCF intellectuals in the thirties.

IV

In the domain of constitutional law, F.R. Scott was acknowledged to be one of the pre-eminent teachers, writers, and advocates of his time. His fine mind, his gifted pen, and the broad sweep of his scholarship united to give his constitutional thinking a far-ranging influence. Scott approached law as a social science; it was to be used to heal the troubles of society and to plan the future deliberately, not merely to express and order the results of past growth. 'A consistent thread of social policy and purpose runs through his constitutional thought. The key ideas are economic planning, social justice, and the protection of human rights,' is the summary of a former student of Scott's, Mr Justice Le Dain of the Federal Court of Appeal. Scott saw clearly that the needs of Canada's nascent and strung-out society called for country-wide social security measures. The deprivations of the depression made such measures all the more necessary, but various Privy Council decisions severely restricted federal constitutional power. From Scott's pen flowed a series of brilliantly crafted articles in which he joined the majority of Canadian academic writers of his time in criticizing the findings of the Privy Council and the narrow methods of constitutional interpretation which led to its conclusions. These results and these methods, Scott argued, were those of a court not sufficiently familiar with a federal system of government and its day-to-day operations, or with current Canadian needs and aspirations. He urged that appeals to the Privy Council should be abolished and the way opened for a new interpretation of the British North America Act in consonance with Canada's more pressing needs.

Scott's arguments were fuelled both by his nationalism and his socialism. He was incensed when the Privy Council disallowed most of R.B. Bennett's 'New Deal' legislation and in the *Canadian Bar Review* of June 1937 remarked sharply: 'That which the builders rejected has indeed become the corner stone. A well-balanced distribution of sovereignty between Dominion and provinces, giving to each residuary as well as specified powers, which was carefully planned by Canadian statesmen knowing the needs of the country, has been scrapped for an alternative theory of a severely limited Dominion but an unlimited provincial residue.' An economic planner, a social engineer, and a Canadian nationalist, Scott was tireless in pressing for ample federal powers to achieve these ends.

It was in the fifties, the decade of concern for human rights and fundamental freedoms in Canada, that Scott's special genius coincided exactly with the need of the country. He pleaded the celebrated case of *Switzman* v *Elbling*, in which the Supreme Court of Canada held unconstitutional Premier Duplessis' Padlock Act, which had been used to repress political and religious minorities in Quebec. In 1959, in *Roncarelli* v *Duplessis*, he succeeded in persuading the Supreme Court to hold Premier Duplessis personally accountable in damages for interceding in a decision by the Quebec Liquor Commission denying a liquor licence to a Jehovah's Witness. He later carried an appeal to the Supreme Court, successfully defending D.H. Lawrence's *Lady Chatterley's Lover* against a charge of obscenity laid in the Quebec Superior Court. Scott versified the process in a ballad with an appropriately punning title, 'A Lass in Wonderland.'

> I went to bat for the Lady Chatte
> Dressed in my bib and gown
> The judges three glared down at me
> The priests patrolled the town.

Scott, as the legal essays demonstrate, expanded the consciousness and recognition of civil liberties in Canadian society. The contribution of his collected legal articles, *Essays on the Constitution: Aspects of Canadian Law and Politics*, was recognized with the Governor General's Award in 1977.

Scott's career as a professor and practitioner of law is discussed by Mr Justice Gerald Le Dain. In 'F.R. Scott and Legal Education' he comments on Scott's role as inspiring teacher and his goals of a stronger federal structure, better social and economic planning, the strengthening of fundamental human rights, and the improvement of legal education throughout Canada. William Lederman's 'F.R. Scott and Constitutional Law' examines some of Scott's legal antecedents, including Roscoe Pound's view of law as social engineering, and outlines Scott's position in relation to the major Canadian constitutional issues. Douglas Sanders in 'Law and Social Change: The Experience of F.R. Scott' weighs the position taken by Scott on social issues within the context of the constitutional problems of the period, noting that it cannot be said that the emergence of the Supreme Court as the final court of appeal for Canada has resulted in a significant widening of federal power. Federal initiatives in social legislation have been realized through constitutional amendment and cost-sharing programs with the provinces. On human rights issues the advocacy of Scott and the judicial leadership of Mr Justice Rand has yielded a rich harvest of judicial opinions giving expression to civil libertarian values in the courts in 1950. These views, however, have remained minority ones and have not been carried forward in the decisions of recent years.

Walter Tarnopolsky's, 'F.R. Scott: Civil Libertarian' is the first essay to set out Scott's role as 'an advocate of civil liberties and architect of modern Canadian thought on human rights and fundamental freedoms.' In early works on the Canadian constitution most analysts ignored basic human rights and freedoms; the fact that this subject now plays such a central role in constitutional studies is largely attributable to Scott as legal essayist. Tarnopolsky's subsequent examination of Scott's writings and the major cases which he has argued also demonstrates Scott's significant contribution to consolidating the 'rule of law' as part of our Canadian constitutional framework.

V

Beyond F.R. Scott the poet, the constitutional lawyer, and the social philosopher, there has always been Scott the Quebecer, the Canadian, and, above all, the fierce believer in freedom and justice. That it was not easy for him to remain loyal to these causes is evidenced by the stand which he has taken in Quebec. With his growing fluency in French, his belief in the law as a force for social change, the social concern of the LSR and the CCF and, last but not least, with his own poetry, Scott often succeeded in bridging the two cultures. He entered actively into the literary culture of Quebec, meeting regularly in the fifties with a small group of Québécois poets. As he explains in the introduction to his translations, *Poems of French Canada* (1977), much of his work on minority rights in the early constitutional essays concerned the problems of Quebecers: 'How to build a Canada that would allow the two principal cultures to flourish freely became an intellectual and emotional challenge, and in this endeavour literature would obviously play an important role.' He had heard the voice of the new Quebec in the poets and in novels like Jean-Charles Harvey's *Les demi-civilisés* and Lemelin's *Au pied de la pente douce* long before the Quiet Revolution had arrived.

Scott was perceived as sympathetic towards francophone Quebec because of a widely disseminated 1942 pamphlet, 'The Plebiscite Vote in Quebec.' During the forties and fifties he moved easily among a group of Quebec intellectuals and artists which included Pierre-Elliott Trudeau and Gérard Pelletier, of the *Cité Libre* group, the late André Laurendeau, editor of *Le Devoir* and René Lévesque, now the Premier of Quebec, as well as the labour lawyer (as he then was) Guy-Merrill Desaulniers, the Laval sociologist, Jean-Charles Falardeau, and the novelist, Roger Lemelin. Through funds left from the estate of Alan Plaunt, Scott in the early fifties organized Recherches Sociales, which published Falardeau's important sociological study *Roots and Values in Canadian Lives* (1961). Scott also persuaded Trudeau, then a young academic, to edit and write an introduction to *La grève de l'amiante* (1956), a study of the important 1949 Asbestos strike. The strike and Trudeau's forthright and passionate introduction to this book signalled for many Quebecers the start of the Quiet Revolution. With Michael Oliver, Scott co-edited *Quebec States Her Case* (1964) and between 1963 and 1971, he was a member of the Royal Commission on Bilingualism and Biculturalism, which recommended sweeping changes in Canada's language laws to facilitate equality between French and English.

The impetus for political justice in Quebec in the fifties was associated with opposition to the repressive régime of Premier Duplessis, but with his death in 1959 a common bond between Quebecers of English and French origin disappeared: of those who had tacitly or openly supported the CCF/NDP, some like Lévesque became identified with the *indépendantiste* movement while others, like Marchand and Pelletier, committed federalists, followed Trudeau to Ottawa under the Liberal banner. Scott's view of social justice for Quebec, common to most English Canadians, presumed that Quebec would remain a province, one with unique language rights and special status, but none the less a province within a federal structure. For the *indépendantistes* this did not go far enough. Many believed that social justice for Quebec could only be achieved when Quebecers were *maîtres chez nous*. Scott, the popular advocate for French-language rights for francophone Quebecers in the forties and fifties, had become by the seventies the unpopular advocate of English-language rights for anglophone Quebecers, a position exacerbated by his support of the War Measures Act. Yet the principle underlying each of Scott's actions was the same: any tyranny of the majority was unacceptable.

Scott's role in the reshaping of Quebec law is introduced by Paul-A. Crépeau, a former colleague and now head of McGill's Institute of Comparative Law, an institute which Scott helped establish when dean of law. Crépeau, in 'F.R. Scott et la réforme du Code Civil,' warmly recalls their joint work on revision of the civil liberties and human rights section of the Quebec Civil Code. Michael Oliver, a close associate in the fifties and sixties, in 'F.R. Scott as Quebecer' speculates on some implications of Scott's position as an anglophone, a Protestant, and a Canadian nationalist within the framework of a francophone, Catholic, and *indépendantiste* Quebec. In this essay we sense some of the dimensions of the clash between the two nationalisms – Quebec and Canadian. Above all, Scott's career indicates the extreme difficulties faced by Quebecers of good will, both francophone and anglophone, in their attempts to reach a common understanding. Differences in language and education, and differing concepts of religion, government, and society have not been easy to reconcile. Yet, we are led to recognize, and to be grateful, that F.R. Scott has gone further than most Canadians of this century in his attempt to find common ground.

VI

In 'F.R. Scott and the Idea of Canada,' Mr Justice Thomas Berger of the Supreme Court of British Columbia, a former leader of the NDP in British Columbia and Scott's junior in 1963 in the Supreme Court in the case of *Oil, Chemical and Atomic Workers* v *Imperial Oil*, places Scott's social vision within the context of Canada's cultural mosaic. He emphasizes that Canada's constitutional legacy from England may be seen as that of parliamentary institutions and the common law and her legacy from France that of egalitarian ideals and the rights of man. Quebec culture, which has drawn most heavily from pre-revolutionary France, has traditionally been less of a hierarchical society than this analysis implies, yet it is certainly true that egalitarian ideas have characterized Quebec since the early sixties. The idea of Canada which Mr Justice Berger associates with Scott's life and work is that of a free and pluralistic society: 'May we not erect on the structure of freedom bequeathed to us a régime of tolerance where the place of minorities and the rights of dissenters are secure?'

Not included in this book is a pre-conference entertainment organized by two of Scott's former students, Donald MacSween, Director General of the National Arts Centre, and Timothy Porteous, Director of the Canada Council. In the fifties they were best known, along with another law student, James Domville, now President of the National

Film Board, as collaborators on *My Fur Lady*, the satirical 1957 McGill revue which took Canada by storm. Their taped skit is a dramatic reconstruction of 'a decision of the Supreme Universal and Eternal Court of Spiritual Justice and Divine Mercy,' concerning the life of F.R. Scott, from the perspective of one Wilbur Throckmorton, Cherubim Second Class. Fired from the Celestial Civil Service for his role in creating Scott, he appeals to the Celestial Supreme Court. His advocates, the Archclerk Michael (Michael Pitfield, then Clerk of the Privy Council) and St Peter (Prime Minister Trudeau) advise Jehovah, J., the presiding judge, to 'hold his nose' and grant the appeal. Jehovah (Chief Justice Bora Laskin) reinstates Throckmorton, observing that the issue turns on the question of 'whether or not Scott has been good for Canada.'

Many of Scott's contemporaries shared his nationalist vision of Canada as a self-governing nation north of the 49th parallel. A lesser number shared his socialist vision of a humane society where all Canadians might be equal. But few had his range of concern, the force of personality, and the gift of language to convey this vision, in all its diversity, to all those with whom he came in contact. Apart from the poetry, the legal and political articles, the lectures, the humour, the generosity with ideas and insights, F.R. Scott has become a beacon in Canadian society. His struggle for the democratization of that society and for universal human dignity has turned many current issues into matters of conscience, on which Canadians have been obliged to exercise intelligent choice. He has not forgotten the first principle of a university – 'That all truth is relative / And only the obligation to search for it is absolute.' Nor has he forgotten its correlative, the courage to act. 'The positive formation of opinion, / The essential choice that acts as a mental compass, / The clear perception of the road to the receding horizon.'[4] The heritage that F.R. Scott leaves us is, above all, one of courage and commitment.

SANDRA DJWA

NOTES

1 'New Paths,' *The Collected Poems of F.R. Scott* (Toronto: McClelland & Stewart 1981) 37; see also Sandra Djwa, '"A New Soil and a Sharp Sun": The Landscape of a Modern Canadian Poetry,' *Modernist Studies: Literature and Culture 1920-1940* 2 (1977) 3-16.
2 Interview with A.J.M. Smith by Sandra Djwa, November 1975; see also 'F.R. Scott: A Canadian in the Twenties,' *Papers of the Bibliographical Society of Canada* 19 (1980) 11-21.

3 F.R. Scott to W.B. Scott, 8 January 1928.
4 Excerpts from 'Good-bye To All That,' and 'To Certain Friends,' *The Collected Poems*, 212, 77.

PART ONE

THÉRÈSE CASGRAIN

The Achievements of
F.R. Scott

Le bonheur le plus grand, le plus digne d'envie,
Est celui d'être utile et cher à sa patrie.
                              Boissy, *Le Sage Etourdi* II: ii

F.R. SCOTT is a great Canadian who has always stood for human rights and justice, and who has had an important unifying influence on French and English Canada through his work as a writer, poet, and professor of law at McGill University. He also played a tremendously important role in the Royal Commission on Bilingualism and Biculturalism. Looking at all these achievements, I am concerned about how to do them full justice, for I have always considered Frank and his wife Marian as very dear friends. If all Canadians from coast to coast had possessed some of Frank's admirable qualities, our country today would be united instead of having to deal with the severe problems facing us at present.

When I was in Vancouver in 1980, speaking to the Women's Canadian Club, I was presented with a scroll, written in French and English, entitled: 'Je suis heureux d'être un Canadien' / 'I am proud to be a Canadian.' I would like to quote you one paragraph from it which strikes me as particularly apt in connection with Frank Scott:

Nous avons hérité des lois et des traditions basées sur la foi en Dieu et dans les hommes, sur un amour sans bornes de la liberté et sur le respect des droits d'autrui.

We have inherited laws and traditions built on faith in God and man, on an unflagging love of freedom, and on respect for the rights of others.

My friendship with Frank Scott dates back to 1942. At that time, I was running as an independent candidate in Charlevoix-Saguenay. In my electoral platform, I had spoken out against conscription. Though opposing compulsory service overseas, I had urged the people of my riding to do their duty and respond voluntarily to the call of their country. Needless to say, a large proportion of the English public censured me, and, alas! very few French Canadians were prepared to defend me.

It was then that Frank came to my assistance. He wrote an open letter to the Montreal *Gazette* (13 November 1942), in which he stated that no one had the right to insult me for expressing my views candidly, and that my opposition to conscription certainly did not mean I was an enemy of my country. I cannot say how grateful I was for the support he gave me, at a time when I needed it so much.

As a friend, I watched, with deep interest and admiration, his determination to uphold the liberties of the citizen in the *Roncarelli* case. Those who knew the Duplessis régime in Quebec will understand what it meant to defy the then premier of Quebec, who was also attorney general of the province, or even to be associated with such an attempt at defiance. I remember going to Frank's home after this case had been won. All his friends were there to rejoice, including Roncarelli.

In 1946, I officially became a member of the CCF party, of which Frank was then president of the National Council. He had also been one of the authors of the Regina Manifesto, published in 1933. Frank and Judge Guy Desaulniers signed my CCF membership card. For many years, we worked together for the same aims, aims today probably taken for granted, such as old-age pensions, unemployment insurance, and health insurance.

Frank is a native Quebecer and has worked for years towards making Quebec citizens understand the necessity of favouring measures for the common good. He protested and fought the Duplessis government many times in order to preserve the rights of Quebecers. The *Roncarelli* and Padlock Law cases were the two most famous instances of this, but by no means the only ones. Perfectly bilingual, Frank Scott has often served as a link between the members of the CCF in Quebec and those in English Canada. He is a founding member of the Canadian Human Rights Foundation, a member of the Royal Society of Canada, and winner of a Guggenheim scholarship.

For me, Frank Scott is also a great friend and now one of my near neighbours. He is modest, serene, and understanding, and I find it a great help to talk things over with him. Often, when I go to his home, he'll be playing the piano. He doesn't claim to be an accomplished musician, but he loves music, and I think this love contributes to his intellectual serenity. Marian, Frank's wife, is also a dear friend. She is a distinguished painter besides being a charming woman who always tries to see the good side of people and things. They have been married since 1928 and are a wonderfully devoted couple, warm and hospitable. They have a son, Peter, a professor of English at Berkeley, California, who, like his distinguished parents, is a strong supporter of the causes in which he believes.

I hope I have been able to convey to you my admiration, esteem, and friendship for Frank Scott. For me, this man is not only a great friend, companion, and neighbour, but above all, a great Canadian.

LEON EDEL

The Young Warrior
in the Twenties ✓

LOOKING ACROSS the decades and remembering the young Scott as best I can – for I was then even younger than he was – I am reminded of Max Beerbohm's brilliant series of cartoons called 'The Old and the Young Self.' I recall in particular a cartoon of the old Arnold Bennett saying to his Young Self: 'All gone according to plan, you see,' and the Young Self responding immediately '*My* plan, you know!'[1] The young self of Frank Scott wasn't as sure or as smug as that, but somewhere in the depths of his large imagination there lay strong feelings, a strain of poetry, and a love of his land and its peoples. If the Young Frank didn't consciously write a blueprint for his old self, we can still trace his growth and development over the years into the Old Frank, so admirable in the fulness of his victories and defeats. During his three years in the Law School at McGill he challenged authority on the very issues he would later take into the public arena – to the Supreme Court and to the halls of the United Nations, and in the form also, and perhaps above all, of verse published then in college papers but later reprinted in all the provinces of what we then called the Dominion of Canada.

I met Frank Scott during the fall of 1925, when he was twenty-six and I had just turned eighteen. I was entering my junior year in arts. Scott was a law sophomore, lately returned from Oxford, where he had been a Rhodes scholar. And I can happily affirm, longevity and hindsight aiding, that the Scott of the present time is the uncorrupted and incorruptible descendant of the tall, angular young man, who with uncommon use of words and a brilliant and often searching gleam in his eye, confronted, and I have no doubt affronted, Montreal. He was saying in effect at the time that Canada was too promising a land, in spite of its youth, to harbour old feudal wealth and privilege, and military restrictions on freedom, the hangover from the recent war, and the caste sys-

6

tem of the Victorians. He insisted that a nation as rich in substance, with only nine million persons in its vast expanse (for the population of all Canada then was about the same as that of New York City), needed new institutions, new ways of thinking, in short new kinds of democracy that went beyond the limited privilege of the ballot box. There had to be some use of so much resource for the many, not the possessive few. I find, in a paper written by Sandra Djwa on this very subject, a passage which eloquently suggests Scott's state of mind and emotion at the time, that is, in 1926. These are his words:

I was in a palatial mansion this evening. All that wealth could purchase of beauty in pictures, hangings, carpets, furniture, china – all that was there. Not a chair, but would sell for enough to feed a slum family for a month: not a picture but would provide a home for every beggar in Montreal.

In the house was a little, tired woman, with a magnificent gown and necklace of large pearls.

She had a cross as a pendant. And down in the Railway Shops men toiled half-naked round roaring fires, and beside clanging machinery, for hours a day at cents an hour. And whenever he wanted to do so, the husband of the tired woman with the pendant cross, would tell these men there was no more work.[2]

This brief note might have become, with a few more touches, a poem in prose or a passage in Dickens or Zola – the richly furnished house, the endowed tired woman with her pendant cross, symbol of love and suffering, within a city in which wealth, entrenched and conserved, exercised a power akin to life and death over the lives of the workers. And in the middle of this city, the new Canadians, exiled from their European homes, and beyond the then slumbering French in the vast expanse of Montréal Est. Such passages describing human inequities filled the pages of nineteenth-century novels. What was relevant in Scott's neo-Rousseauism was the intensity of feeling he expressed in that time and that place. Scott looked with open eyes at what so many of his generation had come to take for granted: the hegemony of the CPR, the great riches still buried underground in mines but already yielding large revenues, the bulwarked St James Street and comparable streets in other cities, and in particular the small and powerful establishment in Montreal that had appointed the former head of Canada's wartime army to be principal of McGill University. General Sir Arthur Currie was a large man, an imposing man, with a deep resonant voice that rang with sincerities and platitudes of the time. He presided over the university for much longer than, in a later time, a noted general named Eisenhower presided over Columbia University. Currie thought of McGill as a kind of military backwater after Vimy Ridge and Mons. He had his staff of ex-officers and his executive assistant, Colonel Bovey, a man of journalistic skill, one of his former colonels. What we said and what we printed in the ways of college students was carefully read in the East Wing of the old Arts Building and an agreeable old-fashioned conformity was sought and imposed on the students.

This is the background for my memories of the young Scott. The returned Rhodes scholar, reading his law during his first maturity, began to write and to talk to his peers about what was going on in Montreal. And although I speak of him, and our lately dead friend A.J.M. Smith, as students of that time, we must remember that both Scott and Smith were grown men, in their twenties. They brought to McGill a greater degree of maturity than the younger prep school students, or someone like myself. McGill, like most universities on the continent, was a place of college yells, initiations, juvenilities. Even the young John Glassco, who said of Sir Arthur Currie that he had brought to McGill his army leadership and a good high school education, even that young wag of seventeen, also lately dead, wore in his sophistication one of those bulging racoon coats that were the rage at the time. The students were addicted to rugby and hockey, as they should be, but not to criticism and to poetry – or to thoughts of the nearby slums. Still, in every college, there is always a little group that, sports aside, wants to read poetry and to discuss ideas and finds some way of discovering its fellows, and voicing the common rebellion of the young that exists alongside the common conformity.

Scott brought to McGill his sense of the Old World, but even more his deeply rooted Canadianism and his belief in the country's liberal future. He was two or three years older than Smith, who was less dedicated to social change than to a vigorous aestheticism and the life of poetry. Both had a fine critical spirit and they provided leadership for younger men like myself. Scott's father had served as a padre, a famous padre, during World War I and was descended from several generations of Scotts in Canada. Smith was first-generation English Canadian; he had been exposed to the passionate war poems of Julian Grenfell, Wilfred Owen, Siegfried Sassoon, and Wilfred Gibson.[3]

I too was a first-generation Canadian: my Jewish parents had immigrated from a European ghetto and we had lived in Saskatchewan. How can I tell you of the isolation of those prairie towns in the days before radio and television, before the airplane? Only the train in the morning across great distances from Winnipeg and the train returning from Saskatoon across twilight snowy space in the evenings. The Winnipeg *Free Press* in the morning and the Saskatoon *Star* in the evening brought to my young self echoes of the world beyond, the cruel headlines of the first war. For the rest, we were self-contained in Yorkton, Saskatchewan, in the main street and the flanking avenues along which I bicycled. What, I ask myself, carried me from my parochial setting into the presence in 1923 at McGill of older men like Scott and Smith, and the others who eventually met in a small basement room on Atwater Avenue during winters of heavy snows to read poems, write articles, and make up the dummy of our journal of dissent in a Victorian Montreal and a semi-soldiery McGill University?

I need not answer this question, for my subject is Scott, not myself. But I had even as a boy been made aware of the social forces of which Scott often spoke. I remembered the bitter period of the Winnipeg General Strike and the slogan, long before the CIO, of 'One Big Union.' We knew J.S. Woodsworth, for he had come to speak in Yorkton at a liberal public forum conducted by a Fabian named Knox, who was the registrar of land titles, and other local liberals. In early adolescence I was made aware of the great struggles of our century: war and famine, and industrial strife. I speak of these ancient things so I may describe the steps by which Scott and Smith came together with two others and myself to publish *The McGill Fortnightly Review*, whose pages still reflect the maturity of the senior editors and the poetic gifts that emerged at that time in Montreal, so that Canadian literary history since has spoken of a 'Montreal Group.' In relating this bit of history, however collegiate some of it may be, I am describing the steps by which Frank Scott became an articulate voice, in verse and in law, in our generation, and the voice of those vibrations that had reached me from Winnipeg in 1919 and 1920 when I was thirteen.

The founding of the 1920s literary movement at McGill is often mentioned. The founding grandfather should not be forgotten. He was Felix Walter, son of McGill's professor of German who, when Scott and I were freshmen in law and arts, ran a column in the McGill *Daily* called 'The Dilettante' and signed it 'Ajax.' In the autumn of 1925 he left for Europe and A.J.M. Smith succeeded him. Smith had contributed items to Walter's column; and he commanded enough contributors to induce the Students' Council to let him publish a literary supplement to the daily, a four-page tabloid. I remember the excitement with which I read the first statement of policy. I can hear Smith's voice in it: 'orthodoxy will also be permitted so long as it is cleverly done.' He took the offensive right off. 'We are among those who would rather err brightly than platitudinize respectfully.' And Smith added: 'The gods of respectability and caution will not be worshipped in this church; rather will it be our endeavour to uncover the clay feet of these too popular idols.' We know now that with these words a new era in Canadian literature was announcing itself. I have kept all these years the eighteen issues of the supplement: they are yellow and falling apart but in turning the fragile pages recently I recognized with pleasure that nowhere in Canada could the daily newspapers, the professional journals, have mustered a Saturday literary page as lively or youthfully brilliant as Smith's. He led off with an article on the future of science (having lately taken a B.Sc. himself). Stephen Leacock gave his blessing with an article on 'The Rush to the Colleges.' French plays in Montreal were reviewed and an editorial denounced the library association for taking a strong stand against sex in modern fiction.[4] Smith exposed us to modern poetry in 1924-5 in bits of filler at the end of the columns – poems by Ezra Pound or remarks by Bertrand Russell. Sir Arthur Currie must have shuddered when one issue contained an article on trade unions.

There was a lead article in an early issue contributed by F.R. Scott – it was the first time I saw the name – poking fun at a projected Cathedral of Learning in Pittsburgh. His Wellsian peep at the future was far ahead of Orwell: he gave us, in 1925, an account of his visit to the multistoreyed cathedral in the year 1985. The educational skyscraper reeked of 'tobacco smoke, slang and efficiency.' It had four miles of corridors, nine dance halls, fourteen gymnasiums, and 735 pure Gothic doorways leading, one supposes, into a few classrooms.[5] Scott's imagination assigned theology to the top storeys, putting the theologs closer to heaven or outer space. Smith, in addition to his science series, wrote two long articles on 'From Patriotism to Pacifism,' quoting fully from British war poets. I do not know whether Sir Arthur read these strong anti-war articles. Nothing could have been better calculated to express the disillusion of the time, so rarely voiced then at McGill. However, it was the last issue in the spring of 1925 that produced a tremor on campus, when Smith quoted Aldous Huxley's 'Fifth Philosopher's Song':

> A million million spermatozoa
>   All of them alive:
> Out of their cataclysm but one poor Noah
>   Dare hope to survive.

The spermatozoa were as disturbing to the conservative element at McGill as Walt Whitman's mention of semen was to Ralph Waldo Emerson a century earlier. The conservatives accused the *Supplement* of being highbrow, supercilious, condescending, and mocking. But to a distinct portion of the student body it had been a breath of fresh air.

In the fall of 1925 Smith organized an editorial board that included the literary law student, F.R. Scott. The first issue was prepared, but it did not go to press. There had been rumblings about the *Supplement*'s high tone, the spermatozoa, the anti-war articles: the official reason given was that the *Daily* lost advertising and could no longer afford a literary luxury. The Student Council refused to vote the funds and Smith and his board found themselves disinherited. The Board formally resigned in protest and announced it would found its own publication, *The McGill Fortnightly Review*. It was during this flurry of excitement that Smith, with whom I had a nodding acquaintance, asked me whether I would like to serve on the board of the new venture as managing editor. I felt as if I were being admitted to Olympus. At the initial editorial lunch I met Scott for the first time. With his sharply etched face he seemed to me as if painted by Holbein; he was an attentive listener, he laughed easily and pleasantly, and he possessed a sharp thrust of verbal wit. He always found some phrase in the *Daily* or the downtown press, some platitude in a speech, and turned it into the stuff of irony and paradox. He seemed to think in epigrams. There was an endless debate between him and Smith about the Georgian poets. Scott was beginning to emerge from his Tennysonian self. During the first year of the *Fortnightly* he wrote conventional verse, mainly sonnets.

Smith had in the meantime struck up a friendship with a young English zoology instructor curiously named Lancelot Hogben, who would later gain renown as the author of *Mathematics for the Million*. But at this time he was the author of a volume of verses entitled *Exiles of the Snow*, and in Montreal he played the role of an exile in the Quebec snows, fighting the bourgeois colonials. Hogben was at McGill long enough to make a lasting impression on Smith and to write poems for the *Fortnightly* under the name Philip Page. I lately came on a passage in Virginia Woolf's letters describing Lancelot in 1918 before he came to McGill. 'A youth of genius; a shock-headed but fresh coloured ardent man of perhaps 22, either hiding from the Police or a Commanding Officer,' wrote Virginia Woolf and that's the way I remember Hogben, whom I knew very slightly. Virginia said his hair 'by the way practically grows into his left eye.'[6] With this hindsight, I can see now that Hogben's friendship with Smith gave the *Fortnightly* a kind of indirect pipeline to British post-war radical taste and to the periphery of Bloomsbury. Certainly Hogben gave Smith all the new poetry to read, including a copy of *Prufrock*, and Smith in turn converted Scott from the *Idylls of the King* and sonnets to the free personal style of the moderns, with the results we all know.

The *Fortnightly* set out to be critical and to make the students more critical. We found we could print 500 copies of an eight-page quarto at Ste-Anne-de-Bellevue for about fifty dollars and on coated stock. The price seems astonishing in these days of high book prices. We needed 500 subscribers at a dollar apiece to enable us to publish ten issues during the academic year. A single copy sold for ten cents. The janitors in the various buildings agreed to serve as our news-stand distributors and were paid five cents of each copy, providing the extra service of delivering to our subscribers. In no time at all we had more than our quota of subscribers, and the single copies sold briskly. Smith, in the *Literary Supplement*, had decidedly created an audience for literature and controversy at McGill. Our first issue was a sell-out and we proudly printed a second edition. We were distinctly in business.

We were in the midst of preparing our first issue when Scott arrived with the news that a committee had been appointed by McGill's corporation to investigate us. The question of censorship was avoided: we were asked instead whether we had a right to use the good name of McGill in a private student venture, under control of neither the Students' Council nor the faculty. Colonel Bovey, Currie's executive officer, was quoted as saying that he was afraid 'someone somewhere' might be offended by what we wrote. Scott's rejoinder was 'nothing is respectable at McGill unless it emanates from authority; and then it is infallible.'[7] I can still remember our meeting with some important personage sent by the committee to interview us. Scott then was our pipeline to respectability; apparently this man was an old friend of the Scott family. He treated the entire matter as a joke. It was clear he believed that McGill students had every right to attach the name of McGill to whatever they did as students. He joked with us, poked Scott in the ribs, said, 'this is the one man who's dangerous,' and went back to the corporation to say he didn't think we were a bunch of communists. Stephen Leacock gave us his blessing by writing an article and sending his one dollar subscription. 'A college magazine,' he wrote, 'if it is of the right sort, is born into a life of poverty. It is supported by the alms of the faithful. But it represents a work of the creative spirit fit to rank with any of the activities of a university.'[8] We thought so, too. Our first editorial explained that since we were an independent journal our readers had to expect independent opinions.

Shortly after the first issue appeared, Scott, who had at once assumed the political leadership of our group as Smith had assumed the aesthetic, paid a call on Sir Arthur Currie. He was received, I gather, in that modest front office where the portly principal looked out on his small domain from his red-carpeted and mahogany-furnished chamber. Scott said to the principal he could not understand why students shouldn't be allowed to voice their opinions. Why did they have to defer to the opinions of others? What harm, he said, could there be in having free expression on a campus? Sir Arthur was at his most ponderous. He echoed the doubts of Colonel Bovey. Of course student opinion was welcome, but in print it exposed the university to readers who might be offended. What if the students flew off the handle? What if they gave voice to dangerous ideas? All his efforts, Currie said, had been directed to maintaining an esprit de corps at McGill. What if someone took the notion to turn the publication into a Bolshevik sheet? He would be most unhappy if that happened; it would give him no alternative but to suppress the publication. And this would dishonour McGill. Now, if the *Fortnightly* would accept a group of advisory editors, that would be a responsible way of running an independent publication.

Scott told Sir Arthur that this wouldn't do at all. And suddenly he counterattacked; he suggested that this proposal showed Sir Arthur did not trust McGill's students. The old soldier was caught unawares. No one apparently had ever suggested to him that he couldn't trust his army. Sir Arthur finally said it wasn't a question of mistrust: of course he had every confidence in the student body, but one might run into irresponsibility. The conversation ended with the principal saying he supposed he had to take the risk and judge us by our performance.[9]

A few months later the conversation between Scott and Sir Arthur was transformed by Smith into a poem published in our journal. Smith described the Big Businessman founding a university so that the coming generation could have the 'proper education.' The verses contained a stanza directly echoing the principal:

> We shall instruct our students in
> The value of discipline:
> *Esprit de corps*
> Won the war,
> Did it not?[10]

The *Fortnightly* had various ways of commenting on much that happened at McGill: when the psychology department invited an entertainer like Houdini to deliver his profundities about escaping from locked trunks in the classroom and the deans bowed and scraped before the Queen of Rumania, Scott brought these two incidents together in four lines entitled 'Trivium':

> Masses heard the great Houdini,
> Masses shouted for the Queenie.
> Did you ever see such asses
> As the educated masses?[11]

When the dean of arts refused to allow the Players Club access to the new university theatre, Scott and Smith combined their talents in the writing of a piece of forensic prose so powerful that the dean and his cohorts retreated. The theatre was won for the students. Scott reviewed art shows, and attacked the annual McGill musical review for its shoddiness as against the talent of the McGill players.

It was in the *Fortnightly* that he published his satire on the pseudo-literary Canadian Authors' Association after attending one of its teas. It can be read today in *The Blasted Pine: An Anthology of Satire, Invective and Disrespectful Verse*, a lively collection that Scott and Smith edited in 1957, and also in Scott's *Selected Poems*. We were very sophisticated, as you may judge. What academic literary review on the entire North American continent could boast in the mid-twenties of an article on *The Waste Land* (by Smith), or a brilliant parody of Gertrude Stein (by Scott), or a piece on Joyce (by myself)? We were modern in the *Fortnightly* long before Edmund Wilson put the moderns together in *Axel's Castle* and the avant-garde became a subject of respectable study in academe. We also had articles on Canadian politics by Eugene Forsey, the future senator, on trade unionism by Allan Latham, and a wide variety of reviews and discussions of politics and the arts.

I cannot resist quoting from Scott's parody of Gertrude Stein to suggest how his ear captured her essential rhythms and embodied in them his own genius for satire. He had Miss Stein take tea at the McGill Union:

Then too the games which you play when you play if you play them are certain. A great difference is made by this great difference. It is fine to see so many watching certain games with certainty. Nothing changes from generation to generation except the thing seen and that makes the game. The few who play it as it is played are the few who used to play it as it was played. All the rest are the rest and the more you have of the rest, the less you have of the few. From this time on the problem becomes definite.[12]

I am not sure Miss Stein would have signed her name to this but she would have had to admit that her relentless logic is in it.

I think I can best conclude this sketchy description of the qualities of leadership Scott showed in the 1920s by referring to a measured and highly judicial article he wrote discussing student government at the university. The germs of his future activism may be read in it. He showed the autocratic way in which the McGill student government ran its affairs: the powerlessness of its leaders, the centralization of its finances. He demonstrated that with all the fear of Marxism at McGill the student government had been unwittingly fashioned in a Marxist model. This was not simply Scott's love of paradox:

Even a cursory glance at our constitution makes it evident that we are living under a form of State Socialism. All the essential ingredients are here: the capital levy, a bureaucracy, nationalisation. It is amusing to reflect that in so unfailing a centre of conservatism as McGill every undergraduate forms part of and works through a socialist organization ... The Students Council forms a Central committee of collection and distribution: if one club loses money through bad management, excessive activity or otherwise, the deficit is made up by taking the necessary amount from the pooled profits of the other societies. This is the principle for which the miners fought in the last strike in Great Britain and for which they were called fools by our businessmen and traitors by our patriots. It is not contended that the miners were wrong – far from it. But it is contended that the defenders of the present system at McGill are wrong because the same principles do not apply to both student activities and mining.[13]

The future dean of McGill's Faculty of Law was pleading for nothing more than greater democracy on the campus. And his plea, as in the *Fortnightly*'s editorials, was for student independence, for greater faith in the young, and for reliance by the existing powers on educated voters and enlightened social procedures.

To complete this short bit of literary and academic history, let me say we did nothing to assure the *Fortnightly*'s future. It graduated with us, on the theory that new generations of students could found their own journals (as they did). The generation of A.M. Klein and David Lewis, of Carl Goldenberg and Eric Berne and others, was following fast on our heels. And so it goes from generation to generation. Scott, beyond his years at McGill and into his professorship in law, helped found other journals, gathered round him younger poets, remained in the ensuing decades at the centre of poetry in Montreal and in Canada, and in his role in the Law School at the centre of the kind of political thought his early essay, quoted above, reveals. I believe I have made it clear that the young Scott in the mid-1920s in every way showed his intellectual probity as well as his artistic feeling and vigorous commitment to Canada's future. I have read his beautiful credo set down in the intimacy of his journals: 'disinterestedness, public spirit, political integrity, a consciousness of the international duty of nations, a love of the beautiful, family life, dignity.'[14]

The ideals of a young man? I think not. All men of good will around the world have nourished such a dream within our brutal century, recognizing that the dream becomes reality only if the ideals are constantly pursued. Those of us who have since read Scott's later poems, or remember his remarkable court defeat of Duplessis, or his own defeat in the Lower Court in his defence of Lady Chatt, won in the Supreme

Court - those of us to whom he is a beloved elder in Canadian liberalism look back with gratitude for his active presence, his unflinching sense of rightness and wrongness as submitted to human and scientific logic, and the ceaseless scintillation of his intelligence - his all-enfolding imagination, which touches everything that he contemplates. His career, even in its reverses, has shown a singular unity. Max Beerbohm could indeed draw a sketch of an Older Scott talking to his Younger Self, but he would have to vary his formula. Everything didn't go according to plan. There had been defeats of some of Scott's most nourished activities, and in particular the subversion of his great work for a fuller dialogue between Canada's French and English - the subversion that Lord Acton described in his discussion of the tyranny of a minority. The Old Scott might rather say: 'Well, things didn't always go according to your plans,' and the Young Scott might answer: 'They were still very good plans.'

NOTES

1 This 1924 cartoon is in the series 'The Old and the Young Self' and was printed in Beerbohm's *Observations* (London 1925). The original is at the University of Texas.

2 Sandra Djwa, 'F.R. Scott: A Canadian in the Twenties,' *Papers of the Bibliographical Society of Canada* 19 (1980)

3 'From Patriotism to Pacifism,' *The McGill Daily Literary Supplement*, 11 Feb. 1925, 1

4 Ibid., 8 Oct. 1924

5 Ibid., 19 Nov. 1924, 1

6 Virginia Woolf, *The Question of Things Happening: The Letters of Virginia Woolf*, II, *1912-1922*, ed. Nigel Nicolson (London 1976) 211

7 Diaries of F.R. Scott, edited by Sandra Djwa with an introduction, unpublished

8 *The McGill Fortnightly Review*, 21 Nov. 1925, 3

9 Diaries, 11 Dec. 1925

10 *Fortnightly*, 10 Mar. 1927, 50

11 Ibid., 3 Nov. 1926, 6

12 Ibid., 25 Mar. 1927, 63

13 Ibid., 10 Mar. 1927, 50

14 Diaries, 3 May 1924

J. KING GORDON

The Politics of Poetry

IT WAS MORE than half a century ago. I was a student from Oxford on an Easter vacation in Florence. We were standing in her garden on the road to Santa Margherita, looking out over the Arno valley towards the foothills of the Apennines. It was a scene of great beauty – the contours of the hills, the grey-green of the olive groves, the black arrows of the cypress, and here and there the white walls of villas against the hillside.

My Florentine friend asked me about Canada and when I described some of the wilderness country through which I had paddled and the grandeur of the western mountains, which I had not yet seen, she said: 'I don't think I could stand it. I would be frightened. No matter how magnificent the view, I need a reminder of humanity to be able to relate to it, to find its beauty.'

I thought of that recently when I read Frank Scott's 'Surfaces':

> This rock-bound river, ever flowing
> Obedient to the ineluctable laws,
> Brings a reminder from the barren north
> Of the eternal lifeless processes.
> There is an argument that will prevail
> In this calm stretch of current, slowly drawn
> Towards its final equilibrium.
> Come, flaunt the brief prerogative of life,
> Dip your small civilized foot in this cold water
> And ripple, for a moment, the smooth surface of time.[1]

Frank Scott came up to Oxford a year before I did. His college was Magdalen. I entered Queen's, whose elegant façade, executed by the favourite pupil of Wren's, graced the High Street at the point where it curved towards St Mary's and the Carfax. Magdalen tower, which dated

17

from Wolsey's time, marked the ending of the High Street at the Cherwell River a few hundred yards below Queen's. Some of us, standing on the steps of Queen's, while admitting the splendour of the tower considered it a bit arrogant in its cool domination of the Oxford skyline.

I do not recall meeting Frank Scott at Oxford, which is a little strange since it turned out that we had similar interests and pastimes. We both sang in the Bach Choir, under the exacting baton of Sir Hugh Allen and once under the friendlier wand of Ralph Vaughan Williams conducting his *Sea Symphony*. We both had our comfortable social philosophies shaken up by the likes of Shaw and Tawney and Hobson and Cole and the Webbs either in person or bursting out very much alive from the covers of books or declaiming from the Oxford stage. And as sons of rectory and manse we gravitated towards the Student Christian Movement and experienced new awakenings, Frank in a serious group study of the Anglican bishops' report on 'Christianity and Industrial Problems,' I in my first contact with international realities as Canadian delegate to the European Student Relief conference in Turnov, Czechoslovakia.

We both rowed in our college boats. But Magdalen was so near to the top of the river and Queen's so near the bottom of the first division that we were not on speaking terms: Queen's I had to settle for bumping Magdalen II. And we had friends in common, including John Farthing, a great Florentine who had introduced me to Renaissance art, and who became a lecturer in economics at McGill. I met him on a visit to Montreal in the late twenties. He was very excited about plans for the formation of a new group, the Leonardo Society, which was committed to introducing some culture to Montreal through the importation of Medici prints of the Renaissance masters. 'Frank Scott, the poet, is a member. You must know Frank Scott: he was up at Oxford with us.' No, I did not know Frank Scott. But we were to meet in the fall of 1931.

That was the opening of the third year of the Depression. I still find it difficult to establish an identification between some of the very real social and economic problems we face today with those the majority of Canadians experienced in the thirties. With the notable exception of a privileged few, most Canadians had no floor to stand on - no wage floor, no job floor, no trade union floor, no health services floor, no civil liberties floor. On the western prairies, the devastation of drought, which preceded the collapse of the world economy, compounded the suffering of farmers and their families.

I had been doing graduate work at Union Theological Seminary in New York under two professors, Harry F. Ward and Reinhold Niebuhr, for whom Christian profession called for a radical analysis of the social situation and appropriate personal and collective action. I did my field

work in Christian ethics in the strike-ridden mill town of East Marion,
North Carolina, where striking textile workers had been shot by police;
in New York's Union Square, where we could witness at close or more
discreet range the efficient crowd control of Grover Whalen's cossacks;
or in South Street at night, on New York's waterfront, among stranded
and hungry seamen with no place to sleep.

When I was named professor of Christian ethics at United Theological College, I received letters from two old friends. John Farthing wrote:

Your coming to Montreal to teach Christian Ethics is like going among canni-
bals to teach them Christian charity. One of the leading lights of your college is
a leading and wealthy merchant of Montreal who has turned off employees of
thirty years' standing for a week's holiday without pay. It seems to me that
there is a smallness about that which is even worse than the hardness.

Graham Spry wrote: 'You will find a splendid group of congenial spirits
in Montreal and very agreeable circumstances in which to work and
there is ample opportunity for your dangerous radicalism.' As it turned
out, both my friends were right.

It was in my first week in Montreal that I was invited to 3653 Oxenden Avenue to meet Frank Scott and a small group who were planning
to form a society that might play a similar role in Canada to that played
by the Fabian Society in Britain. The Montreal group was in close correspondence with a group in Toronto. Frank and Marian Scott met me at
the door and led me into a living room dominated by books and paintings. There were a number of people there. I can recall Eugene Forsey, a
lecturer in economics at McGill; Joe Mergler, a labour lawyer; Jacques
Bieler, an engineer, whose father, a Swiss theologian, taught at my college; and David Lewis, a fourth-year McGill student who was president
of the campus Labour Club.

Frank explained the task of the group for my benefit. Earlier in the
summer he had met Frank Underhill, a professor of history from the
University of Toronto, at a conference in Williamstown. In the course of
an afternoon's walk over the hills, they had come to the conclusion that
the time was right for the establishment in Canada of an organization
devoted to critical social and economic analysis. The Montreal group
had been working on a statement of purpose and prescription which
would be transmitted to the Toronto group for discussion. It had been
decided that Frank Scott, a professor of law and constitutional law at
that, was most qualified to do the drafting.

We made good progress. On 11 November 1931, Frank Underhill
wrote Frank Scott a letter saying he was coming to Montreal to give a
couple of lectures and would like to see him:

I want to see you and talk over the League for Economic Democracy and such things and I'll be free all Sunday ... We had a good group meeting here this afternoon where we discussed your draft and also a more elaborate one prepared by a few people here ... There was general agreement that your draft, as being shorter and more concise was more satisfactory. We are now trying to make a draft based on yours which I shall have with me also. The general criticism of yours was that the paragraph detailing the evils of the present system has not enough direct reference to Canadian conditions, and that the paragraph giving the proposed policy of the League should be a little more specific and concrete. About the name of the baby, all the parents have their own ideas.[2]

The LSR Manifesto that emerged, based on the Scott draft, reveals more than the nicely balanced arguments of the trained legal mind. It turns out to be more than an overview – an appreciation and evaluation of the human condition within a universal frame of reference. It is an oversimplification to say that man is central in this frame of reference – as the eyes of my Florentine friend sought out the white-walled villa in the Tuscan landscape. Man himself is part of the scheme, part of the order and disorder, part of the justice and injustice, a contributor to the beauty while sharing in the beauty. And perhaps beyond it all, there is an order within ineluctable law, positing a divinity because it includes man.

The evil in the capitalist system, to which the Manifesto points, is more than injustice, more than the human suffering which it causes. It is the almost blasphemous defiance of the spiritual principles in an order in which man can find sustenance and fulfilment. The spectacular collapse of the gilded house which the system erected, with the resultant intensified human suffering, presents the challenge to rebuilding on firmer foundations. Or, to put it more concisely:

> This is an hour
> Of new beginnings, concepts warring for power
> Decay of systems – the tissue of art is torn
> With overtures of an era being born.[3]

The new beginnings in Montreal were well under way when the League for Social Reconstruction was formally constituted in Toronto in January 1932. They manifested themselves in a group that gathered from time to time in various combinations and permutations in the house on Oxenden Avenue, in front of which an ancient Franklin was usually parked. The LSR did not consider itself as essentially a political group. It included painters, poets, professors, lawyers, students, business people, and, occasionally, a politician. It was a great group for talk – and laughter. Sometimes the talk would be on writers and their ideas and James Joyce might have to share a bench with John Strachey and Lady Chatterley sit down with Moral Man in an Immoral Society.

Recently, I have been calling the roll of the group that gathered around Frank and Marian Scott – more than calling the roll, but, in a sense, visiting them one by one. I was trying to discover what single shared idea made them a group. It wasn't literature. It wasn't art. It certainly wasn't socialism. And then it came to me: it was ideas. And the times in which we were living had a lot to do with it. The old orthodoxies were unravelling. The sacred cows were out of their pasture and cluttering the highways. And, as Frank perceived, the Social Register had become a marvellous source of mirth.[4] But beyond the drama and absurdities of a world in change there was the common concern for the human condition, the human tragedy, itself the result of outworn orthodoxies enforced by power. And there was the search for new answers – not one answer, many answers from the poets and painters and professors and lawyers and students and business people and even the politicians. Perhaps, shared, there was a common view: a deep concern for man, a being capable of love and creative effort in an ordered world.

Now, when I think of that group, I find myself focusing on one person, Pegi Nicol, of whom Frank wrote at the time of her death:

> She lived her art in her motion and speech
> As her painting spoke and moved.
> She entered a room like a self-portrait
> And her language cut quickly.
> Everything that was ordinary became extraordinary
> Through her vision and touch,
> And what she approached grew bright colours.
> She started songs and joys and bells
> And gardens of pigeon and children.
> ...
> She was a Canadian of these difficult days
> When greatness is in our thoughts[5]

Even when the LSR took on a well-defined shape and an active program, we remained wary of the doctrinaire, on the left as well as on the right. I recall an exciting Sunday morning at Oxenden Avenue when we welcomed John Strachey, freshly arrived from London with the definitive plans for the coming struggle for power. Somehow, they didn't quite fit into our perceptions and priorities and we ventured with some audacity to give battle to the great John Strachey in the course of which a number of chinks were revealed in the Marxist armour.

But this did not add up to dilettantism. Frank later wrote of some of our friends who 'make a virtue of having an open mind':

> Above all they fear the positive formation of opinion,
> The essential choice that acts as a mental compass,
> The clear perception of the road to the receding horizon.
>
> For this would mean leaving the shade of the middle ground
> To walk in the open air, and in unknown places;
> Might lead, perhaps – dread thought! – to definite action.[6]

The inaugural meeting of the Montreal Branch of the LSR took place in Salon B of the Mount Royal Hotel on 11 March 1932. It had been called by an organizing committee composed of F.R. Scott, G.S. Mooney, secretary of the Verdun YMCA, J.K. Gordon, and David Lewis. An invitation had been sent out to interested persons with the suggestion that 'if you know personally of any others who should receive this notice as being probably ready to subscribe to the League's aims, you are asked to communicate with F.R. Scott, 3653 Oxenden Avenue, Harbour 9912.'

The meeting was successful. Sixty persons signed up as members. Plans for meetings were discussed: public meetings with outside speakers, membership meetings to discuss policy matters in the Manifesto, reading material and pamphlets. As speakers, first in demand was J.S. Woodsworth, the LSR's honorary president, leader of the farmer-labour group in the House of Commons. I came across a note, the other day, written in a familiar copperplate hand and signed with the initials, JS. The note read: 'Tell Mrs. Scott that it's time the artists "did their stuff".' Other members of the Ottawa group came down to speak: E.J. Garland of Alberta and Angus MacInnis from British Columbia. From New York came Harry F. Ward and Reinhold Niebuhr, who spoke to packed meetings in the Church of the Messiah, whose Unitarian minister was sympathetic to our aims. Later, Stafford Cripps was to visit us from London and Walter Nash, Labour prime minister of New Zealand.

It was a time of pamphlets and pamphleteering. Over a period of several years we had two committed and eloquent pitchmen, Stanley Allen and Frank Aykroyd, who could have gained fame and fortune in the world of media advertising today. League for Industrial Democracy pamphlets from New York and Labour Research pamphlets from London met our needs until the LSR began putting out pamphlets of its own. And by the winter of 1932/3, four members of the Montreal Branch were engaged in doing the preparatory work on the book which was to appear in 1935 as *Social Planning for Canada*.

Perhaps of more profound impact were the studies in contemporary social conditions in which members of our group were engaged. A Committee on Social and Economic Research was established by the Montreal Presbytery of the United Church. Its members were J.K. Gordon, E.A. Forsey, and J.A. Coote, a member of the engineering faculty of McGill. Through its *Bulletin*, the Committee reported on minimum wages in Quebec, the conditions of unemployment relief in Quebec, women's wages and wages in the textile industry in Quebec, and other relevant social and economic issues. The focus of some of our work was a little sensitive since the chairman of the Board of Governors of United Theological College was president of Canada Cottons. A study of labour conditions in the men's clothing industry in Montreal was carried out by Frank Scott and Harry Cassidy of the University of Toronto. Leonard Marsh, an active member of the Montreal LSR, did research in unemployment and health and welfare services.

A sure sign that profound social change is on the way is when the establishment mounts a counterattack. And this was true in the decade of the thirties. Government, the business community, the press, the police, and certain sections of the church opened fire on all who, in their minds, were constituting a threat to the right-thinking community. And this came as an interesting discovery to many who entered into the activities of the new League for Social Reconstruction.

It is not that the LSR itself was regarded as constituting a threat. It was considered to be dangerous because it was articulating the deep concern and widespread unrest occasioned not only by the catastrophe of the Depression but by the normal working of the system which consigned to poverty a large proportion of Canadian wage-earners and their families. Quite correctly, the leaders of the establishment estimated that the public meetings, conferences, reports based on studies of social conditions, pamphlets, and books were something more than a Fabian exercise for slightly offbeat academics.

Moreover, it was not just the LSR. It was in the churches, which were becoming very vocal in their denunciation of the 'un-Christian' aspects of the established system and had recently spawned a radical group calling itself the Fellowship for a Christian Social Order. There were uneasy rumblings in the trade union movement – in the garment trades and even in the obedient Catholic syndicates. Moreover, there were signs, even in respectable middle-class circles, of growing concern about the suppression of civil rights.

In June 1933, the Montreal Conference of the United Church, by a large majority, passed a resolution demanding the repeal of the infamous section 98 of the Criminal Code, which, as the Montreal *Gazette* explained, had been enacted 'in consequence of the communistic uprising which took place in the city of Winnipeg in 1919.' Holding its fire until March 1934, the *Gazette* blasted off with an editorial entitled 'Friends of Sedition,' in which it berated the churchmen for offering advice on an issue utterly foreign to the mission of Christian teaching and suggested that those favouring the repeal 'are not very far removed, in spirit at least, from the seditionist himself, and Section 98 is fairly broad in its scope.'

A few days after this editorial, a nasty incident of police violence occurred. A Polish unemployed worker resisting eviction with the encouragement of some of his friends was shot in the back of the head by a policeman's gun. A large but peaceful funeral procession for Nick Zynchuck was broken up by plainclothes police with considerable brutality. A number of civic organizations, including the Montreal LSR, called for an inquiry with no result. The coroner declared: 'We have never had any trouble with French-Canadians and it is always the foreigners who start the trouble.' The premier, solidly behind the chief of police, said there would be no inquiry, he would see that the law was respected, and 'foreigners who are not satisfied to breathe the air of the Province of Quebec have but to return to other lands.'

Events on a larger stage were moving fast, events which would produce in Quebec a convergence of temporal and spiritual powers to suppress any vestige of suspected subversion. The LSR, primarily concerned with domestic exploitation and inequities, was increasingly alarmed between 1933 and 1936 by the threatening march of Fascism and Nazism in Europe. The Falangist rebellion against the freely elected government of Spain, with its apparent support from the Roman Catholic Church and active military backing from Italy and Germany, was a tragedy of immense consequence. When it became known that three representatives of the loyalist government of Spain were in North America, the LSR joined other organizations and invited the Spanish group to address a public meeting in Montreal.

On the morning of the meeting, French- and English-language newspapers carried a letter from the archbishop co-adjutor warning local Catholics that a Basque priest in the party was a man of questionable credentials whose opinions were at variance with those of His Holiness the Pope. The same papers warned of the dangers of riots instigated by francophone students and fascist sympathizers. Later in the morning a group of Université de Montréal students who waited on the representative of the mayor were assured by him and the chief of police that no meeting would be held.

A small luncheon meeting with the three representatives took place quietly. So did a well-attended meeting at the McGill Union of the university's Social Problems Club, although it had been threatened by violence. Refused the use of the mid-town hall where the public meeting was originally scheduled to take place and later, under threat of invasion, a Westmount hall that had been promised, a limited gathering met in a salon of the Mount Royal Hotel. A hundred guests had just begun to listen to one of the speakers, Signora Isabella Palencia, when the management suddenly announced that the meeting was cancelled and turned out the lights. Outside, a crowd of students shouting 'A bas les communistes!' harassed members of the audience as they made their way out.

Two days later on Sunday, the Feast of Christ the King was celebrated. One hundred thousand crowded the Craig Street armoury and the adjacent Champ des Mars. They listened to the archbishop co-adjutor denounce communism, deplore Canadian support for 'those barbarians who have covered the soil of unhappy Spain with ruin and blood,' and express gratitude to the civil authorities in Quebec and Montreal for proclaiming their intention of eradicating all subversive propaganda and organizations. In Quebec, Cardinal Villeneuve and Premier Duplessis raised the anti-communist refrain to a higher level of authority.

Frank Scott was to write:

> For these our hearts are bleeding: the homes burning,
> The schools broken and ended, the vision thwarted,
> The youths, their backs to the wall, awaiting the volley,
> The child staring at a huddled form.
>
> And Guernica, more real than our daily bread.[7]

The launching of the CCF in Calgary in August 1932 was greeted with enthusiasm by the LSR. But it posed some problems in regard to the relationship between the two organizations. We settled it in Montreal by interpreting the LSR Manifesto to mean that since we were an educational organization there would be no formal affiliation but that members in their own capacity were free to take an active part and that local branches could give whatever assistance seemed desirable short of affiliation.

In a letter dated 1 December 1932, Frank Underhill wrote to Frank Scott describing the overflow meeting in Toronto's Hygeia Hall to launch the CCF, with J.S. Woodsworth, William Irvine, Gardiner, Agnes McPhail, and Salem Bland all speaking. He spoke of the likelihood of a third group, in addition to farmer and labour, since there are 'such hosts of unattached sympathizers here that something should be done for them.'[8]

Then he wrote: 'He (Woodsworth) wants a draft of a CCF manifesto ready by the end of the year to be submitted in January to their Council. I propose to try a draft of my own unless I hear that you have made progress with one of yours. I could submit it to you for revision and to our inner group here. It must not be very long since it is for general public consumption.'

A good many LSR members were to enter active politics. Some were even to get elected. Frank Scott, active in the early organization of the CCF in Montreal, was to become national chairman. David Lewis was to become national secretary. But the beautiful irony was that perhaps the greatest contribution of the LSR, primarily an educational organization, was the CCF Manifesto, drafted by Frank Underhill, based on the LSR Manifesto, drafted originally by Frank Scott. Call it poetic justice!

On 11 August 1937, Frank wrote me after another CCF convention. I had been elected to a position on the executive and Frank was generous in his congratulations:

I am extremely glad it was offered to you and that you accepted. I think that it is your job to see that the people do not perish for lack of vision. Old J.S.'s power in Canada has come from his vision and there is no political cunning or tactic which is a substitute. The objective of a good society, which is all that socialism is, must be clarified and stated simply to this baffled generation ... It seems to me we have to express through the C.C.F. the idea that our people came to North America to build a fair city, so to speak, and that we have obviously fallen down lamentably on the job. This sense of purpose, I am sure, is a more cohesive force than any detailed program. It is latent in the Regina Manifesto but buried under blueprints.

Frank reported that he had taken on a big job for the Canadian Institute of International Affairs, preparing Canada's position paper for the forthcoming British Commonwealth Relations Conference in Australia.

I have twinges of conscience about doing this kind of work, though they tend to disappear when I think of the possibility of a trip round the world. My rationalization, however, is a feeling that I may perhaps be able to get the poor baffled delegates to ask themselves what they think they own the Empire for. It needs a theory for itself even more than Canada does.

And then came a closing paragraph of pure poetry referring to family life at Lachute where Frank and Marian Scott and their son Peter shared a cottage with their good friends Raleigh and Louise Parkin and their daughter Elizabeth:

Lachute life continues as usual. Marian spends most of her time up in her bed-room painting the interiors of street cars. To some it might seem an odd use for a farmhouse but you know Marian. Occasionally she will break away to paint a flower, but only if it has some ungodly shape. Everyone is well, and the standard of living is constantly rising. There are now two open cess-pools instead of only one. The children's house is almost completed, and is so airtight that it is like an oven most of the day. Peter and Elizabeth are planning a vast marriage ceremony, in which Raleigh is to be Archbishop and I am to be best man and organist, playing the wedding march on the sweet potato. Marian is to be flower-girl 'because she knows so much about flowers.' It will be a positive orgy of sacrilege, as far as I can make out.

I left Montreal not long after and that letter with its blend of politics, constitutional process, and poetry reminded me of much of what Montreal had meant to me for those six years.

I thought of the Laurentians, of the summer at Lachute, of the winter at St Sauveur in front of André Bieler's cottage with its true fresco which he made as Giotto made frescoes, mixing pigment into the wet mortar. And Frank's remark on the slopes of the Marquis's Hill: 'If someone were to ask you, say for a *Who's Who*, what your recreations are, tell him: "Skiing and changing the social order".'

And I thought of the talk and the music – the Sunday afternoon radio series, Toscanini conducting the Philharmonic in the Beethoven symphonies from Carnegie Hall. And the parties at Oxenden Avenue, dancing to Cole Porter's 'Night and Day' and Jerome Kern's 'Smoke Gets in Your Eyes,' which found its way into *Social Planning for Canada* when we needed a subtitle for labour conditions in the tobacco industry.

Then, suddenly, I remembered that evening when there was a group of us at Oxenden Avenue. Frank was out at a reception given by Principal Morgan of McGill for Carl Sandburg, poet and biographer. He came back, amused and delighted. It had been a good party and the conversation had been lively. Frank got up to leave and as he moved towards the door, Carl Sandburg came across the room. He took him by the hand and said: 'You know, there is something about you that reminds me of Abe Lincoln.'

NOTES

1 *Overture* (Toronto 1945)
2 Underhill to F.R. Scott, 11 Nov. 1931
3 'Overture,' *Overture*

4 'The Canadian Social Register,' *Selected Poems* (Toronto: Oxford University Press 1966)

5 'For Pegi Nicol,' *Selected Poems*

6 'To Certain Friends,' *Selected Poems*

7 'Spain: 1937,' *Overture*

8 Underhill to F.R. Scott, 1 Dec. 1932

PART TWO

LOUIS DUDEK

Polar Opposites in F.R. Scott's Poetry

THE CANADIAN POET F.R. Scott may appear to be composed of a complex and irreconcilable mixture of elements, but he is also a writer of extraordinary lucidity, the working parts of whose mind lie visible to the eye as in the poetry of no other writer I know. The mind of most creative writers is a pinball machine, bouncing the ball of ideas off the various polar opposites built into the system. That's why I often feel we should not ask what an author believes or thinks but rather what opposite beliefs and attitudes he is pulled by – there we will discover a whole field of force.

I first saw Frank Scott in person at a public lecture around 1941, at the Museum of Fine Arts in Montreal. He was showing some slides of paintings done under the Federal Art Project of the Work Projects Administration (WPA), a part of the New Deal recovery program in the United States – in other words, a kind of 'socialist' or government welfare program that helped to produce art by unemployed artists – and I recall his saying something like 'Would these fine paintings be here if we did not have this government-sponsored project? See what can be done!' Since then, in Canada, we've had the CBC, the Canada Council, various provincial arts councils, the Humanities Research Council, and conferences to show that Frank Scott was in the prophetic vanguard of an idea. I lived for some days after our first meeting in the aura of his personality and sharp intelligence, cooped up as I myself was in the offices of an advertising agency, writing copy for BC Apples, for whisky and gin, and for the Quebec war effort, feeling that drive of his social criticism in the day-to-day deceptions of advertising and publicity, as well as in the distant thunder of war.

At the same time, Frank Scott was a poet whom I soon met at the get-togethers of *First Statement* and *Preview* magazines. He came down to Craig Street in Montreal, where we had set up a printing press, and sat with A.M. Klein, John Sutherland, and Irving Layton, drinking beer out of a bottle and talking of the needs of poetry. He turned to me on leaving and said he had liked some of my poetry, the sort of casual remark one does not easily forget. Later I met him at joint meetings of *Preview* and *First Statement*, and increasingly at his home as the years went by. He was entirely the poet, so far as I was concerned, but there were two Frank Scotts, or more, as everyone knew. And here the contradictions begin.

For Frank Scott, an evening of poetry might well be followed the next night by an evening with social scientists, historians, and party organizers, where poetry would be on the far side of the moon, so to speak, completely hidden from view. At those times, at home and at the university, where he was teaching law, poetry might become almost a secret activity – as it is for most of us – while the 'serious' and 'real' life goes on. I have often seen him come refreshed to poetry, as if it were something he had rather neglected, something he would much prefer to any other business, something he must now find room for at last.

A typical escapade I remember with pleasure was our group trip to Kingston on a Saturday in the early fifties. Arnold Edinborough had just brought out a new literary magazine, the *Cataraqui Review*, the sort of effort that brought warmth to the cockles of our hearts in those days. A group of about eight or ten of us had decided to go to Kingston, a distance of about 180 miles, to look up this new editor and encourage him. We piled into two automobiles and drove most of the day, stopping for coffee and lunch, laughing and talking madly all the way, and finally knocking Arnold Edinborough right off his feet by this surprise visit. He was then a professor, teaching English at Queen's. He was very modest, not aware that his little magazine was worth making so much fuss about, not sure he had any great program to announce, but I am sure he was also pleased and flattered to see us. We got home late that night, feeling we had had a great literary day. Frank Scott was certainly the leader on that expedition. But such experiences were rare.

So that, although his home was often the meeting place of poets, and he played the host for various magazines and publishing ventures – *New Provinces, Preview, Northern Review* – not all his energies went to these little magazines and books. It was mainly as master of ceremonies and as social mover that he presided over the poetry scene, not as printer, editor, or publisher of books. Patrick Anderson took care of the production of *Preview*, as John Sutherland did of *First Statement* and *Northern Review*. (The case may be somewhat different with *The McGill Fortnightly Review* and *The Canadian Mercury* in the twenties, but that was before my time; I came to know him in the days of *Preview*, and that is where I derive my impressions.) Frank Scott was rather an intellectual guide and mentor, not an active editor in these ventures. He was a divided man, perhaps more fully active in his political and social work than in his literary activity.

But now a deeper division, one of the mind, concerns us. It is that between politics - or perhaps law, with its manifold real social connections - and poetry as a reaching towards a further reality. Take the poem 'Laurentian Shield,' with its magnificent opening:

> Hidden in wonder and snow, or sudden with summer,
> This land stares at the sun in a huge silence
> Endlessly repeating something we cannot hear.

This 'something we cannot hear' promises a true poetic sounding of nature, of the meaning of the land and the earth in the north - 'inarticulate, arctic' - for which we have been waiting. We have other poems, his best, in which this is Scott's main concern. But here the poem remorselessly descends, by measured steps, to a more didactic message:

> It will choose its language
> When it has chosen its technic,
> A tongue to shape the vowels of its productivity.
> ...
> Nouns of settlement
> Slowly forming, with steel syntax,
> The long sentence of its exploitation.
>
> ... monopoly, big with machines,
> Carving its kingdoms out of the public wealth.

The ultimate promise is '... millions whose hands can turn this rock into children.' Of course, the first kind of meaning I was hoping for is (in Archibald Lampman's words) "Voices of Earth," and it belongs to the Romantic nineteenth century. We must translate it into twentieth-century terms. But the second kind of meaning, Scott's meaning, has the accent of modernism, with all its traps and delusions, and its extraordinary vitality for the present.

That is why the very defect of much of Scott's poetry, as poetry, its cocksureness, its socialism, its witty but quickly dated satire can also be the very mark of its modernity, a key to its historical value in opening new doors and windows for poetry in Canada. Even the slightest of social satires, 'Company Meeting,' strikes me now as using that political didactic reductiveness to make poetry wonderfully concrete and down-to-earth:

> The Chairman called the proxies to order at ten
> And opened proceedings with a short greeting.
> The Secretary read the minutes of the last meeting.
> The Vice-President doodled with a ball-pointed pen.

It all comes down to 'dividends' and hopes that 'the inverted pyramid could so easily overturn'; but we have had a taste of modern objectivity, the unpoetical raising its ugly head in poetry, and much will now be expected from that quarter. A pull towards the trivial and the ephemeral is one persistent characteristic of modern poetry.

In other words, F.R. Scott's political didacticism, as most critics would now admit, is at odds with his best poetry. That is part of his internal conflict. But even his politics is at odds with itself. I heard him say recently to a young audience that one danger for the modern world is that governments might take too much power unto themselves, that all power in one set of human hands might be a danger. That is a contradiction to much that we find in his poetry.

The democratic socialism he has espoused envisions a kind of rational utopia on earth, in which technology and social purpose combine to overcome the ancient ills and man will achieve a glorious future, a realization of all that had been stifled and frustrated throughout the centuries by private greed and self-seeking – in short, the dream of perfectibility that we have inherited from the Enlightenment.

And yet the poem 'Mural' is a satire on just such a technological utopia:

> Then, on the Eden air, shall come
> A gentle, low, electric hum,
> Apotheosis of the Wheel
> That cannot think and cannot feel,
> A lingering echo of the strife
> That crushed the old pre-technic life.
> Then poverty shall be a word
> Philologists alone have heard,
> The slightest want shall know its fill,
> Desire shall culminate in skill.
> The carefree lovers shall repair
> To halls of air-conditioned air
> And tune-in coloured symphonies
> To prick their elongated bliss.

Man shall arise from dialled feast
Without the slaughter of a beast;
His conscience smooth as metal plate
Shall magnify his stainless state;
His bloodless background shall be blest
With a prolonged, inventive rest.
All violence streamlined into zeal
For one colossal commonweal.

Here poverty is abolished, but alas, the Wheel that governs 'cannot think and cannot feel.' We have reached the earthly Eden promised in another poem, entitled 'Eden.' But now it is an Eden where 'conscience [is] smooth as metal plate'; that is, where man has lost his humanity, which for Scott lies in the power to choose, and to choose good. The technological utopia is 'one colossal commonweal,' a vague echo of the Co-operative Commonwealth Federation, which Scott helped to establish, but here it is not a state much to be desired.

I bring out these little contradictions to sharpen our zest for this complex poetry when seen in its totality, a poetry where many things are happening at once, and where a very humane poet presides. Political conviction with Frank Scott is not a dry intellectual choice but a deep, abiding commitment that springs from his profound moral nature, even religious nature, reaching back to the roots of childhood. You must learn to love him, also, to appreciate him, for he is a most ethical man and entirely true to himself, else he would never show such easy contradictions.

The ultimate conflict in his poetry, of course, is that between science and religion. It is common now to say that there is no quarrel between science and religion, but that is only because many people are reluctant to engage in 'mental strife.' They just do not want to pursue the issue. The current problem about teaching evolution in schools reveals that there is a problem. The scientific and the religious world-views are radically different; they demand different orientations to reality, and even different kinds of poetry. Frank Scott was caught up in this central modern problem.

There is a kind of ritual poem that he sometimes writes, very much like a prayer, made up of abstract-sounding words. 'Lesson' is one of them. It ends:

He gave into our hand
New seed for every land:
We did not understand.
These innocents Thou starvest,
O Lord, Thou soon shalt harvest.

Here the explicit invocation, 'O Lord,' reveals a profound religious feeling of an orthodox kind. But it is untypical of Scott, and quite out of place.

Yet, at the very heart of his poetry there is a priestly cast of mind; his entire career and his ethical vocation, as a political thinker and poet, suggest the priestly mission. The life is highly serious, and it is unflinching in its humanistic commitment:

> The world is my country
> The human race is my race
> The spirit of man is my God
> The future of man is my heaven.

This little poem is a rebuttal to the motto that appeared under a map of the world, showing all the British possessions in bright red, in the Quebec high school which Frank once attended:

> The Empire is My Country,
> Canada is My Home.

But clearly this is not conventional Anglicanism. I believe it owes much to his father, Canon Frederick George Scott, also a Canadian poet, but it is something new and something enlightened in a modern way. For each of us the father is an archetype, who must be accepted and recreated in some new affirmative expression, but who also must be countered and opposed by some affirmation entirely one's own.

The counter-effort for Scott is science, and with it socialism, for socialism has much in common with a scientific mentality. This dualism appears in various modern poems where biological history and the physical background of inanimate nature are presented. 'Everything is matter,' is the implication, or 'Everything is rock.' I have called such reductive poets in Canada the 'Hard-Rock Poets,' a phrase often misunderstood by students. Thus in the poem 'Old Song' we have a picture of non-living nature:

> a quiet calling
> of no mind
> out of long aeons
> when dust was blind ...

And in poems like 'Mount Royal' and 'My Amoeba Is Unaware' we have a recapitulation of geological and biological history. This is the ground, for Scott, of a new definition of man and nature, in religious terms. But it is one that is not easy to achieve.

The central imaginative device is to interpret the new scientific reality in terms of the older religious mythology. Sometimes this is done tongue-in-cheek, as when the airplane is sustained by 'the everlasting arms of science.' The phrase is in fact blasphemous, unless science is somehow a way to a revised view of religion, which I doubt that it is here. Similarly, in 'Company Meeting,' but on a lower level of poetry, secular trivia are turned on a religious reference:

> ... It would be tragic
> If this Church were found not to be built upon rock.

A more disturbing shock of this kind occurs in the well-known 'The Canadian Authors Meet':

> Shall we go round the mulberry bush, or shall
> We gather at the river, or shall we
> Appoint a Poet Laureate this fall,
> Or shall we have another cup of tea?

Here, jammed between deliberate absurdities, as just another absurdity, we find the familiar church hymn 'Shall We Gather at the River' – which Scott was clearly poking fun at in this poem. And this reminds me suddenly of a deleted stanza with which the poem concluded when it was first published in *The McGill Fortnightly Review* in April 1927.

> Far in the corner sits (though none would know it),
> The very picture of disconsolation,
> A rather lewd and most ungodly poet
> Writing these verses for his soul's salvation.

I hardly need to point out the contradiction between an 'ungodly poet' and one 'writing verses for his soul's salvation.' In dreams, Freud tells us, contradictions simply co-exist, and the same is true of poems.

However, there are more significant examples of this mock-heroic formula, most significant when it ceases to mock. In the poem 'March Field,' a spring poem, we have the closing verse:

> But no seed stirs
> In this bare prison
> Under the hollow sky.

The stone is not yet rolled away
Nor the body risen.

It is the earth itself which is equated here with Christ's body, so that the Christian myth is entirely secularized. The physical world as we know it is primary, and the Christian story is merely laid over it as a gratifying metaphor.

Apart from youthful iconoclasm, which Scott certainly passed through, there is a peculiar relevance to these ironic and high-metaphoric passages. The ultimate purpose for poetry at this time was not merely to present a strong secular version of reality, nor to present a revised version of religious orthodoxy, but to achieve a successful confrontation between the two. We know that this was T.S. Eliot's program, in his most effective early poetry; as it was also W.H. Auden's. The meeting of the high and the low, with a sardonic effect of shock, is almost a definition of modernism in poetry, following the Victorian half-century, at least as far as ideas are concerned. It was for this juxtaposition that seventeenth-century metaphysical poetry often served as the model.

Frank Scott is our first modernist, the most varied and experimental, both in exploring new poetic forms and in shaking up the ideas out of which poetry is made. His early essays, 'The Decline of Poesy' and 'The Revival of Poetry,' modernist manifestos, appeared in *The Canadian Forum* in May and June 1931. It is fascinating, therefore, to watch the effects of collision between the scientific and traditional points of view in his poetry. Note in the following two stanzas, from 'Paradise Lost,' how a high seriousness collapses into light verse as the scientific ideas are pushed to their conclusion. Indeed, a verse of very high poetry is followed by one of near bathos:

The clean aimless worlds
Spun true and blind
Unseen and undisturbed
By mind,

Till some expanding molecule
Of odd construction
Learned the original sin
Of reproduction

If this scientific picture is accepted – the 'aimless worlds,' 'blind, unseen ... by mind' – how can we take seriously the reference to original sin that appears here and at the end of the poem?

> This was the turn of the tide,
> The fall from heaven,
> The spear in the side of God,
> And time's division.

I would say that here, as in 'March Field,' the Christian mythology is used as a mere emotive metaphor, an ancient pattern imposed upon the secular and scientific reality. One must surely ask, 'What is God, here?' Or, aesthetically, 'Can these metaphors work?'

Actually, a complete reinterpretation of the Christian myth is called for. By this I mean, *not* a statement of modern reality in which the real belief implied is an orthodox Christian view of man and nature, nor a reductive satirical joke at the *expense* of Christianity, but a serious, or even religious view which emerges from the acceptance of science and fact, and which is therefore entirely modern, entirely original, a genuine raising of modern consciousness. At his best, I think this is what Scott achieves.

In the poem 'Resurrection' we have

> Christ in the darkness, dead,
> His own disaster hid.
> His hope for man, too soon
> Sealed with the outer stone.

which might make you believe that this is a transcription of accepted Christianity, the Christ of divine incarnation and redemption. Not so. For Scott, this Christ is but one example of humanistic and social enlightenment:

> All saviours ever to be
> Share this dark tragedy;
> The vision beyond reach
> Becomes the grave of each.

And the redemption, which in orthodox Christianity has an eschatological or supernatural significance, is for him merely secular and practical:

> And that of him which rose
> Is our own power to choose
> Forever, from defeat,
> Kingdoms more splendid yet.

The conclusion is entirely humanistic, on a par with the human Christ of Ernest Renan and David Strauss. It combines Christian terminology with a wholly rational and positivist doctrine:

> Play Easter to this grave
> No Christ can ever leave.
> It is one man has fallen,
> It is ourselves have risen.

One would have to call this an ethical religion, not anthropomorphic, but anthropocentric. Yet the contradiction between traditional Christianity, built into the bones of this poet, and a scientific-humanistic ethical faith is held in fine tension, although of course it is the secular and the scientific which was served by the revised Christian myth.

The conflict between science and religion is presented in a variety of ways. In the great poem 'Last Rites,' science, which is the 'known roadway,' and religion, which is the 'unknown,' are seen as reconciled and compatible positions at the moment of death:

> And straight toward me from both sides of time
> Endless the known and unknown roadways run.

In contrast to this reconciling stance, another notable poem, 'A Grain of Rice,' presents the issue differently, and in a way that points beyond this contradiction to that truly original and, for Scott, ultimate direction of religious exploration. 'Religions build walls round our love,' he says – seeing the limitations of historical creeds – 'and science / Is equal of error and truth,' which may mean that science contains as much error as it contains truth; or that, like religion, it is also a mixture of error and truth. In any case, both science and religion are here set aside. The poem goes on to state the core of a religious attitude which contains both the spirit of science and the spirit of religion:

> ... Yet always we find
> Such ordered purpose in cell and in galaxy,
> So great a glory in life-thrust and mind-range,
> Such widening frontiers to draw out our longings,
> > We grow to one world
> > Through enlargement of wonder.

The word 'wonder' will not satisfy everyone. It would not have satisfied T.S. Eliot. But we need only think of the great modern writers, in all their variety, and in their common concern with this question – D.H. Lawrence, Henry Miller, Dylan Thomas, W.H. Auden, Wallace Stevens, W.B. Yeats, T.S. Eliot, James Joyce – to realize how central, and how original, how Canadian, and moderate, this answer is.

I will conclude by noting a final complexity and contradiction in Scott's account of the meditative and mystical experience towards which all religions and metaphysical thinking tend. In a very early poem, 'Vagrant' (1928), we have a satirical picture of the meditative visionary:

> he fled beyond the outer star
> to spaces where no systems are
>
> beyond that last accepted norm
> the final vestiges of form
>
> the compass of his mind   astute
> to find a polar absolute
> patrolled a mute circumference
>
> the present seemed the only tense
>
> there was no downwards for his feet
> even his lust was obsolete

The absurdity of this seeker after the absolute is caricatured in his lack of social connection, his self-centred egotism, and his final isolation in a dismal real world very far from the absolute he is so foolish as to pursue:

> infinity became his own
> himself the sole criterion
>
> and he   the last dot in the sky
> did but accentuate an i
>
> now you may see him   virginal
> content to live in montreal.

I assume it must be the failure of such a seeker after the absolute to engage in socially responsible activity that rouses Scott's ire.

Quite contradictory to this, and much later, is a poem like 'Autumn Lake,' where the absolute – undefined, as it must be – is actually indulged in, as a momentary experience:

> I was drawn
> to that point on the far shore
> where image meets reality

one and one form one
and conflict
ends

so   calmed
I entered
into the wholeness
the still centre

And in 'Japanese Sand Garden,' the same momentary experience yields a
flash of philosophical wit, wisdom, or foolishness, take it as you will:

suddenly
horizons vanish
in this vast ocean
where the most
is made from the least
and the eternal relative
absorbs
the ephemeral absolute.

Since the relative is all we have, it is the '*eternal* relative.' The absolute,
I suppose because it is vouchsafed to humans only occasionally, and only
as a brief illumination, as in these two poems of Scott's, is the '*ephemeral*
absolute.' But of course it is ironic that the 'relative' must be honoured
by using the word 'eternal,' which never can be taken quite seriously, as
'the eternal relative,' while the absolute must be ticked off with the
word 'ephemeral' ('the ephemeral absolute') – that 'ephemeral' to which
the writer is wholly committed. As Scott has it in the poem 'Mount
Royal':

... Pay taxes now,
Elect your boys, lay out your pleasant parks,
You gill-lunged, quarrelsome ephemera!

The ephemeral, so modern, so desirable, is never quite satisfactory,
although we persist in saying that *that is all there is*!

But how beautifully these opposites come together, how beautifully
the discordant elements are reconciled, or made to live together in one
society, sometimes in a moment of wit, sometimes in laughter, sometimes in wisdom or illumination. This is the virtue of Frank Scott's
enlightened poetry, that it has brought to Canada the materials of

modern intelligence, and some of the new experimental forms that this diversity of ideas demanded. He is the Canadian poet whom I would place at the top as the clearest poetic voice of this century in Canada.

NOTE

References to F.R. Scott's poems are all to *Selected Poems* (Toronto: Oxford University Press 1966).

D.G. JONES

Private Space
and Public Space

IF IN THE lives of colonial cultures as in the lives of little ducks and chickens there is a moment of imprinting, that moment for Canada is located in the latter half of the eighteenth century. To make a point of being absurd one might locate it, especially in a discussion of F.R. Scott, in the period 1769-70. Those years saw the publication of Sir Edmund Burke's *Observations on the Present State of the Nation* and *Thoughts on the Cause of Present Discontents*, of Sir William Blackstone's *Commentaries on the Laws of England*, and of Oliver Goldsmith's pastoral elegy, *The Deserted Village*. Unlike most people, Canadians have approached a continent with a mind-set, to use a Scott phrase, defined by this moment.

When Scott looks out from the plane window in 'Flying to Fort Smith,' he sees below:

> An arena
>> Large as Europe
> Silent
>> Waiting the contest.
>
> Underground
>> In the coins of the rock
> Cities sleep like seeds.[1]

Throughout most of the longer poems of the nineteenth century, British North America is seen as a wilderness to be transformed by what E.J. Pratt called 'the civil discipline of roads.'[2] It was a vision in which the pioneer, moving across the continent, creates clearings, which become villages and towns, which become cities or nodes in the larger network of the nation, and, beyond that, of the Empire. Despite Pratt's epic *Towards the Last Spike* and Pierre Berton's more recent *The National*

44

Dream, writers since Lampman have tended to present the road-builders and the city-planners, the railway and the expressway, in an increasingly demonic light.

When Scott speaks of the land as 'waiting the contest,' it is not a contest between man and nature he envisages – the cities already sleep in the rock – but between different conceptions of society. It is a question of whether the cities are to be the result of a marriage between man and the land or of a rape, and of whether they are to be primarily centres of community or centres of power. Scott's life, in politics, in law, in poetry, has focused on this argument.

It is an argument that goes back to Goldsmith's *The Deserted Village*, which marks the decline of the traditional, small-scale community and the rise of the new mercantile society and the metropolitan mass. In effect, Canadian poetry begins when Goldsmith's namesake in Halifax borrows the pattern of *The Deserted Village* and reverses its theme. *The Rising Village* proclaims that the traditional Old World community will be reborn in the New. Goldsmith's poem, not unlike his society, has its ambiguity. It ends with a celebration of imperial England and the suggestion that British North America may yet emulate her urban splendour, wealth, and power. Later writers become more aware of the contradiction. Alexander McLachlan and Isabella Valancy Crawford explicitly inveigh against capitalist individualism and the vision of empire, whether political or commercial, as posing a threat to their vision of community. Throughout most of the century, however, the poets remain basically optimistic in their celebration of a collective project which, though vast, is also remarkably domestic. In part, the optimism of these poets is grounded in the character of the central protagonist, the pioneer, who is both axeman and husbandman, both technologist and lover. At the centre of his world we find his cabin and his garden, and more centrally still, a feminine presence.

However, even before the end of the century, it becomes evident that the pioneer-axeman has become obsolete. With the rapidly changing technology, expanding commerce and industry, the pioneer hero is, in effect, split in two. The technologist is separated from the lover, the public space is separated from the private space, and the feminine presence is no longer central but peripheral. The rising village becomes, in Archibald Lampman's vision, 'The City of the End of Things.' In reaction, the Confederation poets abandon the collective project, the cities, and cultivate an intimate and particular relation to the natural world. They do so at the price of increasing isolation from the human community. Pratt, on the other hand, continues to celebrate the collective project, and in his poetry romance veers towards epic. More normally, however, as we proceed from Roberts' 'The Tantramar Revisited' through Birney's 'November Walk near False Creek Mouth' and *The Damnation of Vancouver* to Dennis Lee's 'Civil Elegies,' we proceed from pastoral celebration to pastoral elegy. We move full circle back to Goldsmith's *The Deserted Village*.

The poetry of F.R. Scott develops at the ambiguous centre of this argument between a pastoral vision of community and the epic of power. The argument is implicit in two lines from a series called 'Impressions':

> In the former garden the looming skyscrapers crush in
> their shade the trees laden with apples.

Scott is pre-eminently a public man. He shares something of Pratt's energy and constructive purpose, his global, almost cosmic vision, his initial impulse to celebrate the collective project. Yet his conception of that project is closer to that of the earlier nineteenth-century poets than to Pratt's. It is a vision of the earth made articulate in human terms, its resources husbanded, its benefits shared by all men, in an ever-expanding, ultimately global, civic space. Temporarily dismayed by the advance of skyscrapers into orchards, he tends to remain optimistic. Like McLachlan or Lampman, but more vigorously, he opposes the forces of capitalism with those of democratic socialism. More broadly, he tends to believe that reason and imagination, science and sensibility, disciplined by will and organized in political action, can reverse the trend to empire and realize in the end that essentially pastoral vision of an organic society. This is the end anticipated in the conclusion to 'Eden':

> As the Flaming Sword receded
> Eve walked a little ahead.
> 'If we keep on using this knowledge
> I think we'll be back,' she said.

Not surprisingly, Scott's evolutionary optimism is not constant; nor is his own stance free from ambiguity.

The bias of the public F.R. Scott, his emphasis on the collective project, is so great it hardly leaves room for the private man, or the artist. In the title poem of Scott's first book, *Overture*, the speaker contemplates a lamplit room where his companion plays a Mozart sonata, the 'ten careful operatives' of the pianist constructing 'harmonies as sharp as stars.' But as the speaker turns from private to public space, he rejects those harmonies and his personal delight. In a world increasingly characterized by decaying systems, warring concepts, the 'overtures of an era being born,' Mozart's music becomes merely 'A pretty octave played before a window / Beyond whose curtain grows a world crescendo.'

More seriously, Scott's pioneering enthusiasm with regard to the collective adventure has its potentially sinister aspect inherited from the nineteenth-century myth of progress, the romance of science and technology. It is that impulse that drives the Tennysonian Ulysses ever outward, beyond the Pillars of Hercules and the point of no return. Homer and Joyce insist on the *nostos*, the return to a domestic centre, whether it is Penelope's bed carved out of the living tree or merely Molly's brass bed from Gibraltar. It is very much an element of that liberal technological culture which, even more than capitalism, George Grant in *Technology and Empire* and Dennis Lee in *Civil Elegies* regard as the enemy of any humane, organic society. Even if it does not aim at empire it requires it. To feed its dream, as to fuel some Space Odyssey 2001, it would exhaust rather than husband the earth. As seductive as its opposite, the Siren's song, it is an element in Scott's vision which he must also resist.

Much of Scott's best poetry develops out of the tension between two voices and two movements, that of the public man caught up in the centrifugal movement of the collective enterprise and that of the private man who insists on a centripetal movement back to an intimate, domestic space, the space of Eros and of death. By and large, Scott maintains a balance by means of his ironic lucidity. Three poems, 'Laurentian Shield,' 'A Grain of Rice,' and 'Trans Canada,' illustrate the progressively expansive movement in Scott's vision and his attempt to retain a balance between public and private, empire and the pastoral vision.

Except that it looks north rather than west, 'Laurentian Shield' recapitulates in miniature the nineteenth-century long poem: its pioneering theme, its basic figure whereby the land becomes articulate in a material syntax which will yet be a civil sentence in the pastoral mode.

> Hidden in wonder and snow, or sudden with summer,
> This land stares at the sun in a huge silence
> Endlessly repeating something we cannot hear.

Though it appears mute, empty as paper, the land has its own identity. It is not merely raw material to be exploited, though Scott's diction allows for that possibility; its own character should dictate the manner of its development.

> This waiting is wanting.
> It will choose its language

47

When it has chosen its technic,
A tongue to shape the vowels of its productivity.

A language of flesh and of roses.

The isolated, italicized last line (taken, I gather, from Spender) forcibly tilts the balance in favour of the pastoral. Yet the more technical, distinctly metonymical, and familiar figures of grammar and pioneer building return with ominous overtones:

Now there are pre-words,
Cabin syllables,
Nouns of settlement
Slowly forming, with steel syntax,
The long sentence of its exploitation.

The poem acknowledges the facts of Canadian history to date. Sketched in four lines, it is a history of exploitation by individual and corporate capitalism. But the future, we are told, promises a more democratic, socialist development, the developers no longer anonymous particles but part of a community. Now, the drone of the plane 'Fills all the emptiness with neighbourhood / And links our future over the vanished pole.'

The last verse emphasizes that it involves a grass roots movement, a 'deeper note,' that springs from the 'mines, / The scattered camps and mills.' While the ambiguity of any such development is acknowledged in the combined military and domestic overtones of the word 'occupation,' the poem shifts back from mechanical to more distinctly organic metaphors. What is now making itself heard is 'a language of life.'

And what will be written in the full culture of occupation
Will come, presently, tomorrow,
From millions whose hands can turn this rock into children.

'A Grain of Rice' makes explicit what the phrase 'the vanished pole' implied, that the collective enterprise is no longer national but global. It also emphasizes that it is domestic, not imperial. Man and his environment form one community, what Gary Snyder calls 'earth house hold.'[3] Survival requires an ecological imagination, an intimate knowledge of its daily moods and domestic economy. The speaker is in Asia. His awareness of the importance of the local rice crop precipitates a more general meditation.

Such majestic rhythms, such tiny disturbances.
The rain of the monsoon falls, an inescapable treasure,
Hundreds of millions live
Only because of the certainty of this season,
    The turn of the wind.

The frame of our human house rests on the motion
Of earth and of moon, the rise of continents,
Invasion of deserts, erosion of hills,
    The capping of ice.

The precarious balance of this household is threatened by internal differences, national and ideological conflicts, the struggle for power. Yet it is a measure of Scott's evolutionary optimism that the poem implies their inevitable defeat – the global organic society will emerge as inevitably as 'a great Asian moth, radiant, fragile,' emerges from its cocoon, 'incapable of not being born.'

With 'Trans Canada' the expanding frontier widens to become not merely global but galactic. And here the tension between public and private space, between technological adventure and human community, is stretched to the critical point. The opening lines are both triumphant and a little ominous. As the plane leaps into a wider prairie, the speaker, playing on the Indian name for Regina, notes that the city is dropped behind 'like a pile of bones.' He recovers immediately, defining the enterprise in more vital terms.

Sky tumbled upon us in waterfalls,
But we were smarter than a Skeena salmon
And shot our silver body over the lip of air
To rest in a pool of space
On the top storey of our adventure.

Neither west nor north, the collective enterprise enters a new space characterized by 'A solar peace / And a six-way choice.' The roads have changed as well.

The plane, our planet,
Travels on roads that are not seen or laid
But sound in instruments on pilots' ears,
While underneath
The sure wings
Are the everlasting arms of science.

Here the poem turns: wit and confidence falter. With their rhetoric and dubious appeal to a religious vision, the last lines are the least sure element in the text. (Science, as 'A Grain of Rice' tells us, is no saviour but the 'equal of error and truth.') The two lines that follow sound less like Francis Bacon than Ecclesiastes.

> Man, the lofty worm, tunnels his latest clay,
> And bores his new career.

The public voice attempts a recovery, insisting that 'This frontier, too, is ours,' that 'This everywhere whose life can only be led / At the pace of a rocket / Is common to man and man.' Nations are 'I lands,' individual voices within this larger space, whose exclusive claims to sovereignty invite Donne's retort that 'No man is an island entire of itself.' Yet, in the vacuum of outer space, in this purely secular everywhere, even Donne might be undone; his words cease to reverberate. The private man registers the fact, noting at nightfall that the stars 'seem farther from our nearer grasp.' In the end, as Elizabeth Brewster has pointed out, the collective 'we' disappears, displaced by the first-person singular.[4]

> I have sat by night beside a cold lake
> And touched things smoother than moonlight on still water,
> But the moon on this cloud sea is not human,
> And here is no shore, no intimacy,
> Only the start of space, the road to suns.

There are limits to the mere articulation of space. Without intimacy, the adventure of Man leaves us untouched.

The compensating centripetal movement may itself become so extreme as to reverse the normal perspective of Scott's poetry. Some twenty years after *Overture*, Scott introduces a volume of selected poems with 'Lakeshore,' which would, in effect, annihilate the whole laboriously articulated civil space in one apocalyptic gesture.

The heavens, the speaker discovers, are below, not above. Here stones float 'upon their broken sky,' and fish enjoy all the advantages of the traveller in 'Trans Canada' without the benefit of an alienating technology; moving at something less than the pace of a rocket, they too have 'doorways open everywhere.' And here the roads lead to orchards, pastoral forests. They draw the naked swimmers home, downwards and inwards, as to the original garden, 'their pre-historic womb,' each stroked 'by the fingertips of love.' Though erotic, it is also 'too virginal for speech,' an ultimate intimacy and privacy.

'Lakeshore' reverses the symbolism normally associated with evolutionary optimism. Emerging from the sea, man has merely risen to 'the prison of our ground,' becoming more isolated from the source of his erotic vitality. Unlike Freud, the speaker sees the rational, willed, laboriously maintained civil order as not only repressive but wrong-headed. It creates an abstraction, a world, to borrow a phrase from Marcuse, of one-dimensional man.

> This is our talent, to have grown
> Upright in posture, false-erect,
> A landed gentry, circumspect,
> Tied to a horizontal soil
> The floor and ceiling of the soul;
> Striving, with cold and fishy care
> To make an ocean of the air.

It is ironic that the only fishy thing about us is our gentility, our circumspection, our caution, calculation, and puritanical reserve. However general, the passage has a nice application to Canadian poetry and culture with its overwhelming emphasis (as Northrop Frye and Margaret Atwood have emphasized)[5] on the horizontal, spatial, and metonymical – on maps and survey lines, roads and railway lines, communication lines and corporate lines and fine lines of all sorts – legal, social, moral. Notoriously we do nothing rash, whether in our banks or our churches. 'Lakeshore' parallels or anticipates various poems, by P.K. Page, Irving Layton, Margaret Avison, and Atwood, poems in which the ordered public space is presented as arbitrary, impersonal, demonic, the world of Atwood's insane pioneer which is finally invaded by the green whale, swept away in the sea of organic life. Even so, the speaker in Scott's poem envisions Flatland being washed away as effectively as if it had been Sodom and Gomorrah.

> Sometimes, upon a crowded street,
> I feel the sudden rain come down
> And in the old, magnetic sound
> I hear the opening of a gate
> That loosens all the seven seas.
> Watching the whole creation drown
> I muse, alone, on Ararat.

So much for empire and even the discipline of roads. The voice of the private man and, one may suggest, the poet takes a measure of revenge on that of the lawyer, politician, public man. For 'Lakeshore' is surely one of Scott's best poems, a nice combination of wit and feeling, clarity and complexity, the incidental and the archetypal, convincing throughout.

Scott, as Milton Wilson and Northrop Frye have termed him, must be one of our most 'urbane' poets. Yet there is a real identification with the purely natural world. In 'Mount Royal,' it is the fossil remains of the Champlain Sea under the urban pavement that serve as a touchstone of reality; the mountain marks time in geological units, within which our urban politics and history become merely the tale of 'quarrelsome ephemera.' It is especially an identification with the elemental landscape of the Shield and with the Mackenzie, a river that is primitive, dangerous, self-cleansing, which moves 'purposefully / to a cold sea':

> A river so Canadian
>   it turns its back
>   on America.

It gives the lie to the extreme optimism of a liberal technological society, that vision of progress and of man's ever-expanding empire over nature.

Scott is too much a maker, of poems, of laws, of a civic order, to rest in the extreme pessimism of 'Lakeshore.' The final note in 'Mackenzie River' is struck by 'the single plume of smoke' that in the context is 'a scroll of history.' It is Scott's clear recognition of the fragility and integrity of earth, of the ecological interdependence of all things, of limits and of entropy, that tempers the expansive optimism of other poems and gives to his overall vision of the collective project its weight and conviction. It requires that any satisfactory articulation of nature within a civil space must be pastoral, not imperial, a husbanding rather than an exploitation of the earth. Even the poet can write: 'It is the farmer sows our crops of words.'

The emphasis in Scott's poetry shifts from the centrifugal to the centripetal, towards a greater recognition of the particular and the private. Ultimately, it is the individual who is the embodiment of all creativity, and morality. In his *Selected Poems* (1966), Scott chooses to end with 'Caring,' a poem which makes the domestic space of love and death, of intimate relationships, once more the 'centre of all we mourn and bless.'

> Caring is loving, motionless,
> An interval of more and less
> Between the stress and the distress.

> After the present falls the past,
> After the festival, the fast,
> Always the deepest is the last.

It leads to the explicit recognition that

> This is the circle we must trace,
> Not spiralled outward, but a space
> Returning to its starting place.

Generally, it is a question of balance. In a world of increasing extremes, Scott is an *équilibriste*. 'Desire first, then structure / Complete the balanced picture,' he remarks in 'Dialogue.' He remains, one might suggest, an eighteenth-century man. As he says in 'Poem for Living,' 'Free the old / from its mould / yet be beholden / to the proven.' He is becoming, one might argue, a good Taoist. Looking at a Japanese sand garden, he concludes: 'the eternal relative / absorbs / the ephemeral absolute.' He is, one must insist, a poet. The critic Tzvetan Todorov makes the point that while language structures reality in terms of *this* and *the contrary*, literature refuses to accept such division as absolute. 'It is, within language, that which destroys the metaphysics inherent in all language.'[6]

Ultimately, the poet is of a piece with the political man. A poem demands liberty, it also requires restraint, and each poem is a special case. Scott is a libertarian, but I suspect he would agree with Edmund Burke, who writes:

The extreme of liberty (which is its abstract perfection, but its real fault) obtains nowhere, nor ought to obtain anywhere; because extremes, as we all know, in every point which relates to either our duties or satisfactions in life, are destructive to both virtue and enjoyment. Liberty too must be limited in order to be possessed.[7]

Burke continues that one can never know beforehand just what degree of restraint will be appropriate but that wise council will seek to arrive at the minimum required. For liberty 'is not only a private blessing of the first order, but the vital spring and energy of the state itself, which has just so much life and vigor as there is liberty in it.' What is said of the state could be said of the poem – or of the dance. In the title poem of a volume published in the seventies, Scott tells us that when he went dancing as a younger man he always led, and the dance was best when the lady was least herself. Now, however, the lady dances on her own,

D.G. Jones

with the happy result that Scott no longer dances with himself. As he says, 'We are two / not one / the dance / is one.'

NOTES

1 References to F.R. Scott's poems are all to *Selected Poems* (Toronto: Oxford University Press 1966) except for the following: 'Impressions,' 'Poem for Living,' and 'Dancing,' in *The Dance is One* (Toronto 1973).
2 E.J. Pratt, 'Towards the Last Spike,' *Collected Poems*, 2nd ed., edited and with an introduction by Northrop Frye (Toronto 1962) 375
3 Gary Snyder, *Earth House Hold* (New York 1969)
4 Elizabeth Brewster, 'The I of the Observer: The Poetry of F.R. Scott,' *Canadian Literature* 79 (Winter 1978) 23-30
5 Margaret Atwood, *Survival* (Toronto 1972); Northrop Frye, 'Conclusion,' *Literary History of Canada*, III, 2nd ed. (Toronto 1976)
6 Tzvetan Todorov, *The Fantastic*, tr. Richard Howard (Ithaca, NY 1975) 167
7 Edmund Burke, 'A Letter to John Farr and John Harris, Esqrs., Sheriffs of the City of Bristol, on the Affairs of America,' *Enlightened England*, ed. Wylie Sypher (New York 1947) 1093

F.W. WATT

The Poetry of Social Protest

WHILE FRANK SCOTT was a young man, still in his twenties, he claimed to feel a certain disdain for the kind of exalted social status which, in fact, he himself has now achieved. 'Let the poet beware,' he wrote, 'when all men praise him.' Scott even then left the door open for a degree of public celebration – but only at an appropriate stage in a poet's life: 'I am quite certain that it is bad for him to be too respectable and too revered, at any rate until he is over sixty.'[1] Now that Scott is some twenty years past that permissible age, I suspect he would still rather be judged personally by the standards of his brash, younger self. In any case, he probably could not have imagined, then, what it was really like to be a fifty- or a sixty-year-old smiling public man – even one who, unlike W.B. Yeats, decided *not* to accept a place in his country's Senate.

There is always a degree of ambivalence in the relation of an artist, particularly that most private of artists, a poet, and the society in which he or she works. Scott himself was well aware of the tug towards social involvement that must be a part (however minimal) of any creative motivation, but which especially marked his own nature. As he said in 1965, while reminiscing with old friends and colleagues about the gregariousness which has characterized his whole life:

The question I have often asked myself is, can the individual of creative mind, just being by himself, develop fully, without some such experience as meeting with others? As far as I am concerned, when I was left alone I don't think I moved forward very much. It was only when I ran into other groups of similar minded people that things happened. My first case, of course, was the *McGill Fortnightly Review.* I ran into A.J.M. Smith and met a whole set of new ideas, and that was to me the first, great, tremendous experience. It seems to me I shifted about ten or fifteen points on the compass from an old attitude to a new one.

Then I had another similar type of group experience, and that was meeting the people who founded the League for Social Reconstruction, and all the new ideas about Canada and socialism and the world in that sense. Then another group of people founding the C.C.F. It was always a group, but live minds and marvellous people, and that carried me mostly through the 1930s. And then came *Preview*, which was poetry again, and another group, in a different context. I didn't have quite the same tremendous sense of the whole world opening afresh, and so many new ideas coming in, but nevertheless, it had that great spirit of creative minds thinking about themselves and the world and the movements around them, and attaching themselves to them. But it was a group experience and in some respects I somehow wish I had been able to act more on my own, because I have always been working in groups and working in joint operations, and editing group magazines and writing books for which I was only one of the many editors. There is too much of this mixing in with the others. On the other hand I sort of depend on it. If I don't have them around, I don't think I would go very well on my own. My car must be full.[2]

It could hardly be a surprise if a man so aware of communal values and so strongly, though ambivalently, motivated by 'group experience' – a man so socially oriented – should spend a good deal of his poetic energies writing about society, even in the writing of 'satire, invective, and disrespectful verse,' to use the subtitle of one of those books of which Scott was 'joint' editor (*The Blasted Pine*). But it would not be surprising either if he should sometimes exhibit intense feelings about privacy and solitude and their terrible fascination, if he should sometimes listen to the voice that cries, 'there is too much of this mixing in with the others.'

The necessity for withdrawal and isolation was evidently every bit as real for Scott as the necessity for social involvement, and indeed was at the core of his first compulsion to write poetry. It was Canadian nature, he tells us, not Canadian society, that inspired him when he arrived back in Canada from Oxford in the 1920s:

I was shocked by the ugliness of the cities and buildings by comparison with those that I had recently lived in, and there seemed so little that one wished to praise or draw inspiration from in our social environment or past history. But the Laurentian country was wonderful, open, empty, vast, and speaking a kind of eternal language in its mountains, rivers and lakes. I knew that these were the oldest mountains in the world, and that their rounded valleys and peaks were the result of long submersion under continents of ice. Geologic time made ancient civilizations seem but yesterday's picnic. This caught my imagination and I tried to express some of this feeling in what I call my Laurentian poems. It was a form of 'internalization of the wilderness,' and it sufficed me at first for poetic inspiration.

Scott goes on to say that it was only after 'the great financial crash of 1929, the ensuing depression and the emergence of revolutionary and reform political movements,' which led him to become 'more involved' in human society, that he turned to the writing of satire.[3]

From that time on the social and political realities of the day began to enter his poetry, and indeed that of other Canadian poets, as never before. Scott was a realist, and for all his awareness of the 'ugliness' of cities he intended to write about modern civilization realistically, where it was lived, in the streets, the railway stations, restaurants, courts, legislatures, board rooms, cocktail parties, beverage rooms, bars, drugstores, universities, schoolrooms, churches, airports, stores, factories, prisons and hospitals – in short, about the city life he knew most of his days, as well as the life of nature to which he also happily withdrew when he had the chance, and which first 'sufficed' him, as he said, 'for poetic inspiration.'

I have quoted passages of self-analysis by Scott at some length because I think that here, with his considerable self-awareness, he brings us close to a central paradox in his work as a poet, a paradox which has caught the attention of readers in differing ways, and sometimes tested the range of their responsiveness. The poet who is drawn or driven to the empty, inhuman, everlasting immensities of the northern wilderness is also the poet who is nourished by 'group experience' and preoccupied by the spectacle of society's abundant and challenging, but trivial and transitory, chaotic and self-destructive life. The poet of the Laurentian vision is also the poet of the socialist vision.

The Laurentian vision, even in the expanded sense in which I want to use the phrase, is the easier to understand, perhaps, though its ultimate reach remains mysterious. The primeval purity and awesome beauty of the wilderness of northern North America are liberating, exhilarating to contemplate. Compared with the confused, often painful babble of human voices, what more seductive than the austere music of the north Scott catches in some of his most familiar lines:

> ... in the deep
> Laurentian river
> an elemental song
> for ever
>
> a quiet calling
> of no mind

out of long aeons
when dust was blind
and ice hid sound

only a moving
with no note
granite lips
a stone throat   'Old Song'

To cast oneself to brood in this vast Canadian emptiness is like travelling into outer space, or like entering the ancient paradisal or heavenly
universe of pure matter, that existed before there ever was an 'inner'
space, before conscious human life emerged: 'The clean aimless worlds /
Spun true and blind / Unseen and undisturbed / By mind ...,' as Scott
describes them in his version of *Paradise Lost*. How often he is imagina-
tively ready to take that flight 'beyond the outer star / to spaces where
no systems are' ('Vagrant'), to 'take off quietly into space' ('A Hill for
Leopardi'), to travel where there is 'no shore, no intimacy, / Only the
start of space, the road to suns' ('Trans Canada'), to climb to an Olympian height from which to look away from, or down upon, the fallen
human world. Perhaps I should say Araratian height, remembering the
mountain peak on which Noah's ark landed, and the ending of the
poem 'Lakeshore,' in which the poet imagines himself in solitary contemplation of a terrible and yet wonderfully emancipating spectacle, the
biblical flood: 'Watching the whole creation drown / I muse, alone, on
Ararat.'

The Laurentian vision is also, however paradoxically, a source of comfort and courage in face of more specifically identifiable occasions for
withdrawal from human society, personal deprivations, loneliness, grief,
especially the experience of the loss of love:

Always I shall remember you, as my car moved
Away from the station and left you alone by the gate
Utterly and forever frozen in time and solitude
Like a tree on the north shore of Lake Superior.
                                        'Departure'

What better way for lovers to try to anaesthetize the pain of dying love
than to set it, like that, against a background of even greater, more universal desolation, to 'Stand still awhile ... and hear / How from old hills
the wind / Blows cold ...' ('Autumnal').

The speaker in 'A Hill for Leopardi,' who could be the solitary poet at
his work, takes daily flight away from terrestrial society to a still rarer

and lonelier elevation where 'the world becomes worlds, suns pass, distance / Curves into light, time bends ... ' But soon 'the thrust dies' and 'Another journey ends where it began / Shipwrecked on ground we tread a little while.' The return to the ordinary world, to society, to human love, to realism is not so much a matter of choice as of necessity. We are humans, committed in whatever degree to 'mixing in with the others,' not birds, trees, or rivers; flesh and blood, not gods or heavenly bodies. It is not fear of flying that requires the return. Scott's poetry, however high and far it travels, never takes that further step, short as it might seem, beyond awe to terror in face of inhuman cosmic nature, the abyss of infinity and eternity. But the intense life-long need for 'others' that so obviously fills his actions and his writings may be sufficient evidence in itself that he knew and feared that fear. Certainly when terror does threaten to invade his poetry, as it does in 'Passer-By,' the form it takes is the spectacle of the 'irrevocable' temporal flowing away of human companionship, 'receding footsteps,' 'endless departure,' 'the years passing' not necessarily any sense of specific personal loss, but the 'pure form of going into the distance.' And significantly the only anodyne this poem offers is the matching spectacle of what Scott might have called (I suppose) the 'pure form of coming near':

> ... always the footsteps recede, the stone crumbles,
> The tide flows out and does not return,
> And from this terror we find no safety in flight
> But only in faces turned to the flood of arrival.

One strength of Scott's poetry is the force with which he presents his Laurentian vision in all its chilling, inhuman reality, without sentimental or ideological alleviation, most explicitly in the familiar lines of 'Surfaces':

> This rock-bound river, ever flowing
> Obedient to the ineluctable laws,
> Brings a reminder from the barren north
> Of the eternal lifeless processes.
> There is an argument that will prevail
> In this calm stretch of current, slowly drawn
> Towards its final equilibrium.

The voice that comes down from the Laurentian Shield, or the Araratian heights, of this poem's vision sounds a sardonic challenge for the ears of the diminished mortal (possibly the speaker's own terrestrial self) who hesitates at the river bank:

> Come, flaunt the brief prerogative of life,
> Dip your small civilized foot in this cold water
> And ripple, for a moment, the smooth surface of time.

Once having gazed from high above at the 'majestic rhythms' of the cosmos, as the poem 'A Grain of Rice' terms them, how can we take seriously the comings and goings, the rise and fall, the 'tiny disturbances' of human civilization? 'Mount Royal' itself, that seems to stand as a sturdy landmark for the politicians of Montreal to chart their movements by, is caught up in the vast geological flux of a rhythm that dwarfs the merely human priorities, timetables, and petty wranglings of urban life:

> ... Pay taxes now,
> Elect your boys, lay out your pleasant parks,
> You gill-lunged, quarrelsome ephemera!
> The tension tightens yearly, underneath,
> A folding continent shifts silently
> And oceans wait their turn for ice or streets.

The poetry of social engagement is hardly possible from so far away in the chilling wilderness of the Laurentians, or so high up the empty slopes of Ararat. Where does the socialist vision belong in Scott's imaginative world, and how is it reconciled with the Laurentian vision?

The most direct way to an answer may be through a work to which Scott gave a position of prominence in his *Selected Poems*, a poem not primarily about society at all, but about an individual ('individuality / lies beneath collectivity,' Scott says in 'My Amoeba Is Unaware') – an individual at the crucial moment of death. From the Laurentian vantage point, dying is an unimportant phase in an endless cycle, a reluctant acknowledgement of the individual's place in the 'eternal lifeless processes,' a yielding of human illusions in face of nature's irrefutable final argument. But in the poem 'Last Rites' a human scene, the hospital deathbed, becomes the chief focus of reality. A dying old man is watched over by Nurse and by Priest. Each has a role to play: the latter with his symbols and rituals of faith which try to answer the 'perpetual, unanswerable why,' the former with her scientific skills stubbornly pushing back the boundaries of death – 'How far? She does not ask.' Priest must worship at the altars of the infinite mystery; Nurse must comfort and sustain the diseased and dying with the ever-growing temporal powers of human knowledge. And the brooding poet-watcher at the old man's bedside exists at the intersection of the known and the unknown, recognizing both the 'rites' of human limitation and the 'rightness' of human knowledge, surrounded by that 'holy spirit' which the compassionate ministry of Nurse and Priest have brought into the death-room. In this scene – in this father, son, and holy spirit – Scott wants us to see (perhaps) the only kind of holy trinity that has reality for him:

> And I who watch this rightness and these rites,
> I see my father in the dying man,
> I am his son who dwells upon the earth,
> There is a holy spirit in this room,
> And straight toward me from both sides of time
> Endless the known and unknown roadways run.

Here, I think, at this point of intersection, the Laurentian vision and the socialist vision meet. Life is a journey, and the traveller has directions and aims but not a final destination. The wise man gives neither Nurse nor Priest total jurisdiction over his passage, but recognizes the necessity of both. They must share, since in his time he must travel both the 'known and unknown roadways,' and these are 'endless.'

Although his poetry is rich in Christian allusion, it is clear that for Scott the Christian message of the priest is a human moral fable, teaching mortals the courage to rise again from the graves of their defeats: 'It is one man has fallen, / It is ourselves have risen,' Scott writes in 'Resurrection.' No divine redemptive sacrifice is necessary, or at any rate possible, to rescue man from his fallen condition. As 'Resurrection' says:

> All saviours ever to be
> Share this dark tragedy;
> The vision beyond reach
> Becomes the grave of each.

If Paradise is to be regained, it will be through the exercise of human reason; or so Eve argues, to end Scott's poem 'Eden': 'If we keep on using this knowledge / I think we'll be back,' she said. Eve may hope, but Scott's highway is not marked by biblical absolutes: there is no paradise either behind or ahead, and, despite Scott's strong critical awareness of the failures of civilization through history, evidently no dark force of evil at work which is incomprehensible to human reason and which calls for miracles. Nurse will never cure the disease of humanity, but neither will Scott abandon his faith in the value of her rational and compassionate ministry.

It is the sense that the human condition is essentially one of always travelling but never arriving that makes Scott's poetry of social conscience 'satiric' rather than 'revolutionary': 'quite a different thing,' as

Scott says, 'though somewhat allied.' Satire is the 'holding up of the existing society against standards one was formulating in one's mind for a more perfect society.' On the other hand, Scott seems to imply, revolutionary poetry attempts not merely to attack the shortcomings of 'existing society' discovered by this comparison, but also to imagine and to advocate the 'perfect society.'[4] But when Scott turns his imagination towards the future, the end of the road, the goal of a social ideal on earth, he reverts to satire once again. And he produces, in the poem 'Mural' ('as near as ... [he] can get to a credible Utopia,' according to Scott)[5] a mocking vision of 'one colossal commonwealth,' a place where 'poverty shall be a word / Philologists alone have heard,' which is closer to the negative Utopias of Huxley and Orwell than to any actual world we might choose to live in.

The message this active socialist sends out in his poem 'To Certain Friends,' those conscience-stricken, thoughtful, liberal-minded, indecisive men of goodwill who are 'now standing about me, bemused, / Eyeing me dubiously as I pursue my course,' is not one of final social goals and destinations to be achieved. It is of the need for local decisions and actions that will define and establish a direction for themselves in an inconclusive and everlasting journey.

> Above all they fear the positive formation of opinion,
> The essential choice that acts as a mental compass,
> The clear perception of the road to the receding horizon.

Obviously for Scott the travelling is intensely real, whether it is earthbound on the road to the socialist ideal or worming outwards and upwards through man's latest clay, the stratosphere, on the road to suns. But in neither case is it humanly possible to complete that journey.

When Scott addresses himself to the familiar fallen world of social man, he has a range of stations, on that imaginative journey, to choose to view it from: the lonely top of Ararat, the intimate personal plains of compassionate involvement, and all the distances, near and far, in between. The voice we hear in the poetry of social reference is varied, though it is often a somewhat Olympian, or Araratian, voice: hard, clear, rational – sunny but with a touch of cosmic chill; edged with lightning-sharp irony or weighted with thundering sarcasm. 'The efficiency of the capitalist system,' this voice will pronounce, 'is rightly admired by important people' ('Efficiency: 1935'). Or it will invite us to

> Come and see the vast natural wealth of this mine.
> In the short space of ten years,

It has produced six American millionaires,
And two thousand pauperised Canadian families.
                                    'Natural Resources' in 'Social Notes'

Or from its lofty perch it can draw our attention to the educational
value of experiences like the Great Depression, which might, from the
lowly human perspective, seem merely distressing:

General Election, 1935

There is nothing like hard times
For teaching people to think.
By a decisive vote
After discussing all the issues
They have turned out the Conservatives
And put back the Liberals.   'Social Notes'

Not all readers, even those in third parties, will find this voice entirely
sympathetic; it has its godlike, arrogant tones, it allows little room for
subtle resonances, differing judgments, or ambivalent feelings. Readers
may feel that it sometimes goes beyond (or falls short of) making us *see*,
and is pressing us to *do*, as it were, from above.

There are several ways in which Scott the social poet comes down
from the heights and draws closer to the plane of ordinary mortals. In
'Dedication' the speaker takes up his place with his fellow man, in the
solidarity of the shared socialist cause. Since poetry cannot compete with
dogma or ideological debate, even a poem like this that springs from the
controversies about revolutionary Marxism and Christian socialism and
all the myriad shades of left-wing belief in between that filled the 1930s,
it may come as close as we can get to providing a sufficient definition of
'socialism' in the context of Scott's verse:

From those condemned to labour
For profit of another
We take our new endeavour.

For sect and class and pattern
Through whom the strata harden
We sharpen now the weapon.

Till power is brought to pooling
And outcasts share in ruling
There will not be an ending
Nor any peace for spending.

But the tone of universalized, passionate, socialist commitment is only one of many more human notes, some closer to the comic than the fervent. What we hear in the comic squib, itself a kind of commercial jingle, called 'Command of the Air,' is an exasperated daily radio listener, like ourselves, suddenly realizing (and making us realize) that the absurdities of commercialized radio, and the society that perpetrates and tolerates it, are every bit as surreal as anything in the paintings of Salvador Dali:

> This sweet music that I hear,
> Is it Soap, or is it Beer?
> Do I owe the string quartet
> To Foulness of the Breath, or Sweat?
> When the Chopin Prelude comes
> Will it help Massage the Gums?
> And will Serkin play encores
> Mixing Bach and Baseball Scores?
> Damn! They've cut the Brahms finale!
> Your world's my world, Mr. Dali!

Verses like these contain no divine protestations or imperatives, and leave entirely up to us what we choose to do about the kind of society that would produce such cultural enormities. When they work, we see and laugh before we are called upon to judge.

The same capacity to make us see (or in this case, 'hear' would be better), and the same kind of intimate involvement – in fact, identification – between the poet and his subject, and therefore between the poet and the reader, charges the serious, much darker poem called 'Prison' with its painful immediacy, its sense of personal responsibility, its cry of guilt and shame:

> In Fullum Street gaol
> In the nineteen hundred and fiftieth year of the Christian
>   era
> Insane women, locked in filthy cells,
> Scream and howl unattended.
> (See the *Montreal Herald* for February the second.)
> At the Ritz the Bach Partita
> Is the more exquisite because it can come
> Out of such a world.
> I too scream in my cell,
> For my own inattention
> Built their gaol, my prison,
> In the far reaches of the inner mind.

In much of the poetry of social engagement the voice we hear is a more public voice, without this intimate personal urgency, but one which nevertheless invites the reader to stand and perceive from the same plane as the poet. Sometimes the conclusion is not the catharsis of laughter or of clear and simple protest, but astonished, half-baffled observation, ironic recognition of the contradictory ways of the world. Sometimes there is far more to be seen than can be readily explained. In 'Picture in *Life*,' there is an irony that cuts in two or three directions. The photograph in *Life* magazine of the American schoolgirl and her hunting trophies from an African safari epitomizes the curious modern mixture of innocence and casual destructive power that characterizes American civilization for some twentieth-century observers. At the same time, the stature of the great European mythmaking empire-builders, with their historical mission combining heroic conquest, Christian evangelism, and commercial exploitation, is mockingly undercut by the picture of the 'girl-child' who could so easily do a 'man's job.' And behind the social contradictions of waning and waxing imperialisms that make up the foreground of the 'Picture in *Life*' are the profound mysteries of nature, the dark realities of Africa and the 'fabulous Nile,' which underlie both the old, fading myths and the advancing destructive forces of twentieth-century civilization:

Here is a child, a small American girl-child, age fourteen,
Who has shot a lion. In Africa.
Far from her home in Morriston, New Jersey.
And she has shot a gnu, a wart-hog, and an elephant.
How shall we deal with her? Sir John Myrtle-Jenkinson
Shot lions in Africa in the days of the British Raj,
But he was building an Empire. It was a man's job,
And he was a man, firm and philistine,
The Rule of Law in the deepest jungle,
And a black tie in a crisis.
Even the lions were proud
To pose with him for the *Illustrated London News*.
His was no idle slaughter, but the planting of the Flag,
The erection of the Cross, and the sale of cotton pants.
But this slip of a girl was on holiday from school.
She had not yet entered grade ten.
She killed innocently, unconsciously, as a tourist
Might stop to buy a postcard of Notre Dame.
She does not understand her summer trip
Dries up the sources of the fabulous Nile
And shoots great holes through all the myths of Europe.

65

Scott does not allow us to forget the power of the unknown in the encounter between man and nature. As 'A Grain of Rice' says, the millions of Asia live, and die, by the 'certainty' of the monsoon season, by the 'turn of the wind,' and for all of us

> The frame of our human house rests on the motion
> Of earth and of moon, the rise of continents,
> Invasion of deserts, erosion of hills,
> > The capping of ice.

Again the imagination is pulled in opposite directions, along the known roadways of social man and out over the 'widening frontiers' of the unknown. At moments in his poetry Scott seems simply to alternate between the two directions, the 'downward' look and the 'heavenward gaze.' 'Reminders,' the short poem from which this way of phrasing the dichotomy is taken, is about that very fluctuation between earthly and heavenly perspectives; between social conscience and aesthetic delight; moral compassion and spiritual liberation:

> Some things surface
> Suddenly, without colour –
> The old shoe on the snow-pile,
> The broken toy in the trash-can,
> The bent figure, alone, on the park bench –
> Forcing us to look downward
> Against the 'uplift of art,'
> To tear ourselves free
> From the inflation of greatness,
> To face the immediacy
> Unfocussed in the heavenward gaze.

Although, as we have seen, Scott can write powerfully out of either way of seeing, the Laurentian or the socialist, the eyes of Priest or Nurse, his most rich and durable poems rise out of the most intense fusion of the two visions: when the breathtaking immensities of the non-human universe loom behind the short urgent movements of earthbound men and women. Scott can be both socialist and spiritual astronaut in his poetry when he sees social life and the life of nature as part of the same endless journey, the roads stretching from the finite to the infinite, directly through the living (and dying) present of each individual.

It is out of this fusion that we get the eloquent socialist dream of a poem like 'Laurentian Shield,' in which the hard, empty, inhuman vastnesses of the Laurentians are transmuted, humanized: the rock itself made into children, with all their innocent limitless promise for the future of civilization. This dream is the fulfilment of Scott's early prophetic response to Canadian nature, as an 'innocent' young man returning from Europe in the 1920s, struck by the 'feeling that we could start afresh in Canada,' seeing in the barrenness of the wilderness not the Wasteland of post-World War I disillusion but a 'waiting' land: 'newly arrived from Oxford,' as he recalled forty years later, 'and deeply impressed by the northland, its great lakes and rivers, its old mountains, and *its sense of something waiting to be made.*'[6]

And finally, at the opposite extreme from 'Laurentian Shield' - moving from objectivity to subjectivity, from the social to the individual, from impersonality to the intensely personal - it is this same coming together of visions that underlies, I think, the concluding metaphor of that late poem of autobiographical summing up, 'On Saying Good-bye to My Room in Chancellor Day Hall.' This poem dwells fondly on the memorabilia of 'group experience' and the commitment to small and great causes, the relics of many trips in a car that 'must be full,' the cluttering personal and social trivia that go to make up a long, ample life - but ends with still another turn, in nakedness and singleness, towards the challenge of the unknown:

> ... I stand again on new frontiers.
> Forgive this moment of weakness, this backward
>   perspective.
> Old baggage, I wish you good-bye and good housing.
> I strip for more climbing.

We need not ask here whether the 'climbing' is to be still farther over the crowded wayward routes to that ever-receding horizon of the ideal society on earth, or up into the solitude of the old Laurentian hills; towards the cruel peak of Ararat, or out to the start of space and along the road to suns. It is perhaps all these at the same time, and more - which only the poetry itself can hope to express.

NOTES

References to F.R. Scott's poems are all to *Selected Poems* (Toronto: Oxford University Press 1966) except for the following: 'On Saying Good-bye to My Room in Chancellor Day Hall,' 'Reminders,' in *The Dance Is One* (Toronto 1973); 'Command of the Air' and 'Prison,' in *Events and Signals* (Toronto 1954); 'General Election, 1935' and 'Natural Resources,' in *The Eye of the Needle* (Montreal 1957); and 'Surfaces,' in *Overture* (Toronto 1945).

1 'Modern Poetry,' an address delivered c1928; one of 'Three Documents from F.R. Scott's Personal Papers,' *Canadian Poetry* 4 (Spring/Summer 1979) 76

2 'Four of the Former *Preview* Editors: A Discussion'; another of the 'Three Documents ...,' ibid. 119

3 'The Poet in Quebec Today,' reprinted in *The McGill Movement*, ed. Peter Stevens (Toronto 1969) 51-2

4 Ibid. 52

5 From the notes to Scott's *The Eye of the Needle* (Montreal 1957) 70

6 'F.R. Scott: Discussing Oxford Study Group ...,' ibid. 92; my emphasis

PART THREE

MICHIEL HORN

F.R. Scott,
the Great Depression,
and the League for
Social Reconstruction

MORE THAN any other event in Canadian history, the Great Depression of the 1930s affected the attitude of intellectuals towards their country. The mounting evidence of distress and social dislocation had a strong impact on a number of educated men and women, most of them working in the traditional or the newer professions. As the effects of the economic crisis, and the inability of business, charitable organizations, and governments to cope with them became apparent, the conviction grew in the minds of some of the younger intelligentsia that there must be change. Canada and Canadians could not go on in this way. To a small but growing group of intellectuals socialism came to seem the way of the future.

Frank Scott was in several ways characteristic of this group. He was young: his thirtieth birthday fell on 1 August 1929, short weeks before the stock market crash that has come to symbolize the start of the Depression. He came from a good family and was well educated; he had recently been appointed to the Faculty of Law at McGill University. For him a secure future lay ahead.

In his ideas, attitudes, and interests, Frank Scott was less characteristic. His religious background and upbringing had left him with a strong concern for human welfare but without a coherent view of the society or the economy. His exposure to the thought of Christian socialists like R.H. Tawney had given him a distrust of capitalism, and had confirmed his disdain for mere moneymaking. He was not yet a radical critic of society, however. Although he could recognize some of the world's stupidities and iniquities, he felt no great desire to try to correct them. His interests, passions even, in the 1920s were the study of history and constitutional law, and poetry.

Scott credits a small circle of friends with his increasing interest in politics and economics as the 1920s came to an end. 'The Group' consisted of a handful of men most of whom, like Scott himself, had studied in Oxford. Among them were Brooke Claxton, Eugene Forsey, Terry MacDermot, and Raleigh Parkin. In this informal discussion group, and in the Canadian Institute of International Affairs, which he joined in 1929, Scott became more aware of Canada and the world. By early 1930 he was helping to plan and draft a book that was intended to propose 'remedies' to the 'political, economic and social problems of the country.'[1]

As the book took shape during the spring and summer of 1930, the original contributors, Forsey, MacDermot, and Scott, were joined by others from outside Montreal, among them Graham Spry and Frank Underhill. For reasons that none of the surviving participants in the project have been able to recall, the book was never published. One possibility is that disagreement developed as to the degree of change that should be proposed. Whatever the case, Scott was among those who were taking an increasingly critical view of Canadian society.

Initially he was struck less by the growing economic dislocation than by mounting evidence that protests against that dislocation met with repression. On 31 January 1931, he made a protest of his own. Its immediate cause was that the evening before the Montreal police had broken up a meeting of the Canadian Labour Defence League and arrested the speakers. That meeting had been called to protest against earlier police interference with gatherings convened to organize demands for unemployment relief. The Defence League was communist-led; in police eyes this sanctioned their interference. But not in Scott's. 'Whether or not these meetings are attended by communists or merely by unemployed labourers makes not a particle of difference,' he wrote to the Montreal *Gazette*, 'for communism is no more criminal than liberalism or socialism.' It was for the courts to decide whether seditious words had been spoken; Scott addressed himself to the legality and wisdom of interfering with freedom of speech and of assembly.

On the basis of newspaper reports, he suggested, the police behaviour at four recent meetings was probably illegal and certainly provocative. 'At not a single one of the four meetings ... has the crowd itself been accused of disorder until *after* the police have arrested speakers and started to disperse the audience.' At one meeting 'the police were gathered in such numbers that the people dared not assemble.' This was a plain violation of the rights to free assembly and speech. 'The British method,' Scott wrote to *Gazette* readers, was 'to let radicals blow off steam to their heart's content.' The inferior method of the Montreal police had simply drawn attention to the meetings. One consequence was that attendance had grown from 250 at the first meeting to more than 1500 at the most recent. 'It would be interesting to know how many converts to communism had been made by this procedure.'[2]

The letter marked a 'turning point' in Scott's life. Suddenly he had come to public notice. The reaction to his letter was mixed at best. The chief of police and the Montreal *Gazette* took issue with him; at McGill University some of the governors were unhappy that he had identified himself as 'associate professor of constitutional and federal law.' The link between him and the university was too obvious. Scott was given to understand that in future he was not to use his title if he should again write to a newspaper about a controversial matter: indeed, such letters in themselves were not particularly welcome. But criticism hardened Scott in the opinion that he was right, and pushed him further along a new course, that of social and political criticism.

He was not the only Canadian academic of whom that could be said. Two weeks before Scott wrote to the *Gazette*, sixty-eight members of the University of Toronto teaching staff had written an open letter to the four Toronto newspapers in protest against police interference with meetings deemed to be communist. Public reaction had been largely unfavourable, and the university authorities treated it as an unfortunate aberration that ought not to be repeated.[3] This failed to intimidate either the letter's chief architect, Frank Underhill, or a small number of younger men and women who belonged to an informal group that had been meeting since the previous fall. 'Radically minded,' their president Underhill called them; among them were Eric Havelock, Harry Cassidy, Joe Parkinson, and Irene Biss. By the spring of 1931, Cassidy, a Vancouver-born economist, informed J.S. Woodsworth that the 'Ginger Group' of labour and farmer members of parliament might soon expect some intellectual support.[4]

At this stage Scott and Underhill had not yet met in person. The two men were acquainted with each other's work, however, not least because both contributed regularly to *The Canadian Forum*. The encounter that both had looked forward to took place in August 1931. It was at the annual Institute on Politics at Williams College, in Williamstown, Massachusetts, a pretty town in the Berkshires. From the very first the two men hit it off together. They enjoyed each other's style. More important, they saw the problems that beset Canada in much the same light and were groping towards the proposal of similar solutions. They had met at the right time.

During a Sunday hike to the summit of nearby Mt Greylock, Underhill and Scott agreed that Canada needed a sort of Fabian Society. Underhill was convinced that a new political party, drawing support from radicalized farmers and urban blue- and white-collar workers, would soon emerge. He argued that a group of intellectuals should help it to formulate its ideas; thus it would not fade away in the fashion of the Progressive movement of the 1920s. Persuaded by the eloquence of his new-found friend, Scott undertook to do what he could in Montreal to get such a group started.

The meeting at Williamstown was the immediate spur to the founding of the League for Social Reconstruction. Upon returning to Montreal, Scott soon found several eager collaborators in the effort to draw up a manifesto for the embryonic organization. Among them were Eugene Forsey, King Gordon, and, younger and more radical than any of the others, David Lewis. In Toronto, Underhill got the assistance of several of his associates in the group of radically minded professors. At least five drafts of the manifesto went back and forth between Montreal and Toronto until finally, on the weekend of 23 January 1932, four other Montrealers accompanied Scott to Toronto in order to iron out some organizational questions and try to agree on a name.

The manifesto finally agreed on was largely the work of the Montreal group. They did not get their way where the name of the organization was concerned, however. They favoured 'League for Economic Democracy' as an adaptation of the League for Industrial Democracy in the United States. The Torontonians preferred 'League for Social Reconstruction' over the American-sounding name their Montreal associates proposed. Scott was unimpressed. 'Couldn't some of you devote an evening to heavy drinking in the hope of achieving an inspiration' and a better name, he asked Underhill in February.[5] Evidently either the spirits or the spirit failed.

The first public meetings of the LSR took place on 23 February in Toronto and 11 March in Montreal. There the manifesto and constitution of the League were adopted and the national executive approved. President was Underhill; members-at-large of the executive were Gordon, Havelock, Parkinson, and Scott. Secretary treasurer was a Toronto high school teacher, Isabel Thomas; the honorary president was the 'prophet in politics,' J.S. Woodsworth.

Both the Toronto and Montreal branches soon had a hundred members, and the organization spread westward. With a manifesto that had been consciously couched in terms meant to attract middle-class converts to the cause of social reconstruction, the LSR within a year had seventeen branches in six provinces, two in the Montreal area (French-Canadian members were scarce), four in Ontario, two in Manitoba, three in Saskatchewan, four in Alberta, and two on the west coast. The manifesto described the LSR as 'an association of men and women who are working for the establishment in Canada of a social order in which the basic principle regulating production, distribution, and service will be the common good rather than private profit,' and listed nine (later ten) 'essential first steps' towards this goal. Critical of the operations of capitalism, the manifesto deliberately stopped short of using the term 'socialism' and eschewed political partisanship. Scott and others had no desire to limit the LSR's appeal.

The formation of the Co-operative Commonwealth Federation in the summer and fall of 1932, a development in which the LSR did not participate, led to demands within the League that it affiliate itself with the new 'farmer-labour-socialist' party. Scott opposed these demands. He feared that affiliation would damage the LSR in the eyes of the politically uncommitted. Flying a socialist flag, furthermore, would harm the LSR's chances of attracting Roman Catholic and French-Canadian members. For the time being at least, he told Underhill, the League should stick to its task of public education. Scott was pleased, therefore, when an attempt in early 1933 to affiliate the LSR with the CCF failed. (The British Columbia wing of the League subsequently reorganized itself in order to become a component part of the provincial CCF.)

Scott's attitude did not mean that he opposed the CCF. Far from it! He became one of the party's first members in Quebec, and in July 1933, attended the CCF's Regina convention officially as a representative of the Montreal CCF Council and unofficially as one of the LSR. Joined by three other members of the LSR inner group, Forsey, Gordon, and Parkinson, Scott played an important role in the process whereby the CCF got a manifesto and program that had been drafted by Underhill, Cassidy, and a couple of other members of the LSR's Toronto branch. Scott was also asked to address the convention. Among other things he said that the CCF might well encourage the teaching and learning of French outside Quebec, and support a bilingual currency: remarks that gained favourable comment in his native province. He returned from Regina appalled by his first-hand look at dried-out southern Saskatchewan, but with the comfortable feeling that the LSR had largely got its way with respect to the new party's program, and that the future looked bright for a Canadian socialism.

In the enunciation of that socialism, something the LSR after some early hesitation came to regard as one of its main tasks, Scott was a centrally important person. His contribution to the printed output of the league included *Social Reconstruction and the B.N.A. Act*, a pamphlet published in 1934, his co-authorship and co-editorship of the LSR's main publication, *Social Planning for Canada* (1935), his co-authorship with Eugene Forsey and Leonard Marsh of the LSR's second book, *Democracy Needs Socialism* (1938), and *Canada - One or Nine?*, the League's submission to the Royal Commission on Dominion-Provincial Relations (1939).

Not surprisingly, Scott was the League's chief spokesman on constitutional matters, but his interests went well beyond that. The regard and respect that others in the LSR had for him was great; and in 1935 he succeeded Underhill as national president, holding that position for two years. By this time he was deeply involved in the affairs not only of the League but of the CCF as well. No longer did he hesitate to use the term 'socialism' to describe his beliefs and the League's. The economic and moral bankruptcy of capitalism had become so clear to him that he now saw democratic socialism as the only alternative.

His assessment of capitalism is clearly evident in a series of poems dating from the mid-thirties. 'Social Notes' they are called; there are six of them. They are satirical, even heavily so, and they make two main points. The first is that, in treating human beings as if they were objects, capitalism is inhumane. The second, as the poem 'Efficiency' so clearly proves, is that the system is also inefficient.

> The efficiency of the capitalist system
> Is rightly admired by important people.
> Our huge steel mills
> Operating at 25% of capacity
> Are the last word in organization.
> The new grain elevators
> Stored with superfluous wheat
> Can load a grain-boat in two hours.
> Marvellous card-sorting machines
> Make it easy to keep track of the unemployed.
> There is not one unnecessary worker
> In these textile plants
> That require a 75% tariff protection.
> And when our closed shoe-factories re-open
> They will produce more footwear than we can possibly buy.
> So don't let us start experimenting with socialism
> Which everyone knows means inefficiency and waste.[6]

From the same period dates Scott's essay 'The Efficiency of Socialism,' published in *Queen's Quarterly* in 1935. In it he countered arguments that socialism would be inefficient and concluded: 'Socialism instead of being a likely cause of economic inefficiency and political corruption, holds the promise of being the cure for these evils.' His conviction that socialism could be both efficient *and* humane was a powerful motive for political action.

In concluding, I should note that Scott was led to help found the LSR, to become active in the CCF, and to become one of the intellectual champions of a Canadian socialism, not simply or perhaps even primarily because of the Depression. In a biography that Sandra Djwa is now writing, she emphasizes Scott's early sense of noblesse oblige, a sense that owed much to the beliefs and example of his father, Canon F.G. Scott. Scott was disposed to see himself as a knight *sans peur et sans reproche*. This disposition had little opportunity to express itself during the 1920s, during much of which he was a student, an apprentice as it were. But by 1931 the time was ripe. Scott's apprenticeship lay behind him; the Depression pinpointed abuses that cried out for correction. The knight was ready for the cause: the cause was that of the common man, the preservation of his rights, and the securing of his welfare.

NOTES

1 Public Archives of Canada (PAC), Brooke Claxton Papers, Claxton to Burton Hurd, 21 Feb. 1930, copy
2 Letter to the Montreal *Gazette*, 31 Jan. 1931, published 3 Feb. 1931
3 See Michiel Horn, '"Free Speech within the Law": The Letter of the Sixty-Eight Toronto Professors,' *Ontario History* LXXII (Mar. 1980).
4 University of Toronto Archives, H.M. Cassidy Papers, Cassidy to Woodsworth, 2 May 1931, copy
5 PAC, F.H. Underhill Papers, Scott to Underhill, 12 Feb. 1932
6 'Efficiency,' *The Collected Poems of F.R. Scott* (Toronto: McClelland and Stewart 1981) 71.

DAVID LEWIS

F.R. Scott's Contribution
to the CCF

WHEN, AS national chairman, Frank Scott opened the 1950 National Convention of the CCF, held in Vancouver for the first time, he delivered an address on the meaning and relevance of democratic socialism in the post-war years of economic and technological expansion. He did so partly in the context of the need to restate basic CCF principles and partly because he had decided to retire as national chairman after eight years in that office. He assured the delegates that he was not retiring from the party and that he would be ready to serve it in some other capacity if wanted. In his inimitable way, he expressed it whimsically, saying: 'I am not, however, to be taken as singing my CCF swan-song. I am not a swan, I don't sing, and I am not dying.'

Scott's address at that time was an illuminating example of, and guide to, his political thought and to his contribution to Canadian social democracy. The basis of his presentation was a declaration that 'Socialism is as valid a creed for a prosperous nation as for a depressed one, for it is concerned with the quality of social life, not just with the amount of wealth produced.'[1] Editorialists who periodically wrote CCF obituaries could not understand this sentiment, let alone appreciate it.

Scott went on to articulate in lucid and convincing terms the differences between the priorities governing the notion of the co-operative commonwealth and those shaping the practices of capitalism, driven and controlled primarily by the pressure to maximize profit and power, with little concern for the human goals of society. He also drew a telling picture of the fundamental distinctions between the nature of Stalin's despotic communism and the objectives and achievements of western democratic socialism. He then made another important statement which, in my view, expressed in simple but profound phrases the non-materialist, spiritual goals towards which socialist policies and action are aimed. He said: 'It is evident that this thing we may call the spirit of man, this light of faith and conscience and decency on which all civilization depends, is not primarily dependent on the ownership of property, essential though it is to subject all forms of ownership to social controls ... Socialism is most concerned with the human spirit, with its freedom, its growth, its emancipation, and with ownership only in so far as some of its forms are obstacles to this freedom just as other forms seem essential to it.'[2]

Having thus fashioned the theoretical frame, Scott went on to discuss the immediate concerns of the convention in a way which evoked an enthusiastic response from most of the delegates. He reminded them that socialists everywhere should take stock of their position in the light of post-war experiences, reminded them, in words that were carefully aimed, but difficult to argue against, that 'the socialist must be aware of world trends, and must realize that he is no more free than anyone else from the danger of old-fashioned thinking.' Who could or would argue that becoming old-fashioned is desirable? The main thrust of the speech was the never-ending controversy about the extent of public ownership. He ended his discussion of the subject with the provocative statement that 'for any socialist today to look upon every proposal for nationalization as the acid test of true socialism, an act of faith rather than of reason, is to be a little foolish.' To have said this within the walls of Canada's socialist Vatican, as Vancouver was in those days, was a mark of Scott's forthright approach to internal CCF problems. I can still see some faces cloud over at the sound of this sacrilege.

The speech emphasized that 'socialism expresses in the fullest degree the great traditions of political democracy,' and in relation to the developing tensions between the Soviet and western blocks, Scott had no doubt where he stood. 'Socialists,' he said, 'must fight to preserve those conditions under which socialism may live.'

In an address which took no more than thirty minutes to deliver, including frequent interruptions by applause, Scott dealt meaningfully with most CCF concerns, international as well as domestic, philosophical as well as practical. As long as thirty years ago, this constitutional expert, who had been and still was a supporter of strong central government, recognized the enhanced position and increased responsibilities of the provinces, and concluded that 'in this sphere as in others we must strike a balance, separating out the functions appropriate to federal action from those appropriate to provinces and municipalities.'[3]

Throughout the history of the CCF, Scott guided the party's policies in the area of constitutional arrangements. His concept of a Canada in which the central government had to play the major role of managing the economy, protecting the rights of all Canadians, and promoting equality in relevant spheres across the entire country, was shared by all of us, including the then CCF government of Saskatchewan. The constitution should not be the occasion for a tug-of-war between the federal and provincial governments but an orderly division of competences shaped by functions appropriate to each level of government. This is what we all preached. We have since learned for the umpteenth sad time that collective life does not necessarily respond to logic any more than does that of the individual.

I have dealt at some length with Scott's 1950 speech, which was published and distributed as a pamphlet, because I believe it is still an important social democratic statement as relevant today as it was thirty years ago. More relevant is the fact that it is an excellent example of the combination of tightly knit theory and orderly realism which was the nature of his contribution to the CCF, in the realm of organization as well as of policy.

Scott was one of the leading founders of the League for Social Reconstruction and an author of the Regina Manifesto. He continued to work with the leaders and caucus of the CCF from then on. When I became involved at the national centre of the party in 1936, he, King Gordon, and Eugene Forsey were the persons outside the caucus with whom the MPs and I, as national secretary, consulted frequently. As a matter of fact, Scott and I had been in correspondence about the CCF and LSR while I was still at Oxford, and had known each other at McGill before that. It was thus as natural for me as it seemed to be for the MPs to turn to him for help, particularly in the areas of law and the constitution.

Except for one year, which he spent at Harvard, Scott's participation in the work of the party was wide and comprehensive. No one who served on the special committee which, in September 1939, developed the CCF policy on Canada's part in the war, or who served on the National Council at that time, could fail to be grateful for his contribution. Without him, the wrenching task of finding a compromise that would prevent the party from being torn by passionately held differences, would have proved much more difficult. I was a member of the committee. Scott and I did a lot of the drafting together, and I know how valuable was his part in the entire process and how appreciative were leaders like M.J. Coldwell and Angus MacInnis.

Thus, by the time of the 1950 convention, the delegates expected intellectual excellence and logical analysis from their retiring national chairman. Indeed, those of us who had worked with Scott in the early years had these values in mind when we asked him to be a candidate for the position of national chairman, back in 1942, when Coldwell left that post to succeed Woodsworth as president and leader of the party. However, what we did not realize then was that Scott would also prove to be a practical, effective executive. Even I, who had for years worked closely with him in the political arena and who was mainly responsible for persuading him to undertake the heavy and time-consuming responsibilities of the chairmanship, was as surprised as the others to find that the academic, theorist, satirist, and poet was fully ready to take a serious part in promoting the organizational aspects of the party and in confronting, in a tough and decisive way, the disruptive forces within and without the organization.

Born in 1899, Scott was exactly a decade younger than Coldwell and a decade older than I. The three of us and Angus MacInnis, who was national vice-chairman, were in constant touch, as was natural for the leader, the chairman, the vice-chairman and the secretary, and despite our different backgrounds we were a harmonious team. Scott was totally objective, always. He had no political ambitions whatever and was not concerned about his personal position in the sphere of politics. Party activities were not his sole preoccupation; his mind roamed beyond the confines of immediate problems to the whole complex of the reach and meaning of human effort. His socialism did not derive from a background of working-class protest but from his own observation and study and, above all, sense of order and justice.

As the son of Archdeacon F.G. Scott, a leading cleric in the Anglican Church who was also a writer, our national chairman thus came from a comfortable and established family in the anglophone community of his province and country. I do not recall Frank Scott mentioning it to me or others of his CCF colleagues, but I learned that his father was on a visit to Winnipeg during the 1919 General Strike and took occasion to show his support for the strikers by addressing one of their meetings from a platform which included Woodsworth.

Frank Scott's socialism, as I sensed it during years of close collaboration, derived from a poet's sensitivity to the human condition and a creative intellect's appreciation of man's potential, if he were freed from the crippling inhibitions imposed on the majority by the power and greed of the minority. He affirmed his conception of man's moral compass with typical and touching clarity in a quatrain titled 'Creed':

> The world is my country
> The human race is my race
> The spirit of man is my God
> The future of man is my heaven

He elaborated a similar theme in his draft of the last chapter of *Make This Your Canada*, headed 'The Rebirth of Democracy.' The book was one he and I co-authored in 1943 and, although we edited the chapter together, as we did all parts of the book, and although I did my share of writing other chapters, this important statement was composed mainly by Scott. It contains his conception of an important aspect of the philosophy of democratic socialism, which I share, and of the bond which makes democracy and socialism one. We said, in effect, what he repeated in 1950, that the CCF believed in democracy because 'Democracy believes in people. It proclaims afresh, as it has always proclaimed, the essential value of every man, woman and child on this rich earth.' And the CCF believed in socialism because: 'No man can be really free without the aid of a well-ordered society to provide him with the health, education, and opportunities for useful work and self-expression that he needs.'[4]

I have always thought that the last chapter of *Make This Your Canada* was an eloquent and valid statement of the democratic socialist's political thesis. It was written in the clear, lucid, and logical style which was Scott's literary trademark. Because we both agreed on the fundamentals of social democracy and because we both rejected Lenin's proposition that the ends justify the means, we were able to work productively together. I do not recall one serious discord between us, even though we were, from time to time, on opposite sides of an issue. I was reminded of this when we disagreed about the invocation of the War Measures Act in October 1970.

What was particularly refreshing about Scott was that he was never petty. This meant a great deal to me as head of the National Office and, for many years, the only senior functionary. He never complained that he had not been consulted; never considered anything from a purely personal point of view; never looked at any policy question or organizational matter in isolation, but related it to the entire range of issues in the light of party doctrine and policies. He could be, and was, irritating on occasion. Suddenly his good eye and mind would wander off into far-off space while a serious matter was being discussed or when I was in the process of presenting a problem for his attention. Nothing was more frustrating for the earnest national secretary. Scott could also be, and was, aggravating when he refused to take an interest in something which the rest of us considered important – a lack of concern which frustrated and devastated the full-time officer. Too often his tall, cutting aloofness and intellectual impatience caused annoyance and hurt to people who deserved better. Aloofness and impatience are luxuries not permitted in politics. I know because I have been much more guilty of them than Scott. I cannot recall particular instances, but these tendencies caused me, as national secretary, what I thought were avoidable headaches on some occasions. Mention of these irritations illustrates the self-evident fact that Scott was human, but they were inconsequential. His contribution was invariably stimulating and rewarding to his colleagues and to the movement.

My wife, Sophie, and I spent many pleasant hours socially with Scott and his warm, soft-spoken artist wife, Marian, and although he and I consulted almost daily by phone, by letter, or at meetings, I cannot say that I got to know his private person. In this respect, he was a typically reticent WASP. He very seldom spoke about himself or about his family, except in self-deprecating amusement. But he was a great companion. Place a martini in his hand and the ingenious wordsmith would fashion a string of humorous similes, aphorisms, and even puns, always accompanied by his own hearty laugh of appreciation – a laugh and appreciation shared by everyone around him. This delightful talent was not confined to social occasions: it often relieved the tensions of political argument.

However, Scott was far from being disinterested in carrying out his duties as national chairman. If he considered an issue important, he pursued it with determination and decisiveness. In fact, he was more impatient with sloppy thinking and reckless dissent than some of the rest of us, including myself. He was more inclined to suggest or to support decisive disciplinary steps when someone's behaviour caused serious problems inside the party or with the electorate. He was a relatively strict presiding officer: he demanded order, discipline, and tidiness in thought and action, but he did so in orderly, disciplined, and tidy phrases, without offensive shrillness. He was never the hazy, bewildered poet. In my opinion, good poets never are, although their creative perceptions of the labyrinth of human emotions and the varieties of human folly may stamp greater angst and bewilderment on their faces than on those of us who are less imaginative. Although Scott did not have direct experience with the electorate – he was never a candidate for public office – he showed realistic political sense which took into account relevant electoral considerations. Unlike some academics then and now, he never doubted that the CCF had been established by the Regina Manifesto to be a political party seeking to win power by the parliamentary, electoral route: that was the only democratic way to build the co-operative commonwealth in Canada.

I have referred to Scott's work at the national level of the CCF, but much of his time and effort was spent in the Quebec section of the party. For many years he served on the executive and council of the provincial organization at the same time as in the federal organs of the party. For many years there were very few French-speaking members in Quebec, certainly not in the leadership category. There was no socialist tradition in the province and the dominant church prohibited Roman Catholics from having anything to do with the CCF. Scott was recognized as one of the leaders in the French- as well as the English-speaking community.

In 1938, Cardinal Jean-Marie Villeneuve, in a speech to the Junior Board of Trade of Montreal, repeated accusations that the CCF was atheistic, materialistic, and communist and declared support of the CCF to be incompatible with being a good Catholic. These charges were not new: they had been made by Archbishop Georges Gauthier and Father Georges-Henri Lévesque a few years earlier and intoned by lower clergy across the province. This time it was decided to prepare and publish a reply. I remember vividly the three days I spent with Scott in his office at the McGill Law School, studying papal encyclicals, and working with him on a draft answer, which was later published by the party in English and French. In retrospect, I find it incongruous and amusing that the document, replete with quotations from the encyclicals *Rerum Novarum*, 1891, and *Quadragessimo Anno*, 1931, should have been prepared by the son of an Anglican archdeacon and the son of an agnostic Jew learned in Marx and the Talmud. Such was the state of the CCF in Quebec for the first eight or ten years of the party's life. It became better later as far as French-speaking leadership was concerned, but not much better in organizational or electoral terms.

Several years later it was Scott who visited Father Lévesque at Laval University and apparently influenced him to change his mind about the CCF. I had an opportunity to confirm that when, on an organizational visit to Quebec City later in 1942, I had the opportunity of a long and friendly meeting with the good Father. Similarly, it was Scott who accompanied Coldwell to a specially arranged meeting with Archbishop Joseph Charbonneau the following year. These were activities at the top, as it were, but no member as active as Scott could avoid local meetings and commitments in an organization as small and frustrated as the Quebec one. Indeed, reference to the province as a whole is an exaggeration; what there was of the CCF was found mainly in Montreal.

It is important to note that Scott was not the only academic active on many CCF fronts in the thirties and forties. In Montreal there were also King Gordon until he left for New York, Eugene Forsey, Stanley Allen, and one or two others. We had the Havelocks, Grubes, McCurdys, Pembertons in Ontario, the Carlyle Kings in Saskatchewan, and I remember meeting some, whose names I can't recall, in Winnipeg and Halifax. I have no memory of active academics in the CCF of British Columbia in those years; I imagine that the influential doctrinaires were not ready to make room for the bourgeois campus intellectuals. Underhill was in a class by himself. He continued to be friendly and helpful for many years, but mainly through his writing, lecturing, and correspondence with Woodsworth, Coldwell, and Noseworthy, on the latter's election to parliament after his historic defeat of Arthur Meighen in a by-election. Underhill was, of course, also in contact with Scott and, less frequently, with the National Office. However, he was never a member of either the provincial or national executive or council, although he was for a short time active on the executive of his local organization. I suppose his irrepressible iconoclasm made it difficult for him to accept the constraints imposed on members of the governing establishment. Nevertheless, and with full appreciation of the part played by the others I have mentioned, I must emphasize that Scott's contribution was outstanding.

When the CCF won the government of Saskatchewan in June 1944, Scott was often consulted by Premier Douglas and Jack Corman, his attorney general, about the constitutional implications of some of the government's policies. Harold Winch, CCF leader in British Columbia, sought and received Scott's advice on many occasions, as did Ted Jolliffe, Ontario leader, even though the latter was no mean lawyer himself. Scott was a major participant in several federal-provincial CCF conferences organized by the National Office; he was also a leading CCF delegate to two conferences of Commonwealth labour parties – the first held in London, England, in 1944, and the second in Toronto in 1947. Nor did his activities end when he resigned as national chairman in 1950, although they slackened a great deal. Scott continued to be a member of the National Council throughout the fifties and was one of the ten CCF members on the National Committee for a New Party, which gave birth to the NDP. I allude to all these events to emphasize the range and scope of his part in the CCF.

There are a couple of matters that were important to me personally and which are relevant in the context of these remarks. The demands of my CCF job often frustrated me because they left little time for other interests. The relatively small part of the day or month I was able to spend at home rendered it difficult for Sophie and me to listen to concerts or to attend the occasional theatrical performance, or to go to lectures, or even to visit the National Art Gallery. It is true that in the thirties and forties Ottawa did not offer many exciting cultural events, but we were not able to enjoy what was offered. And when I worked in any other Canadian city, the schedule was full of formal and informal discussions and meetings. Sophie and I learned to welcome the fundraising need to travel to New York from time to time, where a union friend obtained concert and theatre tickets for us. Although I always read some poetry, my reading of other literature was limited because of the need to study reports, briefs, and political journals. This I did mainly on trains, which had me as tenant a good part of each month. Since the party treasury could not afford berths, I travelled day coach most of the time and spent most of the nights reading. Not a little of my postgraduate education was obtained this way, but I was often culturally hungry.

One aspect of my personal relationship with Frank and Marian was, therefore, my joy at having the occasional opportunity to discuss, or to listen to conversations about, art and literature, and to do so in the company of close political colleagues. To contemplate the human condition without having to define the place of public or private ownership or the desirable international monetary or collective security system, was to me almost like a release from mental bondage. Since I have always been an activist by temperament, I have enjoyed the search for the pragmatic and practical responses which a socialist must find, if his rhetoric is not to become purely self-indulgent gratification. But it was important for me then, as it has always been, to have the opportunity of pulling the curtain down on the political stage from time to time, and to refresh my spirits and my perceptions by incursions as spectator into the world of the creative arts. My friend, the late poet A.M. Klein, helped me fill this need in my pre-Oxford years; Scott did so in the late thirties and in the forties.

When my father died at the relatively early age of sixty-two in February 1950, there was a lay memorial service in the Workmen's Circle Centre on St Lawrence-Main in Montreal. My father's death was not sudden; he had suffered grievously for almost three years from a form of acute leukemia. Expected as it was, his death left a painful void in our closely knit family, every member of which had loved and respected him deeply. So did my father's friends and colleagues in the Jewish labour movement. His coffin was brought to the Workmen's Circle building twenty-four hours before the memorial meeting and a guard of honour stood vigil over it during those hours. The service was in a packed hall, many friends standing in the rear. The family's sadness was tinged with pride.

I had invited Scott to deliver the main address. He did so in English, of course, while Michael Rubinstein, chairman of the Jewish Labour Committee, spoke in Yiddish. I have always remembered the moving effect of Scott's quietly spoken words. He and my father had met many times in my company, but they couldn't get to know each other well; my father's limited English and their entirely different backgrounds and environments stood in the way. Yet Scott had captured the ethics and spirit which had moved my father throughout his life, and the poet's sensitivity enabled him to weave my father's generous public activities into a sympathetic and colourful pattern.

One other incident belongs here logically even though it occurred many years later. In 1969 or 1970, Scott called me long distance and told me that Prime Minister Trudeau had offered him a seat in the Senate. He had, he said, doubts about accepting, in view of his and the party's opposition to the institution. He had already spoken to Douglas and

Knowles and wanted my advice as well. I told him firmly that if I were in his place, I would not accept the invitation for the reasons he had raised, and received the impression that I was merely confirming a decision he had already reached. Scott did not become a senator.

When my mind wanders back to my first fifteen or so years of activity at the national level of the CCF, I think of two men, other than Woodsworth and Coldwell, whose advice and help were most valuable to my work and to the party: Frank Scott and Angus MacInnis. Except for the fact that they were both tall and that both towered over me, they seemed to have little in common on the surface. In fact, however, there was great affinity between their ethical and practical attitudes to democratic socialism and to the CCF place in Canada. They complemented each other.

MacInnis came to the west coast from a poor Prince Edward Island farm. In Vancouver he worked on the street railways, became a leader in his union and in the socialist movement of British Columbia, went into municipal politics and, finally, was elected to Parliament in 1930 and represented relatively the same working class district uninterrupted for twenty-seven years, until 1957, when his health forced him to retire. His background, education, training, and life experience were typically those of a self-educated working-class leader. But if being educated means, as I believe it does, a capacity to analyse and synthesize ideas, a curiosity to understand and interpret the world around one, enhanced wisdom to guide one's actions, and an appreciation of the worth of human dignity and of things beautiful, MacInnis was a highly educated man. In addition, he had a fierce loyalty to democratic socialism and to the CCF as its carrier in Canada.

When parliament was in session, there was hardly a day that I did not consult MacInnis by telephone or in person about one or another problem, perhaps even more often than I was able to consult Scott in Montreal. The advice of the two men was seldom at variance, and when it was, further discussion produced agreement with continuing respect on all sides.

My theories of history are strictly those of a layman, for which I make no apology, especially after the opportunity of observing academe at close range for six or so years. I have never accepted the 'great men' theory of history; I have believed that objective conditions and events throw up leaders and organizations which respond to them in one or other ideological direction. Despite these views, however, I find it difficult to envisage the birth of the CCF without the prophetic inspiration of Woodsworth, or the acceptability which the CCF gained during the war years without the reassuring empathy and strength of Coldwell, or the establishment of the CCF as an important political force, in defeat as well as in victory, without the philosophic depth and organizational firmness and wisdom of Scott and MacInnis.

Scott helped give the CCF shape because he never failed to take sides or to declare and defend what was right. He had no patience with doing anything by halves, when it could, with commitment and courage, be done decisively as one whole. Scott lent order and dignity to party debates and depth to theoretical discussion. He brought to the CCF a commitment to a united and independent Canada, an expertise in the law of the constitution and of civil liberties, an intense dislike of pretension and sham which too often obfuscate political reality, a philosophical search for the meaning of the human struggle for higher values, and a poet's vision of a Canada in which expanded physical and spiritual freedom derives from and is welded to material and spiritual equality. In fact, Frank Scott's contribution to the first difficult, formative years of the CCF – almost two decades – is simply immeasurable. I say this from personal knowledge, as his co-worker during most of those years.

NOTES

1 F.R. Scott, *New Horizons for Socialism* (Ottawa 1951) 4
2 Ibid. 6
3 Ibid. 16
4 F.R. Scott, *Make This Your Canada: A Review of C.C.F. History and Policy*, with David Lewis (Toronto 1943) 191-2

KENNETH McNAUGHT

Socialism and the
Canadian Political Tradition

WHEN FRANK SCOTT and five other authors of *Social Planning for Canada* ruminated in 1975 about the political ambience of the decade in which they had first collaborated, they noted both the importance and the imprecision of the word 'socialism' in Canadian politics. There was, they reflected, 'the obvious difficulty that the word socialist ... has such a variety of meanings as to have no meaning, a condition from which succeeding years of world-wide usage has done little to free it. Nevertheless, the term began increasingly to be used, generally with the prefix democratic to distinguish LSR beliefs from Marxian socialism on the one hand and "national socialism" or Nazism on the other.' Perceiving another continuity, this remarkable team also commented: 'Advocating, as it did, a democratic form of socialism of the British and Scandinavian type, [*Social Planning*] was subject to criticism from the Left and Right.'[1]

After about ninety years of interaction with the Canadian political tradition, or mentalité, several things seem evident about this kind of socialism: it is still criticized from the left and from the right; it has become and is likely to remain the predominant expression of socialism in Canada; it has influenced profoundly Canadian attitudes and policies at all levels of government; and it has been the principal creator and guarantor of our now characteristic multi-party political structure. I wish to examine briefly the critical analyses employed by the right and the left and then suggest the hard-core reasons for the survival and renewed growth of Canadian democratic socialism.

Rumbling on the left has come from a variety of syndicalists and Marxists, each claiming scientific purity and each exhibiting a kind of branch-plant ideology, or left-wing colonial complex, which has ensured an exotic and often ephemeral existence for Marxism in Canada. The most audible source of such criticism today is a group of neo-Marxist academics within the Committee on Canadian Labour History.[2] Devotees of the British labour historians E.P. Thompson and E.J. Hobsbawm, these young Canadian scholars profess to be restructuring Canadian history to show that class conflict has been its mainspring and that 'the rich and vibrant culture of the working class' has been the definitive impulse sustaining that conflict as industrial capitalism raged triumphant across the land.[3] The unbroken line of criticism from the left – from Ernie Winch and the Socialist party of Canada through Tim Buck and the Canadian politburo to the New Left and the neo-Marxists of Black Rose Books, *Vanguard*, *This Magazine*, and other sectaries – has always found its principal target to be 'parliamentarism.' Time after time, successive expressions of the Marxist left have come to grief on the shoals of parliamentarism, either in divisive internal debates about the merits of electoral and legislative activity or as a result of an understandable reluctance on the part of Canadians to believe that Marxist analysis and goals do not assign a central position to collective violence.

Both internal fracturing and external perceptions rendered, and continue to render, Marxism largely irrelevant within the Canadian political milieu. The paradox is that Marxists themselves tirelessly reiterate that, as a means to substantive social-economic change, it is democratic socialism that is irrelevant. And to sustain that belief has required heroic, often poignant faith. A recent cri de cœur from Eric Hobsbawm might well be echoed by his Canadian acolytes: 'Being a revolutionary in countries such as ours just happens to be difficult. There is no reason to believe that it will be any less difficult in the future than it has been in the past.'[4]

Right-wing and centrist analysis of Canadian democratic socialism has been more various, if no less censorious, than that of the left. The right-wing critique peaked in the wake of Ontario's 1943 election which made the CCF the official opposition in the province, but rightist depiction of democratic socialists as agents of Moscow (or, in 1943-5, as Nazis) has been embellished and tailored for use anywhere and is, for example, still much in vogue at the Toronto *Sun*.[5]

Probably more damaging, in the long run, has been the centrist appraisal, which is to say the conventional wisdom of the tenured. This takes several main forms. The first is the fatherly, or patronizing, approach and may be illustrated by reference to three widely read historians. The late Donald Creighton, describing the origins of the CCF, wrote: 'Protestants deeply affected by the ideals of the social gospel, school teachers and university professors, other professional people and white collar workers made up the bulk of the party's membership and helped to give it its earnest, slightly sanctimonious air.'[6] Although the socialist party, according to Creighton, failed to attract substantial support from labour and would likely never get such support, it was to be commended for its un-Americanism, its pressure for essential reforms within the system, and above all, for keeping Mackenzie King worried.[7] Closer to the centre of the fatherly assessment, J.M.S. Careless agrees with Creighton that J.S. Woodsworth was a 'high-minded, universally respected leader' and that, while the CCF 'firmly established itself in national politics,' it would not likely gain major party status because 'many trade unionists rejected socialism,' and because it could make no headway in Quebec. In addition, Careless declares that even 'if the CCF followed British labour in ideas, it was distinctly North American in its descent from Progressivism and its deep-rooted western farm support.'[8]

A peculiar variation of the sceptically tolerant attitude, and of considerable political significance, is found in W.L. Morton's account of the Progressive movement. Emphasizing the 'disposition of third parties to shun responsibility,' Morton strongly reinforced the implicit right-centrist view that socialism in Canada is subject to the American law governing all third parties.[9] This law, also endorsed by Frank Underhill in his revisionist period, and enshrined with varying degrees of forthrightness in most school and college textbooks, was first clearly enunciated in the United States by J.D. Hicks in his 1930s study of populism.[10] It was brought to its finest flower when Richard Hofstadter wrote that 'third parties, like bees, having stung, must die.'[11] A simple law, drawn primarily from the seemingly definitive life histories of American populist and socialist parties, it states that the vastness of the American federal nation dictates that a kaleidoscopic sequence of minor parties is required to forfend against a political polarization which would be (and once was) disastrously divisive. Minor parties, thus, are essential stabilizers, providing political safety valves and occasionally compelling a major party to adopt or even enact a reform plank – which success spells their doom.

From the 1930s through the 1950s our value-free textbooks held that the Canadian political system was subject to the same laws. Thus, like the Patrons of Industry and the Progressives, the CCF, having given laudable expression to political discontent and having been mildly pillaged by Mr King, would either die or hang around for a while as a pious conduit for excess political steam. Eager sociologists embroidered this eminently congenial reasoning by suggesting that the CCF served also as a sort of psychiatric treatment centre for the maladjusted. As a womb-like movement, it couldn't really be a political party and thus was hopelessly becalmed. Thousands of CCF canvassers came to know well this elaborate doctrine of the lost vote. Indeed, the notion that the CCF didn't really *want* power and was, in any event, barred from getting it by the supreme law of North American politics, is perhaps the leading anglophone Canadian example of an academic interpretation becoming a major political force.

In the 1960s, a second American law, based on ideology, was added to the centrist analysis of party-based socialism in Canada. The ideological explanation of the failure of socialism in the United States was put forward by Louis Hartz in the 1950s and, with modifications, imported into Canada by followers of Hartz, such as Gad Horowitz and Kenneth McRae.[12] Simply put, this supplementary law proclaims that anglophone North America is so imbued with 'Lockean liberalism,' and so unencumbered with a feudal past, that socialism is, by definition, excluded. The modifications, in applying this ideological imperative to Canada are, of course, a Quebec which rejected the rationalists' revolution, and an English-based 'Tory Touch' which is said to have provided some relief from the presumed Lockean prohibition against any positive, government-sponsored collectivism. The ideological codicil has been gloomily acknowledged by many on the right as well as by approving centrists. On the right, George Grant, Donald Creighton and, to a lesser extent, W.L. Morton, have been so sceptical in their assessments of the future of true-blue conservatism as to concede defeat.[13]

The most striking thing about all this criticism from the right and the left is the happy consensus about the basic irrelevance of democratic socialism in Canada. Only slightly less remarkable in these analyses is their curious disregard of the host of facts which vitiate the conclusion. The benign liberal consensus view circumvents the factual obstacle by pooh-poohing the facts. For example, the Honourable Paul Martin told me as long ago as 1960 that my examination of the events leading to the passage of our first old-age pension law merely perpetuated a fraudulent fable long treasured by the ancients of the CCF.[14] The real explanation, he assured me, lay in Mackenzie King's deep wish to see such legislation enacted.[15]

The far right and far left, conversely, meet the problem of facts by the method of fanciful distortion. Indeed, the paranoid style in Canadian politics is not principally an expression of the outgroups of society, as Richard Hofstadter claimed was the case in the United States.[16] That style has been exhibited at least as prominently by the right wing of our establishment as by the so-called outgroups.[17] While embellishments of the conspiracy theory vary, the essential distortion of the facts remains the same – from the day when Arthur Meighen discerned a conspiracy to establish a soviet on the banks of the Red River to the anti-socialist crusades of a Bennett (R.B., W.A.C., or Bill/Mini-Wac, as the case may be) or a Sterling Lyon, the central bogeyman is a totalitarian socialist assault upon individualism. The first of the Bennett trinity, R.B., illustrated well the continuity of an indiscriminate conspiracy theory when he said in 1932: 'What do these so-called groups of socialists and communists offer you? We know that throughout Canada this propaganda is being put forward by organizations from foreign lands that seek to destroy our institutions.'[18]

Factual distortion by the far left has been less consistent and more subtle, although no less lethally intended. In addition to the extra-parliamentarist theorizing of the working class culture neo-Marxists, Norman Penner has recently attempted an overall Marxist synthesis of the left in Canada.[19] Although he throws up a smoke-screen of approving some tangential CCF-NDP contributions to the cause of Canadian socialism, he never veers far from his central proposition that only Marxism is socialism. Thus, of course, only what he perceives as Marxism in the CCF-NDP is significant; and in this respect Penner has some remarkable insights into the unconscious Marxism of J.S. Woodsworth and the LSR. Despite a devastating rehearsal of the scholastic debates of the Canadian politburo, he retains his faith.[20] He was cheered, he tells us, by 'the spectacular growth of the Waffle as an organized caucus inside the NDP' and, after the demise of that angular Canadian dimension, Penner found consolation in detecting 'a small but growing section of the intellectuals [who] are turning to Marxism not just as an academic exercise, but with the aim of influencing the direction of socialist thought along revolutionary lines.' Well, as was said in a recent American debate, there he goes again. If Penner is right, we may expect to see in the NDP some such helpful development as that which at the moment is so greatly nourishing the cause of socialism in the British Labour party!

But I do not think that Penner is any more correct or realistic now than were Tim Buck, J.B. Salsberg, or Jacob Penner when every month or so in the thirties they appealed to the leaders of the CCF to join in a united front with the communists – on the specious reasoning that a common enemy meant a common goal. The goals never were the same, and the goals themselves dictated the means by which they might be reached. It is the profound misconception about this matter of goals, a misconception perpetuated for different reasons by the right and the far left, that often obscures the real nature and achievement of Canadian democratic socialism.

Put summarily: the Marxists argue that only sharp polarization of society and radicalization of the working class, followed by an indefinite dictatorship, can achieve the socialist revolution; the CCF-NDP has thus been non-socialist to the extent that it has denied the efficacy of violence and relies upon legislative influence;[21] the far right proclaims that there is no substantive difference between democratic socialists and the

Marxist left and that the whole red movement is a foreign-controlled conspiracy; the 'moderate' right also believes that the CCF-NDP goal of socialism is neither attainable nor desirable in our essentially 'Lockean' society, but that these liberals-in-a-hurry nevertheless perform a therapeutic function in a congealed two-party system.[22]

Why have these analyses been proven astigmatic? I think the reasons for the survival and steady growth of socialism in Canada can best be grouped under three headings: humanism, legitimacy, and realism.

The humanism which lies at the heart of the matter is *not* the chilly rationalism of the enlightenment philosophers or of today's power brokers in the Kremlin. It is, rather, a fiery condemnation of social injustice allied to a deep belief, not in human perfectibility, but in the need to strive for a society as just, as egalitarian, as it is possible for mankind to achieve. This is an egalitarianism which has its roots in Judeo-Christianity and whose most basic conception is thus the equality of all people in the sight of God. Expressions of this basically religious component have been, and continue to be, various: from the utilitarian ethics of a John Stuart Mill through the broad reaches of the social gospel to F.R. Scott's poetic conception of rebirth beside the lakeshore.[23] It was this central strain of religious humanism that led J.S. Woodsworth on his unending tours of compassionate contact with the people who suffered in Winnipeg's slums, in Cape Breton's industrial wasteland, and in the murderous coal mines of Drumheller, which still animates the NDP as a movement.[24] And the same strain is what most decisively differentiates Marxism and democratic socialism, accounting for the socialist insistence that the individual must remain the central concern of social action and its equally adamant refusal to accept any dogma as absolute – a refusal to define the furniture of heaven. It is a humanism which cherishes the principle that the means determine the end. And for all this our central symbol remains that lonely, fragile figure rising to record his parliamentary dissent in September 1939.

Legitimacy, which is essential to political survival, has been acquired through a much more complex process than that which has often been depicted. Certainly, it is important that the names of those who brought the 'good news' of socialism to Canada were more often than not British. It is also important that the versions of Canadian socialism were mostly British in origin and that the British Labour party was established in 1906. But, that the names of most Canadian socialist leaders were not readily distinguishable from those of John Porter's 'charter group' élites, is not as definitive as appears at first glance.[25] After all, people such as J.W. Hawthornthwaite, E.T. Kingsley, R.B. Russell, and W.A. Pritchard preached an essentially revolutionary socialism, a doctrine to which even Jimmie Simpson subscribed in his early career, and one which was primarily a British import. It was the experience described by Eric Hobsbawm that was to determine *which* version was to be legitimated in Canada, and this was an experience common to Canada and Britain. In other words, given the essentially evolutionary nature of societies based on the British parliamentary system of customs and precedents, violent revolutionary action, either in doctrine or in practice, is illegitimate.

Of course, both Britain and Canada have experienced explosions of collective violence. But in both countries, while suppressive overkill has not infrequently been applied by employers and by the state, and while redress of grievances and relatively lenient treatment of violent leaders has been characteristic, such occasions have not served to legitimate violence as a political method – except as used by the state, when it is called force.[26] What *has* been learned in Canada from our many experiences of political and industrial violence is the importance of ensuring that legislatures and their executives not be left in the untrammelled control of those business and professional people who benefit most from the cornucopia of socially subsidized and protected privileges.

The realism of democratic socialism is a product both of its humanism and the requirements of legitimation. Those socialists who drew realistic conclusions from the cumulative experience of the long struggle for substantive change and immediate melioration did so because they perceived two fundamentals of Canadian political society: first, basic disavowal of violence as method and, second, the extraordinary opportunities for influence offered by our constitutional system to minimal electoral success let alone substantial electoral achievement. I suspect that the roles of realism and constitutional opportunity have not received appropriate weighting in discussions of Canadian socialism. It is probably the undervaluing of these two factors that has helped sustain the false images fabricated by the right, the far left, and the centre: the images of the alienated, revolutionary conspirator; of the lackey, however idealistic, of the ruling class; and of the self-righteous press-agent of reformism.

The roles of realism and constitutional opportunity have, of course, been noticed.[27] But, especially in comparative discussions of Canadian and American politics, and in textbooks, they are usually glossed over or assigned minimal significance. Martin Lipset, for example, argues that the opportunities offered 'third parties' in the Canadian constitutional system, as opposed to the constitutional obstacles to third party survival in the United States, are relatively unimportant, since the NDP 'remains a weak third party' and Canada 'still ranks with the United States at the bottom of the list in terms of support for Socialist parties.' His argument includes the proposition that 'the United States does have a mass social democratic movement in the form of the trade union, liberal welfare-state planning, and New Politics wings of the Democratic party.'[28] This assessment is part and parcel of American consensus history and is another example of pooh-poohing the facts. It appears to argue that all the American socialists need really do is form caucuses inside the Democratic party.[29] If applied to Canada, and since the Canadian Liberal party is demonstrably to the left of the American Democratic party (now containing most of our 'red Tories'), it might seem to support the statement that the NDP must be a 'weak third party' by definition. But this, of course, is simply not the case.[30]

Democratic socialist realism in assessing and using the parliamentary system and working within the Canadian political culture developed very early. The first instance, for example, of effective use of a balance-of-power situation was in 1903. The balance in the British Columbia legislature was then held by several members of the Socialist Party of Canada. Ross McCormack has noted that on this occasion, 'even though Hawthornthwaite recognized that co-operation entailed compromise, he supported the Conservative government and was able to wring a number of concessions from Premier Richard McBride.'[31] The SPC candidates came to 'accommodate their impossibilism to political realities.'[32] In the same decade in Toronto, Jimmie Simpson was also moving from Marxist impossibilism to democratic socialism and securing similar 'immediate goals' through elective office, union activity, and co-operation with much-maligned 'progressives' in such varied causes as improved education for workers, temperance, inexpensive housing, and Sunday streetcars. As Gene Homel comments, Simpson had entered 'a period of profound political maturation which was catalyzed ... by his immersion in immediate issues and the question of how to *build* a successful radical movement.'[33]

Throughout this century such preliminary experiences with the opportunities offered by electoral politics and legislative influence were repeated and produced a cumulative effect; and it was to be acceptance of the party and parliamentary systems that would decree that the Progressive and democratic socialist streams would *not* form one river to merge in the placid bosom of the Liberal party. Thus, as he had in 1926, Mackenzie King would confide to his diary in the 1940s that the democratic socialists would not go away. 'What I fear,' wrote King, 'is we will begin to have defection from our own ranks in the House to the CCF.'[34]

It is no longer necessary to recapitulate the successive experiences of official opposition, government, and balance-of-power situations that have entrenched the NDP as a *major* party and *consolidated* a multi-party structure in this country. Yet it is not enough, even so, to refer merely to the *threat* from the NDP, as did Mr Trudeau after the 1972 election, when he conceded that 'we are more forced to listen ... probably as a result of that some of our legislation will be better ... we'll have to compromise.'[35] That direct political threat did in fact lead at once to income tax improvements, pension increases, and a foreign investment review board – and, in the longer run, to public ownership in the energy field. But an equally important aspect of the realist strain is the use of *office* to set examples which other jurisdictions find it difficult or impossible to reject. Among the classic illustrations of this essentially Fabian process are the medical insurance program initiated by the Douglas government in Saskatchewan and the massive land purchase program of the Blakeney government, a policy which appears to be slowly enacting the original 'land-use' plank of the CCF's 1932 Calgary program, and which will probably have to be adopted in some fashion by other provincial governments confronted by irate farmers protesting the onslaughts of agribusiness.

The humanism, legitimacy, and realism of Canadian democratic socialism, then, have been the key strains overlooked, played down, or totally misrepresented by critics to the right and to the left. It remains to touch upon the human instruments who have expressed and been animated by these 'ghostly abstractions.' I must avoid the mawkishness which Frank Scott would so rightly abhor. Yet, personal integrity has been a *sine qua non*. Not all the men and women in our democratic socialism have been full-blown prophets; but the vast majority of them have known how to resist the blandishment of easy preferment, outright offers of high office, and the temptation of European-style formal coalitions. And supporting the active politicians has always been a surprisingly wide array of academics, writers and artists – among whom Frank Scott is, to employ an élitist-socialist tag, *primus inter pares*.

NOTES

1 *Social Planning for Canada*, the Research Committee of the League for Social Reconstruction, with an introduction by F.R. Scott, Leonard Marsh, Graham Spry, J. King Gordon, Eugene Forsey, and J.F. Parkinson (Toronto 1975; 1935) ix, xvii

2 For a discussion of the CCLH and recent writing on labour and socialism, see my 'E.P. Thompson vs Harold Logan: Writing about Labour and the Left in the 1970s,' *Canadian Historical Review* (June 1981).

3 Bryan Palmer's *A Culture in Conflict: Skilled Workers and Industrial Capitalism in Hamilton, Ontario, 1860-1914* (Montreal 1979) is the most forthright attempt to apply to Canada the ideas about an evolutionary, autonomous working-class culture developed by E.P. Thompson in *The Making of the English Working Class* (London 1968).

4 E.J. Hobsbawm, *Revolutionaries: Contemporary Essays* (New York 1973) 15

5 For the smear campaign of 1943-4 organized by Gladstone Murray on behalf of the corporate establishment, see Gerald Caplan, *The Dilemma of Canadian Socialism* (Toronto 1973), especially chapter 8. Such calumnious campaigns were previewed in BC in 1933 and Saskatchewan in 1934, and reached a second crescendo in the Saskatchewan doctors' campaign against 'socialized medicine' in the early sixties.

6 D.G. Creighton, *Canada's First Century* (Toronto 1970) 210

7 To Creighton, King also was 'sanctimonious,' but in addition he was 'puritanical,' 'intensely self-centered and ostentatiously public-spirited,' and 'from the beginning a North American continentalist.' Ibid. 162, 268. No opponent of King could be *all* bad.

8 J.M.S. Careless, *Canada: A Story of Challenge* (Cambridge, Eng. 1963) 361-2

9 W.L. Morton, *The Progressive Party in Canada* (Toronto 1950) 148

10 J.D. Hicks, *The Populist Revolt* (New York 1931)

11 Richard Hofstadter, 'Political Parties,' in C.V. Woodward, ed., *A Comparative Approach to American History* (Washington, DC 1968) 229. It is probably correct to say that the most important American 'input' to Canadian socialism has been the populist stress on party democracy – and this is certainly the most important Canadian Progressive legacy to the CCF-NDP, for it has obviated the severe dangers inherent in what might be termed the democratic centralism of the British Labour party's system of bloc voting.

12 Louis Hartz, *The Liberal Tradition in America* (New York 1955) and *The Founding of New Societies* (New York 1964); Gad Horowitz, *Canadian Labour in Politics* (Toronto 1968); Daniel Bell, *Marxian Socialism in the United States* (Princeton 1967). S.M. Lipset makes the point that Hartz's basic conception was clearly foreshadowed by H.G. Wells in 1906 and by Werner Sombart at the same time: Lipset, 'Why No Socialism in the United States?' in S. Bialer and S. Sluzar, eds, *Sources of Contemporary Radicalism* (New York 1977).

13 Creighton, *Canada's First Century* and *The Forked Road* (Toronto 1976); W.L. Morton, *The Kingdom of Canada* (Toronto 1969). Creighton concludes in *Canada's First Century*: 'The review of the Canadian constitution, begun in confusion and irresolution ... was likely to end in futility; and the failure of this unavailing effort was certain to bring continentalism one long stage further towards its final triumph.'

14 See *A Prophet in Politics* (Toronto 1959) ch. 15.

15 Mr Martin said that he would soon write an article substantiating this interpretation. When I recounted this incident recently to a former Liberal cabinet minister he responded with a no-comment chuckle.

16 Richard Hofstadter, *The Paranoid Style in American Politics* (New York 1965). Even in the United States one can scarcely describe Grover Cleveland, Teddy Roosevelt, or J. Edgar Hoover as out-groupies.

17 For paranoia in the Canadian sectarian left, see Roger O'Toole, *The Precipitous Path* (Toronto 1977).

18 *Canadian Unionist* (Dec. 1932), quoted in Walter Young, *The Anatomy of a Party: The National CCF 1932-61* (Toronto 1969) 257

19 Norman Penner, *The Canadian Left* (Toronto 1977)

20 Primarily an account of communism in Canada, Penner's book is useful mainly as a supplement to Ivan Avakoumovic's *The Communist Party of Canada: A History* (Toronto 1975) and William Rodney's *Soldiers of the International* (Toronto 1968).

21 Penner thus ignores the CCF-NDP achievements in office, as official oppositions and in balance-of-power situations. In his index appear Rioux, Vallières, S. Ryerson, Salsberg, Morris, Stewart Smith, Buck, Carr, Spector, Stalin and Lenin, but not to be found are F.R. Scott, Forsey, Spry, Coldwell, Jolliffe, Barrett, Stephen Lewis, or Blakeney. T.C. Douglas, who headed North America's first socialist government, is mentioned once for having 'participated in united front activities,' while David Lewis is mentioned twice – because he allegedly withdrew a CCF candidate in order to help Salsberg in an election (surely apocryphal!), and again because he believed that the CCF should 'effect a marriage with the labour movement' of which communists had been 'the most effective organizers.' The enthusiasm with which the neo-Marxist cultural conflict crowd studies occasions of 'worker violence' as evidence of 'revolutionary potential' also intimates a basic preference for extraparliamentary methods of change and political education.

22 The academic gamesmanship which draws a straight line from John Locke, the enlightenment political libertarian, to 'democracy' and 'free capitalist enterprise' I have always regarded as coming within Thorstein Veblen's rubric of 'deliberate obfuscation.' With respect to the relationship between security of property and political liberty it could more reasonably be argued that today both Locke and Jefferson would find democratic socialism not only agreeable but essential.

23 See, for example, Richard Allen, *The Social Passion: Religion and Social Reform in Canada 1914-28* (Toronto 1971); Michiel Horn, *The League for Social Reconstruction: Intellectual Origins of the Democratic Left in Canada 1930-42* (Toronto 1980); Gregory Baum, *Catholics and Canadian Socialism: Political Thought in the Thirties and Forties* (Toronto 1980). At a recent conference on the LSR, Frank Scott reflected that his reading of the reports of Anglican conferences of the early twenties ranked as an influence on his own thinking about society with the writing of R.H. Tawney.

24 The complementary aspects of movement and party have been concisely depicted in Young, *Anatomy of a Party* 287-302.

25 See John Porter, *The Vertical Mosaic* (Toronto 1965). A recent critique of Porter's analysis upsets, in my opinion, much of his central argument and

adds considerably to an understanding of our capacity to 'Canadianize' both people and ideas: A. Gordon Darroch and Michael D. Ornstein, 'Ethnicity and Occupational Structure in Canada in 1871: The Vertical Mosaic in Historical Perspective,' *Canadian Historical Review* (Sept. 1980).

26 I have discussed this question more fully in 'Collective Violence and the Canadian Political Tradition,' in M. Friedland, ed., *Courts and Trials* (Toronto 1975). The best discussions of the use of force in industrial disputes are: Desmond Morton, 'Aid to the Civil Power: The Canadian Militia in Support of Civil Order,' *Canadian Historical Review* LI, 4 (Dec. 1970), and, 'Taking on the Grand Trunk: The Locomotive Engineers' Strike of 1876-7,' *Labour/Le Travailleur* (1977); David Bercuson, *Confrontation at Winnipeg: Labour, Industrial Relations, and the General Strike* (Montreal 1974); Don MacGillivray, 'Military Aid to the Civil Power: The Cape Breton Experience in the 1920's,' *Acadiensis* (Spring 1973).

27 Especially in Young, *Anatomy of a Party*, chs 7-10; Martin Robin, *Radical Politics and Canadian Labour, 1880-1930* (Kingston 1968) 272ff.; Desmond Morton, *NDP: The Dream of Power* (Toronto 1974)

28 S.M. Lipset, 'Radicalism in North America: A Comparative View of the Party Systems in Canada and the United States,' *Transactions of the Royal Society of Canada* (1976)

29 Or non-party groups such as the League for Industrial Democracy or Michael Harrington's Committee for Social Democracy

30 It is interesting that in a subsequent article (in *Sources of Contemporary Radicalism*), Lipset terms the NDP 'a major third party in English-speaking Canada.' In 1963, Norman Thomas reflected that 'had we had a centralized parliamentary government rather than a federal presidential government, we should have had, under some name or another, a moderately strong socialist party' (Norman Thomas, *Socialism Re-Examined* [New York 1963] 117; quoted in Lipset, *idem*). For a sceptical comment on Thomas's apologia, see my 'Consensus and American Socialism,' *The Canadian Forum* (June-July 1978).

31 A. Ross McCormack, *Reformers, Rebels and Revolutionaries: The Western Canadian Radical Movement 1899-1919* (Toronto 1977) 64

32 Ibid. 63

33 Gene Homel, 'James Simpson and the Origins of Canadian Social Democracy,' PHD dissertation (University of Toronto 1978) 725. See also Homel, 'Fading Beams of the Nineteenth Century: Radicalism and Early Socialism in Canada's 1890's,' *Labour/Le Travailleur* (Spring 1980).

34 J.W. Pickersgill, ed., *The Mackenzie King Record*, I, *1939-44* (Toronto 1960) 571. For a comprehensive background to King's lugubrious ruminations see Laurel Sefton MacDowell, *'Remember Kirkland Lake': The History and Effects of the Kirkland Lake Gold Miners' General Strike 1941-42* (Toronto 1983).

35 J.T. Saywell, ed., *The Canadian Annual Review* (Toronto 1972)

PART FOUR

F.R. Scott and Legal Education

FRANK SCOTT taught law at McGill for some forty years. The profound impression he made as a teacher remains with one for life. By his example as a university man of law with a unique range of achievement he inspired his fellow teachers and made a significant contribution to the recognition and development of the academic branch of the legal profession.

I first encountered Frank Scott in his constitutional law class in 1946. We were for the most part a class of returning veterans, glad to be back, looking forward to careers in civilian life and eager for intellectual stimulation. He made us think, disturbed our complacencies, and enlarged our understanding and perspective. He was then forty-seven, had been teaching since 1928, and was at the height of his powers and creative activity. He himself was engaged in a kind of combat, full of zest, interest, and commitment. His teaching had an energizing as well as an illuminating effect. It was challenging. What he was talking about, broadly speaking, was the nature of Canada and what it meant to be a Canadian, and the role of constitutional law in relation to the supreme values, as he saw them, of Canadian life. As veterans, we had thought much about what it meant to be a Canadian and what the shape of the post-war world should be like. His was one view, and it was a stimulating one.

Perhaps the outstanding characteristic of Frank Scott as teacher and legal scholar was his point of view or philosophic frame of reference. There was no pretense of neutrality in his teaching and writing. He had strong convictions on what should be the broad goals of government policy, and these provided the framework within which he considered the implications of the distribution and exercise of legal power. A consistent thread of social policy and purpose runs through his constitutional thought. The key ideas are economic planning, social justice, and the protection of human rights. As the major themes in his work in public law are examined more closely in other essays in this volume, I shall only touch on them briefly here.

Frank Scott believed in strong, central government capable of stimulating and regulating economic activity and redistributing income in order to maintain minimum standards of welfare. Much of his work in constitutional law was devoted to demonstrating how the judicial interpretation of the constitution by the Privy Council had changed its nature as conceived by the Fathers of Confederation and had so weakened the powers of the central government as to make it incapable of dealing effectively with national problems. He often observed that the failure of democratic government to act would not mean an absence of effective government: the vacuum would be filled by the governmental power of the large corporation. His perception of the corporation as a rival government had affinities with the main thesis of Galbraith's *The New Industrial State*.

In administrative law, Frank Scott sought to explain and justify the growth of modern administration – the positive state, as he would call it – and he expressed concern about the use of judicial control to defeat the policies that the administration was required to implement. 'Judges,' he said, 'must not substitute their notions of social purpose for those of the legislature; indeed, they are there to see that the policy of parliament is carried out, not that it is altered or frustrated.'[1] At the same time, he valued the role of the courts in maintaining the rule of law and the protection of civil liberties, and by his own interventions in this field he helped to affirm that role. One of his themes in administrative law was the importance of making the state and its instrumentalities fully liable for the damage caused by their wrongful acts. He urged elimination of the immunity of the crown and public corporations enjoying the status of crown agents. 'If the state creates risks of damage,' he said, 'it should assume these risks as fully as any private person.'[2]

An important theme in his work as teacher and scholar was the development of Canadian independence. His writing on this subject reveals his deep love of country and his appreciation of the unique nature of Canadian nationhood. Of the political nationalism that inspired confederation, he wrote: 'Its principal aim was to achieve those democratic ends which all true nationalism strives for – the elevation of a whole people to a new status in the community of nations. Canada was to be "redeemed from provincialism"; her public men were to move into a larger world where great duties and great opportunities would evoke great responses.'[3] Some of his most interesting writing discusses the nature of constitutional relationships in the Commonwealth and the question of the patriation of the Canadian constitution.

Finally, Frank Scott was profoundly concerned as teacher and scholar with the problems of Canadian unity, particularly the position of French Canada in confederation. Here his constitutional philosophy encountered a major problem: how to reconcile the emphasis on more power for the federal government with the desire of French Canada for a stronger constitutional basis for the development of its life as a distinct cultural community. Scott was always sympathetic to the claims of French Canada for a fairer opportunity to share in the advantages of Canadian life, but he questioned the identification of French Canada's interests with the provincial government of Quebec as the sole or principal defender of those interests. He contended that 'minority rights' should not be confused with 'provincial rights.' He argued that the larger opportunity French Canada sought could only be opened up by federal action. A closely related theme in his work was the relationship between minority or group rights and individual rights, and how these two kinds of rights are to be reconciled in practice and given adequate protection at the same time.

Scott approached these issues from an historical as well as a contemporary perspective. The historical approach was an important feature of his work as teacher and scholar. He had honoured in history at Bishop's and had continued his study of history while at Oxford on a Rhodes scholarship. He credited H.A. Smith, who taught him constitutional law at McGill, with persuading him of the importance of the historical approach to the constitution. 'It was he,' Scott said, 'who taught me to see the problems which the Act of 1867 was intended to remedy, to look at the conditions in the British North American colonies in the 1860s, and to seek the intentions of the Fathers of Confederation not only in the words of the statutes but also in all the material available to historians, including the Confederation debates and other *travaux préparatoires*.'[4] I have already quoted from his essay on 'Political Nationalism and Confederation,' which is full of historical perspective. There is one very characteristic passage in it, where, speaking of the commercial interests which saw advantages, and in some cases salvation, in confederation, Scott said: 'A fact to which Canadian historians have drawn far too little attention was the union in 1863 through the International Financial Society Limited, of the two largest corporations with a stake in Canada, the Grand Trunk Railway and the Hudson's Bay Company.'[5]

Frank Scott taught law in the liberal tradition. His courses in public law could have been given to arts students as well as law students. They had the broad foundation of learning, the perspective, the range, and the connection with other disciplines, such as history and political science. It is significant, I think, that his articles were published over the years in a variety of learned journals and that, when finally brought together as a collection of essays on the constitution, with the subtitle *Aspects of Canadian Law and Politics*, they were crowned with a Governor General's Award. Scott shared the conviction of Karl Llewellyn as to the value of the liberal approach to legal education. In an address at the Chicago Law School in 1960, entitled 'The Study of Law as a Liberal Art,' Llewellyn said: 'The truth, the truth which cries out, is that the good work, the most effective work of the lawyer in practice roots in and depends on vision, range, depth, balance, and rich humanity – those things which it is the function and frequently the fortune, of the liberal arts to introduce and indeed to induce.'[6] Llewellyn concluded that 'the best *practical* training, along with the best human training' that a university could give a lawyer was 'the study of law within the professional school itself, as a liberal art.'

At the same time, Scott's courses had professional rigour. They were concerned with fundamentals, and they were comprehensive in their treatment of their subject. Scott taught constitutional law in two parts: the first part, given in first year, dealt with the general principles of the constitution derived for the most part from the unitary system of Great Britain, including such matters as the nature of the legislative, executive, and judicial branches of government, the distinction between constitutional law and constitutional convention, the royal prerogative, the legal position of the servant of the crown, the nature and implications of legislative sovereignty, and the meaning of the rule of law. These questions were examined in their distinctively Canadian context. There was, for example, a full analysis of the precise effects of the Statute of Westminster.

The second part of the subject, given in second year, was concerned with the nature of Canadian federalism and the distribution of legislative power. What my lecture notes in constitutional law for the years 1946 and 1947 reflect is Scott's emphasis on a good all-round grasp of fundamental principles. He covered aspects of constitutional law which other teachers and scholars might not have considered deserving of the same priority. Current events have proved them to be of supreme practical importance. There was consideration, for example, of the various theories as to the essential nature of confederation and the extent to which there had been consultation of the provinces in connection with the amendments of the constitution. It is striking how many of the fundamental questions he considered are still living issues today. Scott said once that we had a rendez-vous with the BNA Act, and although he said that with particular reference to the distribution of legislative power, he taught constitutional law as if he wanted his students to be prepared for that rendez-vous, whatever the agenda might be.

When speaking of professional rigour and comprehensiveness, I should observe that, while Frank Scott came to specialize in public law, he had a solid grounding in private law as well. He had taught Obligations at McGill. And it showed in his work. He did not suffer from the limited view and range resulting from premature and narrow specialization. *Roncarelli* v *Duplessis*, after all, was a case that involved the principles of the civil law of responsibility (fault, damage, and causal connection) as well as the principles of public law governing the limits of ministerial authority and the validity of administrative decisions. One of its interesting aspects from the point of view of legal theory was the interrelationship of private and public law principles. It was a fitting focus for Scott's kind of legal breadth.

In *The Aims of Education*, Alfred North Whitehead said that the essence of university education was the imaginative consideration of learning. Teachers, he said, must be filled with living thoughts: they must be able to bring their subject to life. Frank Scott met this requirement pre-eminently. In his case, it sprang not only from his intellectual gifts and general cultivation, but from the nature of his interests and involvement. One of the occupational hazards of teachers in basic courses is that they will grow stale by repetition and lose their inspiration or (what may be as bad for the students) seek to maintain their own interest by moving into increasingly specialized and esoteric areas so that they are really substituting post-graduate teaching for undergraduate teaching. Scott never seemed to lose his enthusiasm for teaching fundamentals. The secret, I believe, was that he continually renewed his interest by relating the fundamentals to contemporary conditions and events. He was what the students in the 1960s used to refer to as 'relevant.' He was not interested in constitutional doctrines and principles as mere abstractions, but in their operating nature and effects. His teaching and scholarship were policy oriented and concerned with functional implications. This emphasis is reflected in his statement: 'While the law of the constitution went one way, the facts of modern industrialism went the other.'[7]

Playing over the whole field was his interpretative perspective, which perceived the underlying significance of things and the connection between them and was capable of throwing fresh light on issues. This was probably the outstanding mark of his scholarship. One could cite many examples. A typical observation was the suggestion in his 1959 Plaunt Memorial Lectures on 'Civil Liberties and Canadian Federalism' that we should celebrate 1 October as our independence day because 1 October 1947 was the effective date of the Letters Patent, which transferred 'all powers and authorities' of the crown in respect of Canada to the governor general.

Perhaps in no other piece of writing is his imaginative perspective more strikingly demonstrated than in his highly original article on section 94 of the BNA Act. This provision, which provided a means by which the federal parliament, with the consent of the common law provinces, could assume legislative jurisdiction with respect to matters of property and civil rights, was generally thought to have become a dead letter. Scott's purpose was to draw attention to the original significance of the provision and to its future possibilities for constitutional flexibility. To this end, he raised the startling hypothesis that the federal Industrial Disputes Investigation Act (the 'Lemieux Act'), as amended (after the decision in the *Snider* case) to provide for its provincial adoption for disputes within provincial jurisdiction, had in fact been adopted by most of the provinces in such a manner as to meet the requirements of section 94: the consequence, Scott argued, was that legislative jurisdiction with respect to the subject-matter of the act had been irrevocably transferred by the adopting provinces to the federal parliament. Scott himself acknowledged that this view was unlikely to be adopted by the courts, but it was typical of the imaginative question that he was capable of raising in his analysis of a legislative provision. This was undoubtedly one of the qualities that made his advocacy, when he finally went to court, so impressive and compelling. His mind ranged freely. He was not hidebound by an exaggerated concern for what was 'sound.' Frank Scott once said to me in a letter that he had 'tried to see the law in the round,' and that was reflected in his approach to teaching. The image I retain of the effect of his teaching is of one holding a precious stone in his fingers and turning it slowly so as to allow the light to play on its many facets.

There was undoubtedly a relationship between Scott's teaching and scholarly vocation and his literary vocation. He perceived the aesthetic quality in the law. It is reflected in the title of one of his essays, 'The State as a Work of Art.' His perception was what Llewellyn referred to as 'the quest and study of beauty in and within the institution of law-government.' His care for form was a valuable example in a profession that lives by the word. Scott spoke and wrote as teacher and scholar with simple elegance, clarity, and force. He had, of course, the poetic power of going to the heart of the matter.

Enlivening all his teaching and writing was his irrepressible sense of humour, expressing itself in epigram and aphorism, delighting in irony and a sense of the ridiculous. The title 'Duplessis versus Jehovah' is only one of many examples. Speaking of 'the growing use of monetary policy, taxation and planned government spending, as factors in maintaining economic equilibrium,' he said, 'Keynes became a kind of post-natal

Father of Confederation.'[8] Writing (in 'The Redistribution of Imperial Sovereignty') on the form which patriation of the Canadian constitution should take, he said:

> To borrow another analogy from the well-known eastern myth, we may say that until now all legal rules in Canada, from municipal bylaws to whole codes of law like the Quebec Civil Code or the Criminal Code, have derived their validity from the elephant of the BNA Act, which stood firmly upon the turtle of the sovereignty of the United Kingdom Parliament. Beneath the turtle nothing further has existed to support a stable universe. Now the various Dominions are getting their own turtles, and we are looking for a Canadian turtle.[9]

Of the validity of the spending power he said, 'generosity in Canada is not unconstitutional' and 'making a gift is not the same as making a law.'[10] My constitutional law notes for 1946 and 1947 show that, speaking of the contribution which Canada's participation in the two world wars made to the achievement of Canadian independence, he said, 'Canada won her independence fighting against Germans.'

Throughout his career, Frank Scott was passionately concerned about the recognition and development of university legal education. It was a subject that came up often in his discussions with fellow teachers, academic administrators, and other members of the legal profession. He knew long periods of discouragement and frustration. For many years progress was painfully slow. But before his teaching career came to a close he saw full-time academic legal education established in Canada on solid foundations. He had helped to keep the faith alive through the difficult years.

Frank Scott had a true vocation for the life of the full-time law teacher, and he remained faithful to it to the end. He tells how he was sitting as a beginning lawyer in 1928 in the Montreal firm of Lafleur, MacDougall, Macfarlane and Barclay, with whom his older brother was associated, when he received a letter from McGill. He says that before opening it, and without any prior intimation of what it contained, he knew intuitively what it was about, and he knew what his answer would be. It was an invitation from the dean of the McGill Faculty of Law to accept appointment in succession to H.A. Smith as professor of federal and constitutional law. He did not hesitate and he never regretted his decision.

The condition of academic legal education in Canada when Frank Scott joined the full-time faculty at McGill in 1928 was far from robust. Before 1900, legal training had been based essentially on a system of articling or law office apprenticeship followed by bar examinations. It was not necessary to obtain a law degree, and little credit was given for having one. The period of articling varied from three to five years depending on the candidate's previous education. The educational requirements for admission to the study of law were modest for a learned profession: in most cases, a senior matriculation. A university degree in arts or some other undergraduate course was recognized by the reduction of one or two years in the period of articles, and a law degree was at first given a similar recognition in some jurisdictions. There were seven law schools in the country, all in the east. They were staffed by a small nuclei of full-time teachers who were heavily outnumbered by part-time instructors drawn from the bar and bench. In some jurisdictions there was a system of concurrent law school and law office training. This was still essentially the picture after World War I, except that by 1921 there were law schools established in each of the prairie provinces.

The underdeveloped state of legal education in Canada was brought forcibly to the attention of the profession in the 1920s by a small but distinguished and dedicated group of full-time teachers who sought through the Legal Education Committee of the Canadian Bar Association to arouse the profession to the need for greater support of full-time academic legal education. In his report in 1923, the chairman of the committee, Dean D.A. MacRae of Dalhousie Law School, referred to the comparative sizes of the full-time staffs of American and Canadian law schools as follows: 'As compared with the better law schools of the United States Canadian Law Schools are sadly deficient in the matter of staff. Harvard has fourteen full-time teachers, Northwestern thirteen, Columbia thirteen, Yale thirteen, Cornell seven, to take only a few instances at random. The maximum number of full-time teachers at any Canadian Law School engaged in teaching common law subjects is at present only three.'[11] Commenting on the system whereby students attended lectures for part of the day and worked in offices for the rest, H.A. Smith said in the spirited discussion which followed presentation of the MacRae Report: 'The needs of the student are thought to be met by giving one lecture after breakfast and another before supper, and he is expected to spend the remainder of the day picking up what odds and ends of information he can in an office.'[12] That was essentially the state of affairs when Frank Scott became one of the three full-time members of the McGill Faculty of Law.

Full-time academic legal education made relatively modest progress in the 1930s and 1940s. Professor Maxwell Cohen, who was one of Scott's colleagues at McGill and who also made a distinguished contribution to the development of legal education in Canada, reported on its condition in 1949.[13] His article drew some comfort from a perceptible improvement in conditions relative to the 1920s, but it revealed that full-time faculties were still very small, library resources, with few exceptions, insignificant, and physical accommodation in many cases inadequate. The number of full-time staff in the eleven law schools of Canada ranged from one to a maximum of seven. There were four at McGill, one more than when Frank Scott had joined the faculty twenty years earlier.

As every report on the condition of legal education observed, the university priorities were a reflection of the relative lack of professional interest and support. What was required was recognition by the profession of the necessity and value of full-time academic legal education. For many years there was uncertainty in the profession as to the best approach to legal education and training. What was being worked out was the proper distribution of responsibility between the universities and the practising profession. It took a long time to reach a satisfactory accommodation. In the process, there was a good deal of misunderstanding and recrimination, and, I suppose, one would have to say, mutual distrust. The practising profession was concerned about the adequacy of academic legal education as a preparation for the practice of law. It was also concerned about its own capacity to provide an adequate system of practical training. For their part, the full-time teachers of law resented the practising profession's lack of confidence and support and felt frustrated by its efforts to control the content of the academic program. Both sides thought they knew what was required. Neither could do it alone. It required an adjustment of responsibility and a renewed dedication on the part of each to do what they could do best. The system that was ultimately worked out was the full-time degree program followed by a period of organized practical training, including systematic instruction as well as law office experience.

Academic legal education can be effectively imparted by part-time teachers. There have been some outstanding part-time teachers, and there will always be a certain number on the staff of a well-organized and well-balanced law school. But the profession requires a corps of men and women who have the ability and the time for research into and deep reflection on the nature and development of the law in its various fields, and to provide critical perspective. This is well understood by the judicial branch, which depends heavily on the quality of the materials that are put before it. The full-time teacher has the independence and the detachment for critical evaluation of the law and the legal process. This is a supremely important function and almost a justification in itself for a distinct branch of the profession. Moreover, the development of suitable teaching materials and an effective educational process in each field is a difficult task that requires the leadership of persons devoting their full time to this objective.

The quality of the academic branch of the legal profession and the respect which it enjoys in the rest of the profession depend, of course, on the quality of its individual members. It has always been difficult to recruit and hold outstanding persons with a true vocation for teaching and scholarship. There are many competing attractions and opportunities for the exercise of legal ability. There is a certain ambivalence about the respective pulls of the life of action and the life of contemplation. Underlying the career decision must be a strong belief in the validity and worth of what one is doing. Frank Scott had that strong belief, and he projected it to a remarkable degree. It was a source of encouragement and inspiration for his colleagues in the academic branch of the profession.

In the late 1940s, Scott initiated the discussions which led to formation of the Association of Canadian Law Teachers, now known as the Canadian Association of Law Teachers. He was elected its first president. The Association helped to strengthen the sense of professional identity and purpose among law teachers. It afforded an annual opportunity for contact and exchange on matters of mutual interest – so important as a means of overcoming the sense of isolation of the individual scholar in this vast country. The report of his committee on legal research, to which I shall refer shortly, alluded to the special problem of getting together in Canada, where, in speaking of the early years of the Association, it said: 'Its chief difficulties at the moment are the usual Canadian ones – too little money and too much geography.'[14] The founding of the ACLT was one of several such university initiatives in which Frank Scott participated during his academic career. He believed in the association and co-operation of teachers for the pursuit of common interests. He was first and foremost a man of the university. He had the respect of his colleagues in the other faculties, and he enjoyed intellectual exchange with them. I can see him now in what we used to refer to as the 'circle' in the McGill Faculty Club, holding forth at lunch. The spirit of the university was in his blood.

The 1950s were difficult and crucial years for legal education in Canada. They were also years of outstanding achievement for Frank Scott. Unlike his great contemporary 'Caesar' Wright at Toronto, it was not given to him to have a position of administrative responsibility and leadership during those years. As is well known, Frank Scott had been repeatedly passed over for dean of the McGill law faculty, when he was the obvious choice, because of his political opinions and activities. When he was finally offered the deanship in 1961, he accepted it, with some misgiving, as much to set matters right, if somewhat belatedly, as because of what he felt he could accomplish in the few years remaining to him before retirement. But the fact that he was not dean during the 1940s and 1950s (when one was appointed dean for life, not for a term) in no way lessened his personal authority and influence in the academic community. And he was, as a result, freer to pursue his wide range of individual and independent activity. In 1952, for example, he spent a year in Burma as resident technical representative of the United Nations. This was a reflection of his devotion to the goal and responsibility of world community, another important aspect of the idealism and conviction that inspired his endeavours.

In 1954, the recognition of the profession was reflected in his appointment as chairman of the special committee established by the Canadian Bar Association to inquire into and report on the state of legal research in Canada. It was a strong and representative committee that included Dean Wright among its members. Its report, on which Scott spent many hours of careful labour, is an impressive document and a forceful statement on legal education as the necessary foundation of good legal research. 'The first requisite for better legal research in Canada,' it said, 'is better law schools. On this point your committee is unanimous. It is in the law schools that the young men and women entering the profession learn the habit and techniques of research. There they will acquire a respect for legal scholarship if they are ever going to, and will meet the instructors who can inspire them with a desire to make their own contribution to the legal thought of their country.'[15]

The report emphasized the great disparity in the comparative support for legal education and medical education – a point that had been referred to in the MacRae Report of 1923 and the Cohen survey of 1949. It was something Frank Scott felt particularly strongly about because he had seen at first hand the striking difference in the support which medicine and law had received at McGill. Medicine was the jewel in the McGill crown. It must be said that it had earned its position by outstanding achievement that had brought it an international reputation. But behind the high level of professional, and therefore university, support for medical education was the individual concern for personal health and survival, which could always be relied on to stimulate the flow of financial support. The individual did not think as much of what he or she owed to the blessing of personal security and freedom under law. As Scott's report put it: 'Is the health of the individual body of more concern than the health of the body politic?'[16]

The report called for a new status for the law schools. It also referred to the central issue in legal education in the 1950s: the struggle in Ontario for the full recognition of academic legal education by the Law

Society of Upper Canada. That struggle began with the departure of Wright, Willis, and Laskin from the Osgoode Hall Law School in 1949 and ended with the settlement of 1957, in which John Arnup and Alex Corry played leading roles. The report of the Committee on Legal Research was written when the controversy was at its height. The bitterness engendered by it was reflected in the observations of Dean Wright, who dissented from the majority recommendation for the establishment of a legal research foundation by the Canadian Bar Association on the ground that it would detract from the support that should be given to the law schools. He spoke of the future in pessimistic terms: 'After nearly thirty years spent in legal education in this country, I regret having to state that the prospects for improvement in educational standards in law are far from bright. Schools that have struggled to preserve and to improve standards have met and are still meeting with opposition from the organized profession.'[17]

As it turned out, Dean Wright's remarks were made when legal education was on the threshold of the breakthrough that was to open the way to the great development of the 1960s. In 1957, the Law Society of Upper Canada surrendered its monopoly over legal education to permit the full recognition and development of university faculties of law. The Society established the present system of legal education and training by which a full-time three-year degree course is followed by a period of practical training called the Bar Admission Course, which consists of twelve months' articling followed by six months of systematic instruction of a practical nature at Osgoode Hall. Although Frank Scott could not play a direct role in the resolution of this conflict, of such far-reaching consequence for legal education in Canada, it may be assumed that the report of his Committee on Legal Research, because of its strong affirmation of the importance of academic legal education and the need for increased support for the law schools, contributed to the climate of professional opinion that furthered its resolution.

It was during the 1950s that Frank Scott took his long-standing advocacy of civil liberties into the courts with striking success. What his participation as counsel in the *Switzman* and *Roncarelli* cases reflected was not just his professional ability but his independence and moral courage. It is difficult for someone who did not live in Quebec at that time to appreciate the atmosphere of psychological intimidation that was created by the Duplessis régime, and the determination that it took to challenge Duplessis in such a direct manner. Prominent counsel felt obliged to decline the *Roncarelli* brief. In my opinion, it is as much for his independence and moral courage, reflected over the years in the strong stands he took on contentious issues, as for his unusual gifts and intellectual achievements, that Frank Scott is so respected in this country. As we may say of someone that he is worth his salt, so we say of Frank Scott that he was worth his tenure. Bora Laskin, who was then the distinguished professor of law at the University of Toronto, expressed one perception of what Scott's example meant to the academic branch of the profession, when, in his review of Scott's Plaunt Memorial Lectures in 1959, he said:

Professor Scott, by any measure, is already a heroic figure in Canadian public life. Both contemplative and active, he has combined careers as law teacher and lawyer, political theorist and party strategist, poet and man of letters, speaker and author. His contribution to Canadian public law has come as significantly from his advocacy before the Supreme Court of Canada as from his law review writings. The debt of the full-time law teacher to Professor Scott is a lasting one. This most academic of lawyers has, once and for all, I hope, laid the ghost of the inadequacy of the law teacher to perform in the practical arena of the court room. His arguments in *Switzman* v. *Elbling* on the validity of the Quebec Padlock Act and in *Roncarelli* v. *Duplessis* on the delictual responsibility of a minister of the Crown (even if he be a premier or prime minister) were delivered as much on behalf of the full-time law teachers of Canada as on behalf of Scott himself.[18]

I end as I began. Frank Scott was a model of excellence for his students and his fellow teachers. He inspired them both. He stimulated the love of law and the professional aspiration of his students, and he stimulated the sense of professional identity and purpose of his fellow teachers. By his example, he enhanced the image of the academic branch of the profession, helped to attract others to full-time teaching and scholarship and strengthened the claim of the academic branch to recognition and support.

NOTES

1 F.R. Scott, 'Administrative Law: 1923-1947' (1948), 26 *Canadian Bar Review* 268, 277
2 Ibid. 282
3 Scott, *Essays on the Constitution* (Toronto 1977) 34
4 Ibid. 390-1
5 Ibid. 4
6 Karl Llewellyn, *Jurisprudence* (1962) 376
7 Scott, *Essays* 142, 147
8 Ibid. 397
9 Ibid. 246

10 Ibid. 297

11 (1923), 1 *Canadian Bar Review* 671

12 8 *Proceedings* of the Canadian Bar Association (1923) 101

13 Maxwell Cohen, 'The Condition of Legal Education in Canada' (1950), 28 *Canadian Bar Review* 267

14 Report of the Committee on Legal Research (1956), 34 *Canadian Bar Review* 999

15 Ibid. 1020

16 Ibid. 1004

17 Ibid. 1059

18 Bora Laskin, book review in 13 *University of Toronto Law Journal* (1959-60) 288-9

WILLIAM R. LEDERMAN

F.R. Scott and
Constitutional Law

IN THE PREFACE to his *Essays on the Constitution*, Frank Scott tells us that he started to teach Canadian constitutional law in 1928, just as the Great Depression was about to close in on all parts of the country. As he tells us, the human misery he soon saw widespread around him impelled him to progressive political activities. And this involvement, he also testifies, sharpened his insight into the nature of law and particularly of constitutional law.

I saw that every legal change involves a choice of values, a selection of objectives, and in this sense I was greatly attracted to the concept of law as social engineering being then advanced by the great American jurist, Roscoe Pound. Changing a constitution confronts a society with the most important choices, for in the constitution will be found the philosophical principles and rules which largely determine the relations of the individual and of cultural groups to one another and to the state. If human rights and harmonious relations between cultures are forms of the beautiful, then the state is a work of art that is never finished. Law thus takes its place, in its theory and practice, among man's highest and most creative activities.[1]

Accordingly, Pound's sociological jurisprudence seems to explain much about Frank Scott's conceptions of the nature of Canadian federal constitutional law. Pound spoke of conflicting human interests and claims that arose from the facts of life in our society, and of how the decisionmakers of the law, whether legislators or judges, must strive to reconcile these opposing claims with compromises that establish tolerable equilibrium points between them. The decisionmakers, Pound said, must strive to make the good things of existence, tangible and intangible, go around as far and as fairly as possible among the people, with the least friction and waste. This effort at distributive justice involved two things we should notice in this context. First, it meant that existing laws must be relevant to the human needs of the society concerned. Hence, Pound emphasized the need constantly to get in the evidence about the actual effects of existing laws for the people concerned, and on then judging the meaning and worth of the laws in the light of those consequences.

This all seems somewhat obvious today, but Pound's approach contrasts sharply with another idea of law that has had much strength: the notion of law as a self-sufficient autonomous system of societal rules with which citizens must conform, without much regard for systematic assessment of what the rules were really doing to them or for them.

But Pound's social engineering was not just a matter of getting in the facts, important though that was. Value judgments, or policy decisions, if you prefer that expression, were also called for from the decision-makers, particularly as they contemplated what lesser or greater reforms of established laws were justified. Roscoe Pound implied that it was the better or more just compromises of conflicting interests that made the goods of existence go around with the least friction and waste, but he was never very clear about what his criteria of value were beyond the rather obvious prevailing standards of the moment. It seems to me that Frank Scott goes beyond Pound in this respect. Usually, in both politics and law, Scott was explicit about the values he accepted and the positions they caused him to take concerning both the interpretation and the reform of the law. Moreover, to this range of vision Scott added the federal dimension: that of conflicting federal and provincial governmental claims to possession of designated areas of legislative jurisdiction.

He always asked not only what changes in the law were needed, but also, which level of government, federal or provincial, would be the better agent to originate, administer, or reform the law. He knew all about the logical overlapping of the power-conferring phrases in the respective federal and provincial lists of legislative powers, and knew that frequently plausible arguments could be made either way. Beyond logic then, there was a choice still to be made, and Scott usually leaned in favour of the power of the parliament of Canada rather than that of the provincial legislatures. In this respect he both influenced and reflected the prevailing centralist leanings of English-Canadian political scientists and jurists in the period 1920 to 1960 – the period that covers the aftermath of World War I, the Great Depression, World War II, and its aftermath in the decade of the 1950s.

One way of ensuring large powers for the central parliament was to advocate a broad interpretation of the federal general power, the so-called 'Peace, Order, and Good Government Power,' found in the opening words of section 91 of the BNA Act. In 1950, Scott the lawyer and

118

Scott the poet came together to give all these factors remarkable expression in a poem entitled 'Some Privy Counsel.' I quote in full:

'Emergency, emergency,' I cried, 'give us emergency,
This shall be the doctrine of our salvation.
Are we not surrounded by emergencies?
The rent of a house, the cost of food, pensions and health,
    the unemployed,
These are lasting emergencies, tragic for me.'
Yet ever the answer was property and civil rights,
And my peacetime troubles were counted as nothing.
'At least you have an unoccupied field,' I urged,
'Or something ancillary for a man with four children?
Surely my insecurity and want affect the body politic?'
But back came the echo of property and civil rights.
I was told to wrap my sorrows in water-tight compartments.
'Please, please,' I entreated, 'look at my problem.
I and my brothers, regardless of race, are afflicted.
Our welfare hangs on remote policies, distant decisions,
Planning of trade, guaranteed prices, high employment –
Can provincial fractions deal with this complex whole?
Surely such questions are now supra-national!'
But the judges fidgeted over their digests
And blew me away with the canons of construction.
'This is intolerable,' I shouted, 'this is one country;
Two flourishing cultures, but joined in one nation.
I demand peace, order and good government.
This you must admit is the aim of Confederation!'
But firmly and sternly I was pushed to a corner
And covered with the wet blanket of provincial autonomy.
Stifling under the burden I raised my hands to Heaven
And called out with my last and expiring breath
'At least you cannot deny I have a new aspect?
I cite in my aid the fresh approach of Lord Simon!'
But all I could hear was the old sing-song,
This time in Latin, muttering *stare decisis*.[2]

That poem leaves me with very little more to say; in it you see revealed the essential Frank Scott as a man of law. Law is for people, it is not the other way around. Moreover, policy choices always face legal decisionmakers, and Frank Scott was in the business of facing up to such issues and taking positions. After the shocks of the Great Depression and the terrible stresses of World War II, it was indeed necessary to look to the federal government and parliament for leadership in providing country-wide social service measures. Unemployment insurance became a federal responsibility in 1940 by constitutional amendment, and in the 1950s and 1960s, health and hospital insurance and income security supports were put in place, largely as a result of initiatives by the parliament and government of Canada. Frank Scott and many of his contemporaries, especially in English Canada, were moved to their centralist theories of Canadian constitutional history and law by the societal needs that cried out for these great social service schemes, and in turn, their theories helped to persuade and encourage the Canadian government and parliament to assume such responsibilities. But the co-operation and collaboration of autonomous provinces was always necessary, and indeed it was my native province of Saskatchewan that pioneered in the fields of public medical and hospital insurance.

In any event, in the 1960s and the 1970s the social service schemes matured and likewise the provinces developed greatly in their respective governmental capacities. These are some of the factors that have been leading recently to a somewhat different mix of federal and provincial tensions and claims, with more responsibility passing to the provinces.

Frank Scott of course always recognized the importance of the essentials of provincial autonomy, especially for his home province of Quebec. Nevertheless, I am not sure that he would approve the extent to which the pendulum has been swinging towards greater provincial powers in Canada lately. I doubt that Lederman and Scott are in agreement about this at the present time.

But that is not really what matters now. The right *answers* are not preordained. What each of us *can* do though is to assess the evidence, ask the right questions in the right order, and then take one's own positions on the current issues of Canadian federalism. If we do this, we will be following the distinguished and courageous example afforded over many years by Frank Scott, Canadian disciple of Roscoe Pound.

NOTES

1 F.R. Scott, *Essays on the Constitution: Aspects of Canadian Law and Politics* (Toronto 1977) ix
2 (1950), 28 *Canadian Bar Review* 780. A slightly revised version was published in *Collected Poems* 80.

DOUGLAS SANDERS ✓

Law and Social Change:
The Experience of F.R. Scott

FRANK SCOTT used law to promote social change. He did this in his constitutional writings and as counsel in a series of court cases in the 1950s. Law is usually seen as a conservative force in Canada. Lawyers are not normally the agents of social change.[1] Canadians expect the courts to pay little attention to current social and political issues.[2] Scott challenged these assumptions. He argued that Canadians had a progressive legal tradition and invited the courts to support human rights and allow centralized state regulation of the economy.

Scott fashioned his arguments in four ways. He held up the English common law tradition as positive and asked 'What have we made of it?'[3] Second, he saw the Canadian constitutional tradition as supporting minority rights. He argued that the rights of French Canadians to their religion and language had been recognized and that Quebec had been accorded a decent measure of regional autonomy. Minority rights were a major theme of the confederation pact (*Essays* 14-17, 82)[4]. Third, he argued that the Canadian constitution had been a nationalist achievement. A strong central government had been created which should properly assume the major directing role in Canadian political and economic life (*Essays* 8-14, 17-26, 187). Fourth, Scott saw unregulated economic forces as working against the nationalist and democratic achievements of Canada. He described the denial of human rights in the 1930s as a reaction to the Depression (*Essays* 51). He saw the decentralist decisions of the courts as favouring business interests (*Essays* 275). Human rights and economic justice could only be achieved by a strong central government. In this way his commitment to human rights, economic democracy, and nationalism were interrelated.

Douglas Sanders

SCOTT IN THE 1930s

The Canadian constitution has not yet recovered from the damaging effects of judicial interpretation in the past. (*Essays* 401)

The most passionate debate in Canadian constitutional law has been over the interpretation of the 1867 BNA Act by the Judicial Committee of the Privy Council. Alan Cairns has called it 'the most significant, continuing constitutional controversy in Canadian history.'[5] There are two uncontroversial ways in which the performance of the Judicial Committee can be criticized. The first is that their decisions were inconsistent with each other. In the *Russell* case they ruled that legislation prohibiting the use of alcohol was not within provincial powers.[6] In the *Local Prohibition* case they ruled it was.[7] In the *Snider* case they ruled that the power over 'Peace, Order and Good Government' was limited to emergency situations.[8] That was rejected in the *Aeronautics* and *Radio* cases.[9] The decisions of Viscount Haldane form a consistent group of judgments, but they are inconsistent with both earlier and later decisions. Scott's writings welcomed the centralist decisions, but do not have as a point of criticism the inconsistency of the Judicial Committee's rulings.

The second criticism of the Judicial Committee is that it did not follow the text of the BNA Act. This point, while I think it can be called uncontroversial, has been argued in very different ways. The Rowell-Sirois Report (1940) argued that the intentions of the framers of the BNA Act and the text of the act itself were ambiguous. No clear direction had been given to the courts and the Judicial Committee, therefore, could not be blamed for putting its own interpretation on Canadian federalism. Scott was highly critical of this part of the report, for he had frequently argued that a centralist intention was abundantly clear in the statements of the framers and in the text (*Essays* 264). To Scott, the Judicial Committee departed from the text and the end result was damaging to the country. To other observers, the Judicial Committee departed from the text but the end result was good for Canada. Cairns has argued that the Judicial Committee's provincialism 'was in harmony with the regional pluralism of Canada.'

Scott's criticisms of the Judicial Committee involved four major propositions: the weakening of central authority in Canada had an imperialist motive; the Judicial Committee was isolated from Canada; its decisions favoured laissez-faire economics; and, the Judicial Committee was less sensitive to minority rights than the Supreme Court of Canada.

In 1942 Scott attributed imperialist motives to the Judicial Committee in the following passage: 'The Fathers made the supremacy of the

Canadian parliament depend, not on provincial consent, but on imperial grant. The provinces did not create the Dominion; "it derives its political existence," as Lord Carnarvon said, "from an external authority." Only because we have neglected this theory, and because the Judicial Committee of the Privy Council had another theory it preferred to impose for imperialist purposes, has the law and custom of the Canadian constitution deviated so grievously from the agreement of 1867' (*Essays* 25-6). The full achievement of Canadian nationalism was: 'frustrated and delayed by the innumerable resistances of imperialism, operating through traditional channels, both in and out of Canada, using at times the blind alleys of imperial federation and retaining always the trump card of judicial appeal' (*Essays* 34).

The Judicial Committee was both praised and criticized for its distance from Canada. To some the distance ensured judicial neutrality. To Scott and others it put the institution hopelessly out of touch with the realities of Canadian life. Commenting on the 'new deal' decisions in 1937, he observed: 'None but foreign judges ignorant of the Canadian environment and none too well versed in Canadian constitutional law could have caused this constitutional revolution' (*Essays* 99). In one of his most recent writings, Scott referred to serious reform in Canada during the 1930s as 'thwarted by the fundamental law of the constitution as seen through distant eyes' (*Essays* ix).

Perhaps Scott's most important criticism was that the Judicial Committee's decisions, consciously or unconsciously, were hostile to government regulation and supportive of free enterprise capitalism. Reform legislation was either defeated by decentralization of powers or by the judicial creation of a vacuum of legislative power. In 1931 Scott wrote of Haldane's 'emergency' doctrine: 'Canadians who desire to improve the quality of Canadian life by sane and progressive legislation, must now work through nine channels in many cases where the Fathers of Confederation would have permitted them to work through one' (*Essays* 42). He recognized that 'wide and powerful sections of the community' favoured 'free enterprise' and supported 'provincial autonomy' (*Essays* 260). It followed that the Judicial Committee was not imposing an idiosyncratic view, but notions prevalent among the élites in England, Canada, and the United States. Canadian courts were unlikely to be any different from the Judicial Committee. After all, the United States Supreme Court had also invalidated 'new deal' legislation, supporting laissez-faire economics, without being 'distant' or 'imperialist.' Fundamentally, Scott was advocating judicial neutrality, which, in his view of the Canadian constitution, would favour the central government. With a strong central government, economic planning and social security programs would be much easier.

Scott argued, as well, that the Judicial Committee was less sensitive to minority rights than the Supreme Court of Canada. He devoted an article to this argument in 1930.[10] It was designed to rebut French-Canadian arguments that the Judicial Committee, because of its distance and neutrality, could be counted on to support minority rights in Canada. At various times Scott noted that the Judicial Committee had overruled the Supreme Court of Canada on the Manitoba Schools Question, enabling French-language education rights to be ended in that province.

The critics of the Privy Council won. Appeals were terminated in 1949. Scott had been involved in the issue to advance nationalism and socialism. While the ending of appeals was a nationalist victory, it is not remembered in those terms today. To modern Canadians it is a change that was inevitable. It is irrelevant to post-war nationalism, which has focused on the United States, not the United Kingdom. And, most significantly, the Supreme Court of Canada did not emerge as a strong national institution in the years after the ending of appeals. In nationalist terms, the achievement was necessary, but produced little change in Canadian society.

The ending of appeals did not advance socialism. Canadian politics did not move to the left in the post-war period. The central government did not attempt economic legislation that would have placed in question the decentralist, laissez-faire Judicial Committee decisions of the 1930s. Whether the Supreme Court of Canada would have charted a new path on regulatory legislation in the 1950s we cannot know. In their decisions over the last three decades they have modified some of the Judicial Committee's most decentralist decisions, but the change has not been dramatic. Social security has been significantly extended in Canada and, as Scott rightly predicted, that required the involvement of the federal government. The change was accomplished with two constitutional amendments and cost-sharing programs. What may be the major piece of federal economic control legislation since World War II, the wage and price controls of the mid-1970s, was justified by the courts as a temporary measure. That justification was formulated in a manner in harmony with the language (if not the spirit) of the most restrictive of the Judicial Committee decisions of the 1930s. Much of the legacy of the Judicial Committee is still with us.

SCOTT IN THE 1950s

Constitutionally speaking, the 1950s was predominantly the decade of human rights. (*Essays* 354)

The 1950s have been described as the 'golden age' of the Supreme Court of Canada.[11] The courts' decisions upheld federal legislative power and supported human rights values. In the 1960s and 1970s the Supreme Court had clearly changed. Any centralist direction ended, and with few exceptions, the court has rejected civil liberties claims. This shift in judicial behaviour by the Supreme Court has puzzled observers. Eight factors can be suggested to explain the court's performance in the 1950s:

(1) The court had been freed from its subservience to the Judicial Committee of the Privy Council. The Judicial Committee had been discredited, a fact that gave an opening to the Supreme Court to carve a new path, if it so wished.

(2) Mr Justice Ivan Rand sat on the Supreme Court of Canada in the 1950s. He was a strong judge who articulated first principles of Canadian political life and remains today the most quotable judge who has ever sat on our Supreme Court.

(3) There was an international climate of support for human rights in the years immediately after World War II. This influenced political and legal thinking in Canada.

(4) Canada emerged from World War II with self-confidence and a new sense of strength. Canadians followed closely the civil rights struggles in the United States and applauded the support that was available through the courts. United States Supreme Court decisions made front page headlines in Canadian newspapers. By the 1960s Canada was more nationalist, more self-protective, and more concerned with countering the economic and cultural impact of the United States.

(5) In both the United States and Canada it has been argued that the courts act in a compensatory role in relation to the legislatures. The United States Supreme Court was active in civil rights cases in the 1950s when Congress was unable to respond to the clear need for social change. That role in promoting civil rights and integration was more and more taken over by the legislatures in the 1960s and judicial activism lessened. As well in Canada, the Supreme Court was activist in the period when we did not have human rights codes or bills of rights. When the legislatures had become active in this area, the courts withdrew.

(6) Just as much of the United States concern focused on the south, much of Canada's concern focused on Quebec. The Duplessis government in Quebec was committed to protecting Quebecers from radical views. It was Quebec's repression of communists and Jehovah's Witnesses that provided much of the grist for the mill. Quebec was being integrated into the economic and political liberalism of North America. Larger social and economic forces were destined to bring broad changes

to Quebec society and the Supreme Court was given the opportunity to undercut some of the more reactionary actions of Duplessis' government.

(7) The Jehovah's Witnesses proved to be an exceptionally well-organized minority. They had pursued a strategy of litigation in the United States which had led to a striking series of Supreme Court decisions in the late 1940s. Their Quebec campaign was well organized (largely from outside the province). They tested the Canadian courts as no other minority has done.[12]

(8) There were as well at least two exceptional lawyers involved. W. Glen How of Toronto devoted his legal career to defending the Jehovah's Witnesses, of which he was a member.[13] He produced a massive, written argument in the *Saumur* case extensively documenting the history of religious freedom in Canada.[14] The other lawyer who is identifiable in the civil liberties cases is Frank Scott. Like How, he was not appearing as a regular practitioner but as a supporter of the principles involved. For at least some of the cases he was not paid.

We do not have a thorough analysis of the factors that lay behind the 'golden age' of the 1950s or the wooden ages of the 1960s and 1970s. Clearly a combination of factors has been at work. Scott's involvement must be seen in the larger context of judicial response in the period.

What did Scott expect of the courts? His criticisms in the 1930s asserted that judges were giving reactionary support to capitalism and imperialism. Judges had shown they were prepared to overrule 'laws of which they disapproved.' Why, in the 1950s, should judges cease to be reactionary? Certain explanations can be suggested. Scott may have believed that the judges would react differently to civil liberties issues than they had to economic issues. He knew that this was not certain. In writing on a fairly scandalous case of abuse of process in the 1930s Scott commented: 'Two judges only out of the six, Robson and Dennistoun, JJA, would have allowed the appeal and awarded damages. Both showed an admirable concern for the protection of personal liberty, and a firm grasp of the duty, clearly imposed on the judiciary by the nature of our constitution, to stand as guardian of the citizen against arbitrary behaviour by the state' (*Essays* 79). In 1949 he commented on the effect of having a constitutionally entrenched bill of rights: 'the inescapable effect is to shift the burden of defining and protecting rights from our elected representatives to our nominated judges. Ultimately the question narrows down to a choice between a faith in the courts and a faith in legislatures. History has shown that either may become the enemy of freedom' (*Essays* 214). There was a chance that the courts might be favourable, but Scott does not suggest that they could be predicted to react to civil liberties issues in ways different from their reaction to other issues.

A second explanation is possible. Scott may have felt that, given the social attitudes of the 1950s, and the need to modernize and liberalize the province of Quebec, the institutions of the state (including the law) would see it as in their interests to have civil liberties values upheld. Tolerance, by this analysis, would secure political and social stability and economic growth more successfully than repression. A third explanation is possible. On civil liberties issues there was a conflict between French and English views. In a direct conflict, the English views would prevail because of an English majority on the Supreme Court of Canada. 'Perhaps nowhere in the public law of Canada is the difference in outlook between French and English more marked than in respect to civil liberties ... The judges in Quebec are far more inclined than are the common law judges to uphold the authority of the state as against the individual, though generalizations here must be used with caution' (*Essays* 319, 322).

In his writings Scott put forward rather simplistic civil libertarian arguments. The rights of Jehovah's Witnesses and communists must be protected, he argued, or everyone is deprived of rights. The infringement of the rights of any is the infringement of the rights of all (*Essays* 321). As well, he argued that tolerance of various opinions was necessary so that there could be a winnowing of ideas in society, in order to test their truth (*Essays* 61). Given the earlier judicial behaviour, of which he was a critic, and the later judicial behaviour, the arguments fail to explain why Scott would have expected positive results in the 1950s. And so I assume that he became involved in litigation that he, himself, saw as unpredictable in outcome.

Frank Scott appeared as counsel before the Quebec Superior Court in *Lazare* v *St Lawrence Seaway Authority* in 1956.[15] Indians of the Caughnawaga reserve, just outside Montreal, challenged the ability of the federal government to expropriate their reserve lands. They relied on an original grant of the land by Louis XIV and on decisions of the United States Supreme Court. The arguments failed and the decision does not feature in current discussions of Indian rights. The case was significant in two ways. Modern Indian rights litigation began in Canada in the 1960s with a series of Indian hunting rights cases. There are only two cases in the 1950s where innovative attempts to advance Indian rights were made. One issue that had to be fought in the period was the willingness of governments to take parts of the remaining reserve lands for public purposes. Given the inadequacy of the reserve land base, the issue was a real one. The fight in 1957 was a significant break from the past. The issue has since been largely won, though the *Lazare* case will not generally be remembered as the first cannon shot in that battle. The case was important in a second way. While the lands were in fact taken for the seaway, the Indian opposition forced a re-examination of the compensation. As a result a new agreement was reached, much more favourable to the Indian band.

In 1957 Scott appeared as counsel in the Supreme Court of Canada in *Switzman* v *Elbling*.[16] The *Switzman* case involved the famous Quebec Padlock Law. In the late 1940s when the Canadian parliament had decided not to ban the Communist party in post-war Canada, Quebec had already moved into the breach with the 1937 legislation which allowed the province to padlock any house which had been used to propagate communism. It was also made illegal to publish or distribute any material propagating communism. The *Switzman* case was deliberately set up to test the validity of the provincial law. The owner of a house brought a civil suit against a tenant to have the lease cancelled on the basis that the tenant was using the house in a manner contrary to the provincial law. Quebec argued that the provincial legislation merely dealt with property and civil rights in the province and was, therefore, clearly within provincial jurisdiction. Mr Justice Rand stated:

The ban is directed against the freedom or civil liberty of the actor; no civil right of anyone is affected nor is any civil remedy created. The aim of the statute is, by means of penalties, to prevent what is considered a poisoning of men's minds, to shield the individual from exposure to dangerous ideas, to protect him, in short, from his own thinking propensities. There is nothing of civil rights in this; it is to curtail or proscribe those freedoms which the majority so far consider to be the condition of social cohesion and its ultimate stabilizing force.

The majority in *Switzman* v *Elbling* held that the provincial law was, in essence, a matter for the criminal law and therefore was beyond provincial legislative jurisdiction. Scott later described the decision as meaning that political activity in Canada was protected against interference by the provinces. That seems accurate in terms of the banning or control of particular ideas or political organizations, though political demonstrators are subject to considerable provincial control in public rallies and parades.

In 1958 Scott appeared before the Supreme Court of Canada in *Roncarelli* v *Duplessis*.[17] This case is one of a series of cases involving Quebec attempts to stifle the aggressive proselytizing of Jehovah's Witnesses in the province. Roncarelli, a restaurant owner, had posted bail for a number of Jehovah's Witnesses who had been arrested on leafleting charges.

Maurice Duplessis, who was both premier and attorney general in the provincial government, ordered the cancellation of the liquor licence for Roncarelli's restaurant because Roncarelli was aiding the Witnesses. Roncarelli brought a civil action against Duplessis personally for the damages caused by the cancellation, which he argued had been done for improper reasons. The decision appears to turn on the particular wording of the Quebec Civil Code section on tort liability, but the plaintiff's success is generally described as a victory for the 'rule of law.' Three judges dissented, including two of the three Quebec judges on the court.

The *Brodie* case, decided by the Supreme Court of Canada in 1962, was a significant landmark in Canadian obscenity law.[18] The case involved D.H. Lawrence's novel *Lady Chatterley's Lover*. The Canadian case came after major obscenity trials in France, the United States, and the United Kingdom had allowed distribution of the book. The case therefore placed our laws in the context of an international liberalizing of obscenity laws by the courts. In this case the Supreme Court of Canada dealt for the first time with a new statutory definition of obscenity introduced in 1959. The new definition was supposed to be an 'objective' definition which would be certain and simple. It was to supplement the older judge-made 'Hicklin' test, which was perceived as 'subjective' and more difficult to prove. The new definition was brought in to 'crack down' on pornography, not to liberalize the law. The *Brodie* decision made the new definition both exclusive and more liberal than previous obscenity laws. The decision is a fairly famous example of judicial interpretation of statutory provisions having a life of its own. Without question the intent of parliament was thwarted in the process. The case also established the relevance of literary merit in obscenity cases. The case is the most fundamental decision in the modern liberal interpretation of obscenity law in Canada.

In 1961 Scott appeared before the Supreme Court of Canada in *Oil, Chemical and Atomic Workers* v *Imperial Oil*.[19] The Social Credit government in British Columbia had passed a law forbidding trade union monies which had been collected by means of a compulsory check-off (permitted by provincial law) from being donated to political parties. For anyone familiar with British Columbia politics, the legislation was blatantly partisan. Only the opposition New Democratic Party received funds from trade unions. Since there was no parallel prohibition against corporate donations to political parties, the expected sources of funds to the Social Credit party were not affected. The legislation had been a piece of political showmanship on the part of the provincial government and the government did not seriously try to enforce it. As in *Switzman* v *Elbling* a test case was created. The province of British Columbia intervened to defend its legislation. Tom Berger and Frank Scott appeared for the union in the Supreme Court of Canada, both, of course, publicly identified with the New Democratic Party. But the 1950s were over. The Supreme Court looked at the form of the legislation and held that it was within provincial jurisdiction. The judgments did not acknowledge the political realities behind the legislation.

CONCLUSION

It seems clear that Frank Scott regards his literature as his major achievement. His legal work has the appearance of failure in that his centralist constitutional views are quite out of line with those of contemporary constitutional lawyers and politicians. Even the New Democratic Party is decentralist by Scott's standards. He did not consolidate his constitutional law teaching and writing by producing a text on the subject. There would seem to be two reasons. First, he used his constitutional law writings to advance certain positions and, in this, found it was useful to use more immediate forms. Second, his strong identification with certain views did not make him well suited as the author of an academic text.

Two of the cases in which he has appeared – *Switzman* v *Elbling* and *Roncarelli* v *Duplessis* – continue to be seen as milestones in Canadian constitutional law. But in many ways they can be seen as part of a bygone era. While civil liberties values prevailed in the Supreme Court of Canada in the 1950s, no civil liberties doctrines were ever clearly adopted by a majority of Supreme Court justices. The legacy of the period was not strong enough to prevent the Supreme Court from changing direction entirely, without being obliged to specifically overrule any previous decision. Like the Privy Council before it, the Supreme Court has also been inconsistent.

In 1960 Frank Scott could say: 'we cannot but be struck by the emergence in our law of a remarkable combination of cases and legislative purposes which we can properly classify under the heading of human rights' (*Essays* 353). Today we have the legislation, and may soon have a constitutionally entrenched charter of rights, but we do not have the cases. Scott's work in the 1950s played, without question, a role in the expanding recognition of human rights values in Canadian society. While that work is not perpetuated in the decisions of the Supreme Court of Canada, it is perpetuated in legislation and institutions in the country and in the large number of supporters of human rights issues. The relationship between Scott and these developments is general, not specific. His influence is in the background, and thus is less clearly understood. In my view it should rank as a clear accomplishment, along with his literature.

NOTES

1 In comparison, at least to the United States, there are no nationally known lawyers in Canada. There seem to be no equivalents to Clarence Darrow or F. Lee Bailey. Current leading lawyers, such as J.J. Robinette and Edward Greenspan are not well-known. Frank Scott, when he was active as counsel, was an ideal candidate for public attention, but received little as a lawyer.

2 Chief Justice Bora Laskin is the most visible person on the Canadian bench, but is often perceived as an isolated figure, dissenting from the more conservative rulings of the majority of judges. As a *Globe and Mail* editorial writer commented a decade ago, the Supreme Court is, strangely, no place for heroics: see Cameron Smith, 'The Highest Court,' *Globe Magazine*, 14 Mar. 1970. Our most famous judges of the past, Lyman Duff and Ivan Rand, are hardly known at all. Even the literature on these figures is scanty.

3 F.R. Scott, 'Freedom of Speech in Canada,' *Papers and Proceedings*, Canadian Political Science Association, 1933, 169, in F.R. Scott, *Essays on the Constitution: Aspects of Canadian Law and Politics* (Toronto 1977), 60 at 64 (hereinafter cited in the text as *Essays*). Scott acknowledged some debt to legal thinkers in the United States: see preface in *Essays* ix. In general, however, Scott did not use material from the United States in his legal writings.

4 His view of the minority rights arrangements in the BNA Act led him late in life to oppose the language legislation of both the Bourassa and Lévesque governments in Quebec.

5 Alan C. Cairns, 'The Judicial Committee and Its Critics' (1971), 4 *Canadian Journal of Political Science* 301

6 *Russell* v *R.* [1882] 7 AC 829

7 *Attorney General for Ontario* v *Attorney General for Canada*, [1896] AC 348

8 *Toronto Electric Commissioners* v *Snider*, [1925] AC 396

9 *Re Regulation and Control of Aeronautics in Canada*, [1932] AC 54; *Re Regulation and Control of Radio Communication in Canada*, [1932] AC 304

10 Scott, 'The Privy Council and Minority Rights' (1930), 37 *Queen's Quarterly* 37

11 See Dale Gibson, 'And One Step Backward: The Supreme Court and Constitutional Law in the Sixties' (1975), 53 *Canadian Bar Review* 621.

12 See M. James Penton, *Jehovah's Witnesses in Canada* (Toronto 1976).

13 See W. Glen How, 'The Case for a Canadian Bill of Rights' (1948), 26 *Canadian Bar Review*, 759; How, 'Religion, Medicine and Law' (1960) 3, *Canadian Bar Journal*, 365. How's work is described in various parts of Penton, *Jehovah's Witnesses in Canada*. How continues to be active in Jehovah's Witnesses cases; see 'Blood, Toil, Tears and Death,' *Maclean's Magazine*, 20 Apr. 1981, 33.

14 *Saumur* v *City of Quebec*, [1953] 2 SCR 299

15 (1957) Que. CS 5 (reported in French)

16 *Switzman* v *Elbling*, [1957] SCR 285
17 *Roncarelli* v *Duplessis*, [1959] SCR 121
18 *Brodie* v *The Queen*, [1962] SCR 681
19 *Oil, Chemical and Atomic Workers* v *Imperial Oil*, [1963] SCR 584

WALTER TARNOPOLSKY

F.R. Scott: Civil Libertarian

IT IS difficult to discuss the attainments of Frank Scott even with respect to civil liberties alone, because he was so much a Renaissance man – constitutional lawyer, law teacher, man of letters, political activist and, above all, in a combination of all of the previously mentioned manifestations, a civil libertarian. I want to concentrate on Frank Scott as advocate of civil liberties and architect of modern Canadian thought on human rights and fundamental freedoms.

Despite impeccable family background and education, Scott was a 'rebel without pause'; and just as Bertrand Russell was perhaps best described as 'the passionate sceptic,' so Frank Scott could perhaps best be characterized as 'the compassionate rebel.' Consistently, for over half a century, he managed to present a minority view, as well as a view of minorities, not only with incomparable perspicacity, wit, and literary style, but with courage, insight, and compassion as well.

I will illustrate my characterizations of him and, perhaps, even some of the ironies associated therewith, by reference to the following specific propositions, determining our appreciation of human rights and fundamental freedoms in Canada, for which he can claim credit: (1) The topic of human rights and fundamental freedoms is not only a legitimate, but an indispensable component of Canadian constitutional law. (2) Within our federal state, there is an important role for the central government in the field of human rights and fundamental freedoms, despite provincial jurisdiction over 'property and civil rights.' (3) The 'rule of law' is as important a part of our 'Constitution similar in Principle to that of the United Kingdom' as is parliamentary supremacy. (4) Although traditionally in Anglo-Canadian constitutional practice our human rights and fundamental freedoms were realized by restraining governments from interference, increasingly we have recognized that some of our human rights can only be realized through assumption of government responsibility. (5) An essential feature of Canadian federalism, unlike the unitary and homogeneous situation of the United Kingdom, is protection of such group rights as those relating to language and religious schools.

Before turning to these topics, I must refer to Scott's role as an advocate and activist in defending the civil liberties of unpopular minorities. This was accomplished not just through legal scholarship, but through more popular writings in such magazines as *The Canadian Forum*, as well as through organizational and counsel work.

FRANK SCOTT, DEFENDER OF
THE CIVIL LIBERTIES OF PERSECUTED GROUPS

Most students of Canadian history, especially students of constitutional law, will be familiar with the contributions of Frank Scott to the defence of the Jehovah's Witnesses in Quebec in the 1950s. What is less well known, among those who have reached university age since then, is that his defence of unpopular minorities goes back to a very difficult and tense time in the 1930s, and continued through an equally difficult time, with respect to the Japanese Canadians, at the end of World War II.

Few causes in the early 1930s could have been less pleasing, not just to those in authority, but even to the majority of ordinary citizens, than defence of communists and leftists, especially if they were 'foreign.' Scott, however, did not hesitate to provide this defence by such means as an essay[1] on 'The Trial of the Toronto Communists,' in *Queen's Quarterly* in 1932 (*Essays* 49), a lecture on 'Freedom of Speech in Canada,' presented the same year at the annual meeting of the Canadian Political Science Association (*Essays* 60), and a comment on the *Wade* v *Egan* case, in the 1936 volume of the *Canadian Bar Review* (*Essays* 76). In these three essays, Scott expressed his objection to police behaviour infringing on the freedoms of speech and association during the years of economic crisis, and his criticism of the absence of judicial or executive control of such infringements. Perhaps the most important symbols of this oppression were section 98 of the Criminal Code and the deportation provisions of the Immigration Act.

Section 98 declared that any association whose purpose was to bring about governmental or economic change within Canada by the use of force, violence, or injury to person or property, or which taught or advocated these methods of securing such change, was unlawful. Membership of, or financial contribution to, such an association was unlawful. Attendance at meetings or public advocacy of such association led to presumption of membership. Furthermore, printing, publishing, circulating, or selling any literature which advocated the use of force to effect governmental or economic change, or advocacy or defence of such violence, were also unlawful. The maximum penalty under section 98 was twenty years.

Scott's attack on section 98 began by pointing out that it extended restrictions for protection of public security beyond those in the traditional criminal law:

The common law crimes of treason, sedition, seditious conspiracy and unlawful assembly have always been considered an adequate protection for public security in any situation short of actual or impending rebellion. Yet Canada in 1919 proceeded to graft on to her Criminal Code a special section – the now notorious Section 98 – which for permanent restrictions of the rights of association, freedom of discussion, printing and distribution of literature, and for severity of punishment, is unequalled in the history of Canada and probably of any British country for centuries past. (*Essays* 49-50)

Not only did Scott impugn the legitimacy of section 98, but he illustrated its oppression with reference to the trial of eight leaders of the Communist party, arrested in Toronto in August 1931. They were all charged and subsequently convicted of being members of an unlawful association, although there was no evidence that any of them engaged in any violent acts. He summarized the effects of the trial thus:

What is most striking about the trial is the fact that the eight accused were in effect sentenced solely on account of their opinions, since there was no reliable evidence adduced to show that they or the party to which they belonged had actually occasioned any acts of violence in Canada. The use of force in which they and the party believed was to occur at some future date. It is also to be noted that they were found equally guilty of the crime of seditious conspiracy, which shows that our normal criminal law on these matters is quite adequate to look after the Communist party even without Section 98, if we wish to proceed against it. Just why it should be necessary to outlaw Communists in Canada when it is unnecessary in all civilized countries that have not turned fascist, we have never been told. Nor are we informed why the policy of persecution will have any other than the normal result of spreading the very doctrines it is designed to suppress. (*Essays* 67-8)

Even more biting was his criticism of the deportation provisions of the Immigration Act. He suggested that as much as certain aspects of section 98 were 'a sufficiently severe break with our traditional freedom,' the deportation provisions, 'because they lead to exile after secret trials, and because they bear most hardly upon the friendless foreign element in Canada, are even more pernicious' (*Essays* 68). He described deportation by a board of inquiry in the following terms:

For the totally different purpose of administering justice to foreigners who have committed certain crimes – for that is what these boards are doing – they are a travesty of everything we profess to believe is proper in the enforcement of criminal law. The accused does not stand a dog's chance. He is tried secretly. He may be whisked away from Winnipeg and be tried in Halifax ... He is not stated to have the right to call witnesses in his own behalf – and the right would be ineffective where long distances intervene between his home and the port of entry. He has no right to refuse to give evidence, but may be questioned. His judges are probably petty officials untrained in the interpretation of statutes and the weighing of evidence, and liable to direct pressure from above. His appeal may be even less a trial than the enquiry: the Minister is not obliged to hear counsel for the defence. And the penalty is the 'cruel and unusual punishment' of exile, as likely as not to a country where further penalties will await the radical deportee. (*Essays* 69)

He went on to show that 'even naturalized aliens cannot feel safe' because the Naturalization Act provided for revocation of citizenship by the governor in council of any person who has 'shown himself by act or speech to be disaffected or disloyal to His Majesty' or when the governor in council was satisfied that the continuation of the certificate was not 'conducive to the public good.' He referred to the fact that, during 1931-2, as many as 239 certificates were revoked or annulled. 'No reasons are given. Naturalization thus gives no security in regard to freedom of speech; even sedition seems an exact term beside the words "disloyalty" and "disaffection," and as for the clause protecting the "public good," what is this but straight permission to cancel certificates at will?' (*Essays* 69).

Scott's advocacy of the need to respect 'freedom of speech' in those difficult times deserves to be repeated today, as his remarks are timeless:

The time for defending freedom never goes by. Freedom is a habit that must be kept alive by use. In times like the present, when mankind is hesitating before a bewildering choice of remedies for its afflictions, freedom of discussion is more necessary than ever. There are two ways of attempting to solve our present economic problems. One is to use the sword; this is the Communist and Fascist technique. The other is to think through the difficulties, to decide a policy, and to legislate it into existence. That is what we like to think is the Canadian technique. It cannot work without the utmost freedom of speech and discussion.

The achievement of a full degree of personal liberty must await the conquest of the economic system by the democratic principle. But much could be done immediately to widen the area of freedom of speech in Canada, and liberal minds of all parties should unite in this endeavour. In particular the repeal of Section 98, the confining of the immigration boards to their proper functions, a restriction of police control over owners of halls, a reasonable granting of permission for parades, and the setting aside in every city and town of specified localities for outdoor meetings under police supervision, are essential steps toward regaining our traditional freedom. Law and order would be more secure in this atmosphere of tolerance, because tolerance induces a respect for authority. The well-tried rules of our normal criminal law would still be available to put down violence and to preserve the public peace. (*Essays* 75)

Nothing could illustrate Scott's defence of unpopular minorities better than 'The Deportation of the Japanese Canadians: An Open Letter to the Press,' which was sent to fifty-five newspapers in Canada early in January 1946, protesting the deportation orders of December 1945 against thousands of Japanese and Japanese Canadians. In retrospect, during the 1970s, many people have claimed that they spoke out against the treatment of these people during and after World War II, but it is difficult to find printed evidence of as bold an indictment as that of Scott:

The Canadian government is about to deport from this country some 10,000 men, women and children, mostly Canadian citizens, for no other crime except that they have a particular racial origin. They are being sent to a land which most of them have never seen, which is too devastated by war to receive them, and where their future is hopeless. Not since the expulsion of the Acadians has such severe treatment been accorded to any social group within our frontiers, and there was at least some military justification for that deportation whereas there is none for this. (*Essays* 190)

Scott claimed that there was hypocrisy in the policy of the government towards the Japanese Canadians, when compared to those of Italian or German descent. He indicated the 'trick or device' of asking the Japanese to sign repatriation forms while the war was still on:

It is like offering a condemned man a pistol so that he may choose swift suicide to a public hanging. Is his death voluntary? Perhaps no one was 'forced' to choose repatriation, but the whole Canadian policy, the extreme racial hatred in British Columbia, the refusal of other provinces to co-operate in resettlement, the long history of deprivation of citizens' rights to people who were Canadian born British subjects, the statement of the Hon. Ian Mackenzie that they could never return to the coast – all this was the compulsion. (*Essays* 191)

His plea on behalf of the Japanese Canadians is all the more poignant in the light of race relations developments during and after World War II:

At the very moment when Parliament is trying to give some secure status to Canadian citizens by the Citizenship Bill, we should not treat fellow citizens in this fashion. It makes a farce of citizenship. We are all immigrants in Canada, except the Indians and Eskimos, and no citizen's rights can be greater than that of the least protected group. Every Canadian is attacked in his fundamental civil liberties by this policy ...

The real problem we have to solve in Canada has nothing directly to do with the Japanese at all: it is the problem of racial intolerance. This problem is only aggravated by the deportations. They mean a victory for intolerance and bigotry. We should be generous to this harmless minority whom we previously admitted to our shores, and apply fully to them the principle that race, religion and colour are no bar to full citizenship in this democracy. (*Essays* 192)

Almost immediately after his defence of the Japanese Canadians, Scott turned his support in defence of another unpopular minority, the Jehovah's Witnesses in Duplessis' Quebec. Since this aspect of his achievements is probably the best known, and since I will be returning to them subsequently, let me merely point out that very soon after Frank Roncarelli had his liquor licence cancelled and his restaurant raided, with policemen carrying away his entire stock of liquor, Scott objected publicly through a *Canadian Forum* article on 'Duplessis v Jehovah.'[2] The essence of his charge can probably be found in the following paragraph:

What Mr. Roncarelli really did was not to promote disorder, but to check Mr. Duplessis' mass persecution of the Witnesses. Because while the laying of a charge – in this case of peddling literature without a license – is not necessarily persecution, it becomes so when we learn that the number arrested reaches many hundreds, and particularly when Mr. Duplessis tries to deny the accused the normal right of every citizen to bail. At the present moment, under a pretence of legal process, and in Mr. Roncarelli's case without even a pretence, a small religious sect has been persecuted and indeed martyred in many parts of Quebec. (*Essays* 195)

However, at the same time, Scott was concerned that the persecution be seen in perspective and not be a basis for anti-Quebec hatred:

And lastly it may be worth warning too zealous defenders of civil liberties against using this incident as an excuse for another attack upon Quebec. The most serious breach of civil liberties in this country is British Columbia's – and the federal government's – treatment of Canadian citizens of Japanese origin. Beside it the case of Jehovah's Witnesses in Quebec is less reprehensible. For the Japanese-Canadians do not insult their fellow citizens by calling them evil names in widely distributed pamphlets. (*Essays* 196)

In the light of his perceptive analysis of the unjustified oppression of unpopular minorities in the 1930s, through the 1940s and into the 1950s, it came as somewhat of a surprise to those who criticized the invocation of the War Measures Act in October 1970, that Scott supported its invocation. In May 1971, in an essay on 'The War Measures Act in Retrospect,' published by the Canadian Association of University Teachers in a 'Symposium on the War Measures Act,' Scott claimed that one week after the proclamation on 23 October 1970, he had written in his diary eight reasons why he 'had supported the application of the War Measures Act to the critical situation in Quebec.' These can probably be summarized in the following excerpts:

No modern industrial society, where a natural disaster or a determined few can imperil millions, can risk drifting along with forethought and foresight. But the Quebec and federal governments had only the War Measures Act to deal quickly with a deteriorating situation. All the evidence pointed, not to a popular insurrection, but to a further erosion of civil government, and to what Gérard Pelletier has called 'uncontrollable civil disorders.' This is how it looked to me.

A shock treatment was needed to restore the balance. It was given, and it worked. There was only one death and it was not caused by the forces of law and order.[3]

For those who would criticize him, however, it should be recalled that by 25 October, when the 'climate of fear' (which is alleged to have been prevalent by those Quebecers who defend the invocation) was such that there was some difficulty in getting legal representation for those arrested or detained, a group of fourteen citizens approached Justice Minister Jérome Choquette to select three of their members to form part of a committee of investigation of the detainees, with complete freedom to visit all prisons in the province. One of those who participated in visiting the prisoners and providing advice and assistance as part of this committee of investigation, was seventy-one-year-old Frank Scott.

CIVIL LIBERTIES IS A NECESSARY COMPONENT OF CANADIAN CONSTITUTIONAL LAW

Although such standard English texts on constitutional law as that of Dicey[4] included discussions of civil liberties before the turn of the century, this was not true of the basic Canadian texts before World War II. Thus, for example, neither W.H.P. Clément, nor E.R. Cameron, nor A.H.F. Lefroy, nor J.E.C. Munro included so much as a mention of civil liberties.[5] Even that perspicacious and influential constitutionalist, W.P.M. Kennedy, as late as 1938, did not consider the topic as deserving of attention in his basic text on *The Constitution of Canada, 1534-1937* (2nd edition). The one exception I have been able to find is that of W.S. Scott who, in *The Canadian Constitution Historically Explained* published in 1918, devoted three chapters to 'Magna Carta,' 'Petition of Right,' and 'The Bill of Rights and the Act of Settlement,' respectively.

Nor was the situation much different among political scientists. For example, as late as 1944 H.D. Clokie, in *Canadian Government and Politics*, did not discuss human rights and fundamental freedoms and, in his appendix, although he listed the Succession to the Throne Act, 1937, and the Seals Act, 1939, made no reference to, for example, the Bill of Rights Act, 1688, or the Act of Settlement, 1701. R.M. Dawson, in *The Government of Canada*, first published in 1946, did devote some five or six pages to 'fundamental liberties,' but by the fourth edition, in 1963, this section had expanded to only ten pages.

After the 1940s, however, although there were still some works on Canadian constitutional law, for example, that of F.P. Varcoe,[6] which did not consider inclusion of a discussion of civil liberties, this trend was reversed when Professor Bora Laskin (as he then was) included a chapter on 'Constitutional Guarantees' in the first edition of his basic text on *Canadian Constitutional Law* in 1951. In subsequent editions this became a chapter on 'Civil Liberties and Constitutional Guarantees.' However, when the late Professor Albert Abel revised a fourth edition of Laskin's *Canadian Constitutional Law* in 1973, he deleted the chapter on 'Civil Liberties.' The reaction among constitutional law teachers was so strong that within a year the publisher engaged John Laskin to reintroduce a special chapter on 'Civil Liberties, Constitutional Guarantees and the Canadian Bill of Rights' at the end of the book. Today, all the standard works, such as those of Whyte and Lederman, and Hogg, invariably include chapters on civil liberties.[7]

What is being implied in this survey is what I want to suggest directly, namely, that the various writings of Frank Scott on human rights and fundamental freedoms, commencing in the early 1930s and continuing through the 1940s, assured a place for the topic in future works on constitutional law in Canada. This influence might be said to have culminated in 1949 when he set out, for the first time, how extensive was 'Dominion Jurisdiction over Human Rights and Fundamental Freedoms' (*Essays* 209).

THE ROLE OF THE CENTRAL GOVERNMENT
WITH RESPECT TO HUMAN RIGHTS
AND FUNDAMENTAL FREEDOMS

Perhaps the best way to illustrate the influence of the 1949 essay by Scott on 'Dominion Jurisdiction' is to refer to a report presented in 1944 to the Canadian Bar Association by the Civil Liberties Section, summarizing its propositions as to legislative jurisdiction in relation to 'liberties and property rights':

1 Civil and property rights proper, which are more in relation to civil law as distinct from the criminal law, and cover:
   a liberty of religion and language;
   b liberty of opinion including freedom of speech, of writing and of the press;
   c liberty of enterprise, including freedom of private initiative and industry;
   d freedom of work;
   e freedom of association;
   f the right to private property;
2 The protection of the person of the subject, which is more or less in relation to criminal law; and
3 The preservation of political institutions under which liberties have been acquired and appear to be guaranteed.[8]

The report went on to state that the first group is in provincial jurisdiction, the second in federal, and the third is divided, some items falling within the jurisdiction of the provinces and some within the jurisdiction of the federal parliament.[9]

Space does not permit setting out in detail how inaccurate this summation would be considered today. Suffice it to say that following Scott's article in 1949 no one would again assert that the first group is in provincial jurisdiction only, because the jurisdiction of the federal parliament is at least as extensive with respect to these rights and liberties as that of the provincial legislatures. With respect to the second group, jurisdiction is not solely federal because the provinces have jurisdiction with respect to the administration of justice, including enforcement of the Criminal Code, as well as their own penal provisions in support of provincial laws otherwise within provincial jurisdiction.

In this essay, not only did Scott set out the argument for an 'implied Bill of Rights' in the BNA Act, first hinted at in the *Alberta Press Bill* case, and subsequently picked up by members of the Supreme Court of Canada in the Jehovah's Witnesses cases of the 1950s, but he also provided the basic argument, since referred to and amplified both by authors and judges, distinguishing between the matter of 'civil liberties' and the subject of 'property and civil rights' within section 92 of the BNA Act. From this he proceeded to show how – through such powers as those over the criminal law; under the peace, order, and good government clause; as a result of jurisdiction with respect to the post office, broadcasting, and telecommunications; in relation to citizenship rights; with respect to the functioning of parliament; in relation to such persons under federal control as the armed forces, the RCMP, Indians, and Eskimos, and federal employees and civil servants; because of unemployment insurance and employment offices; resulting from such spending power projects as family allowances, housing, and health measures; by means of cultural services like the National Gallery, the National Film Board, the CBC, and so on – federal powers over human rights and fundamental freedoms were extensive enough that 'there does not seem to be a single article in the Universal Declaration of Human Rights of 1948 on which Ottawa may not take some positive action if the government so wishes' (*Essays* 211-12).[10]

THE RULE OF LAW IS AS IMPORTANT A PART OF OUR CONSTITUTION AS PARLIAMENTARY SUPREMACY

In the previous topic attention was drawn to Scott's 1949 essay on 'dominion jurisdiction' as including a suggestion that the BNA Act did include some specific, and some implied, limitations on that basic principle, inherited from the United Kingdom, of the sovereignty of parliament. It was not, however, so much in his writings as in his arguments before the courts in *Roncarelli* v *Duplessis*, that he established the importance of the 'rule of law' which, even to this day, forms the basis for the teaching of this principle in constitutional law courses in Canada.[11]

The background to the case, and its importance in Canadian constitutional history, is probably best described in Scott's introduction to his *Canadian Forum* essay on 'Duplessis v. Jehovah':

On 4 December, 1946, Mr. Duplessis, then Prime Minister of Quebec, ordered the liquor license of Frank Roncarelli to be cancelled by the Quebec Liquor Commission because he persisted in giving bail for his co-religionists, the Witnesses of Jehovah, in the Montreal courts. The long saga of his fight for justice, ending thirteen years later in the Supreme Court of Canada, provides an important affirmation of the Rule of Law in Canadian jurisprudence ... But though Roncarelli established a great legal principle, his restaurant was closed, his social status in Montreal undermined, and he was obliged to earn his living elsewhere. The Witnesses of Jehovah, however, now practise their religion unimpeded by the Quebec police. (*Essays* 193)

Frank Scott was co-counsel in the *Roncarelli* case. The principle of the 'rule of law' was outlined, in the arguments submitted to the Supreme Court of Canada, in the following terms: (1) By the public law of Quebec, which derives from English law, public officers including the respondent are personally liable for their delictual acts, whether committed in the exercise of their public functions or outside them. (2) The measure of fault is determined by Article 1053 of the Civil Code. (3) The official who orders an illegal act is equally liable with the person who carries it out. (4) It is a delict or quasi-delict for a public officer to usurp a power that does not belong to him and to act in a manner not authorized by some positive text of law. It is this last argument which summarizes the principle of the 'rule of law.' The brief explained the argument thus: 'This is a fundamental principle of the English and Canadian Constitutions. It is the foundation of the supremacy of the law over the state and over every state official. With us, all officials possess a limited jurisdiction only, which some statute or text of law defines.'[12] In line with this proposition, it was suggested that: 'No statutory or other text of law relating to the offices held by Respondent justified the several acts and omissions which caused damage to appellant.'[13] The brief continued by referring to the fact that the respondent held only two offices to which any public rights and duties might attach, namely, that of prime minister and attorney general, and asserted:

There are no special functions or powers attached to the office of Prime Minister at common law. It is a purely political position conferring *per se* no legal powers or immunities. The only statutory reference to the office in Quebec is found in the Executive Power Act ... Nowhere is the Prime Minister given any right of interference in the administration of the liquor laws of the province, a right to defame citizens or to punish them for giving bail, or to commit any of the other acts which damaged Plaintiff ...

The rights and powers attaching to the office of Attorney General are set out and analyzed in sufficient detail in the trial judgement below ... There is a total absence of any grant of power to order the cancellation of licences or to act as Respondent acted toward Appellant.[14]

As a result, it was submitted that, since Duplessis had failed to show any provisions in the law giving him the authority to interfere with the administration of the Quebec Liquor Commission and to order it to cancel a licence, he was acting outside his statutorily defined functions and therefore had committed a fault causing damage for which he should be held personally liable.

The 1950s was the great decade of the protection given to civil liberties by the Supreme Court of Canada. Among these were three cases which illustrated the 'rule of law': *Roncarelli* v *Duplessis*, *Chaput* v *Romain* and *Lamb* v *Benoit*.[15] In a lecture to the Ontario Branch of the Canadian Bar Association in February 1960, 'Expanding Concepts of Human Rights,' Scott summarized these three cases in the following terms:

You remember the proud boast of Dicey when he said: 'With us every official, from a Prime Minister down to a constable or a collector of taxes [below which, apparently, his imagination could not sink], is under the same responsibility for every act done without legal justification as any other citizen.' The *Roncarelli* case involved the liability of a Prime Minister, and the *Chaput* and *Lamb* cases involved the liability of constables, and all the officials sued were held liable for acts done without legal justification. Only the tax collector was missing to make Dicey's picture complete. So the great principle of the supremacy of the law was reaffirmed, and in situations, be it noted, involving liability under the Civil Code of Quebec. (*Essays* 354)

About a decade later, at the dinner address at the official opening of the University of Windsor law building, Scott defined the essence of the 'rule of law' in 'two basic rules underlying our constitutional structure, which entitle us to say that we live in a free society':

The first is that the individual may do anything he pleases, in any circumstances anywhere, unless there is some provision of law prohibiting him. Freedom is thus presumed, and is the general rule. All restrictions are exceptions. The second rule defines the authority of the state, and places the public official (including the policeman) in exactly the opposite situation from the private individual: a public officer can do nothing in his public capacity unless the law permits it. His incapacity is presumed, and authority to act is an exception. Duplessis, for instance, could not find any legal authority to justify his order to cancel Roncarelli's liquor licence: so he paid personally.

ALTHOUGH THE TRADITIONAL CIVIL LIBERTIES
WERE REALIZED BY RESTRAINING GOVERNMENTS,
SOME OF THE NEW HUMAN RIGHTS
CAN BE REALIZED ONLY THROUGH
ASSUMPTION OF GOVERNMENT RESPONSIBILITY

At the same time that Scott explained how the fundamental protections of our traditional civil liberties resulted from the application of the rule of law (that the private individual is free to do what is not forbidden,

while the government official may not do anything to restrict that freedom unless specific authority can be found in law) he also recognized
that this same fundamental approach did not apply in the realization of
all forms of human rights. It would be otiose for me to repeat what has
already been mentioned concerning Scott's involvement in favour of
economic reforms. From a civil liberties point of view, I would like to
quote briefly from merely one of his 1930s writings, 'Freedom of Speech
in Canada,' to illustrate his early comprehension that impediments to
that free discussion which is necessary to economic reform came not just
from governments, but from those with private economic power as well:

> [T]here is a widespread feeling in Canada today that if a man wants to hold his
> job he had better not talk too much ... Its existence is a fine commentary upon
> the nature of our social life, implying as it does that the person who works for a
> living is owned body and soul by the employers, and that these are unscrupu-
> lous enough to penalize a man for his opinion. It largely explains our public
> apathy in the face of manifold provocations. How often we hear it said of some-
> one that he is in favour of this or that reform, but of course he 'cannot say
> anything.' He cannot say anything, the other man cannot say anything – no one
> can say anything, except the Communist, and he is promptly deported. So the
> leading British Dominion drifts along in this year of grace 1933, frightened out
> of its all too diminutive wits. Our captains of industry are firm believers in
> individual initiative and private enterprise, but they are the first to deny the
> application of their pet principles in the field of freedom of speech. In fairness
> to them, however, it must be admitted that this sense of fear may equally be
> due to a lack of courage on the part of the employee. (*Essays* 75)

That, however, is merely a description of the importance of the traditional civil liberties in permitting the issues of economic reform to be
raised and discussed. Acceptance of government responsibility for the
welfare of its citizens is a further step and one that Scott urged at an
early date. Perhaps his best summation of what is involved comes in his
1949 essay on 'Dominion Jurisdiction over Human Rights':

> 'Human Rights' ... embodies the idea of economic rights and claims to welfare
> services such as the modern state is being increasingly asked to provide. We are
> more aware today of the foolishness of pretending that a man is 'free' when he
> is unemployed and without income through no fault of his own, or when he
> cannot pay for good health or good education for his children. Thus we hear
> today that a man has a 'right' to a job or to maintenance when out of work, the
> children have a 'right' to education and health; and President Roosevelt was
> true to his age when he included in his four 'freedoms' the freedom from fear
> and from want. (*Essays* 218)

In that same essay he went on to indicate that since social security was one of the rights proclaimed in the Universal Declaration, it was not surprising that the federal government had undertaken its responsibility by taking the initiative in the fields of old-age pensions, family allowances, and hospital insurance. At the same time, Scott suggested that much more could be done:

If there is need for a national housing plan to relieve the serious shortage throughout the country, to provide for the progressive elimination of substandard dwellings and slums, and thus to give security and decency to family surroundings throughout the country, it is less constitutional law than political hesitancy which prevents it. Without arguing for any particular plan or policy, it is evident that the field of social security offers wide opportunities for the federal government to fulfill its responsibilities as a signatory to the Declaration of Human Rights. (*Essays* 234)

Perhaps his most eloquent description of the need to take up support of these new human rights came in his 1960 address to the Ontario Branch of the Canadian Bar Association on the topic of 'Expanding Concepts of Human Rights' (*Essays* 353). While commending the legal profession for its role in keeping government under the law and assuring 'liberty against government,' he suggested that in recent times this concept has been supplemented by 'liberty through government':

Certain human rights ... can only be realized through governmental action. This should not surprise us, for government action means the making and enforcing of laws, and we are all accustomed to say that without law there is no liberty. We are not so traditionally accustomed, however, to say that without an unemployment insurance law, or without an old age pensions law, or laws providing for free universal education, there is no liberty. Particularly among members of the legal profession are these newer forms of human rights apt to be either forgotten or neglected, because these social insurances require administration through government commissions and enforcement in administrative tribunals rather than consultation with lawyers and actions in the regular courts. Lawyers tend to pay attention mostly to judicial review over administrative agencies ... Yet this, though of great importance, is not the central issue. The object of these laws is to free men and women from known and certain risks which exist in our industrialized society, and which if not insured against can destroy so much liberty among so many individuals as to make Bills of Rights to them a hollow mockery. The hungry man must be fed, the sick must be attended to, the old must be provided for, the young must have a chance to enter to the fullest degree into our cultural heritage through education. To deprive people of these essentials to the good life, or to allow the still unresolved problems of our economic system to deprive them of them without taking steps to alleviate the deprivations, is to take away human rights. (*Essays* 356-7)

Scott went on to reassert his support for a Bill of Rights, and to indicate that essentially a Bill of Rights is concerned with 'liberty against government,' but, he suggested, 'I would be happier if we also included some words or phrases, if not in the text of the constitution then in its preamble, expressing the now universally accepted notions of social security and human welfare' (*Essays* 358).

AN ESSENTIAL FEATURE OF CANADIAN FEDERALISM IS PROTECTION OF SUCH GROUP RIGHTS AS THOSE RELATING TO LANGUAGE AND RELIGIOUS SCHOOLS

As Scott pointed out in 1959, in four lectures on CBC radio on 'The Canadian Constitution and Human Rights,' although the rule of law principle, and the freedoms of speech and of the press, were part of Canada's inheritance from the United Kingdom, 'freedom of conscience was certainly not one of our inherited rights in Canada.'[16] He went on to show that Roman Catholics and Jews gained a recognition of their religious rights and, more importantly, of the right to participate in public life despite their religion, before this occurred in the United Kingdom.[17] This acceptance of religious and language rights is, to Scott, the essence of Canadian federalism. Even if this were not so, his lifelong defence of minorities would have provided the basis for his defence of French-language rights. When the civil liberties aspects were combined with the historical-constitutional, it was no wonder that he should be one of the earliest and most consistent English-speaking defenders of bilingualism in Canada. In a 1947 essay, in *Queen's Quarterly*, 'Canada, Quebec, and Bilingualism,' he combined civil liberties arguments with pragmatic ones in his advocacy of accepting the bilingual reality of Canada:

Just why so many people in Canada should resist the idea that French should be officially recognized it is difficult to understand. Quite apart from the erroneous view it represents of the actual situation, plain democratic justice and common-sense would seem to indicate that the mother-tongue of one-third of the population of any country has a claim to recognition which cannot be denied ...

... If every Canadian could be brought to realize that the possession of these two languages is a great national and international asset and not a liability, not only would we have more national unity in this country, but our delegates to international conferences would be better equipped. (*Essays* 200)

In view of Scott's lifelong defence of the rights of the individual and, obviously, his position as a Quebec anglophone who felt strongly Canadian, it is no wonder that he has never been sympathetic to the view of many francophone Quebecers today, and especially their governments, whether Liberal, Union Nationale, or Parti Québécois, that language rights should be a matter of provincial responsibility and that the language rights of a collectivity could override the language rights of individuals. In 1957, well before the series of language laws enacted by the Quebec governments just mentioned, although not for the first time as far as he was concerned, Scott asserted the following in 'Areas of Conflict in the Field of Public Law and Policy':

Unless Quebec is to become an independent state outside Confederation, which virtually no one in Quebec seems to desire, the limitation of legislative and executive powers imposed by the present constitution on the Quebec government would seem to make it wholly inadequate as the *exclusive* defender of French culture, even if all French minorities in other provinces are disregarded. The elevation of the government as the sole champion of the race has therefore grave dangers for that race: it might have the unexpected effect of imprisoning the vital energies of the French-Canadian people. (*Essays* 308)

He went on to deal with the position of the French Canadian in Canada, illustrating the dilemma as between relying upon the province of Quebec for the protection of French-Canadian reality, and the cost thereby created of writing off the French minorities in the other provinces:

The French Canadian is at home in Quebec. So is the English Canadian in the province, though some other minorities are perhaps not so secure. The French Canadian wants to feel as much at home when he lives in Ontario; that is, he wants his own language, his own school, his church and parish, and his French Canadian way of life. To some extent he has achieved this in districts adjacent to Quebec. But his minorities farther from the homeland have not achieved it, and the English-speaking inhabitants of other provinces are surprised, if not startled, to discover that they are expected to adapt their local laws (e.g. as to separate schools) so as to make possible the steady development of a French-speaking cultural minority as an island colony in the midst of their already heterogeneous populations. Meeting this resistance, the French minorities look to Quebec for help, which in turn reacts with stronger claims. The fact that an exaggerated provincial autonomy may actually weaken the outside minorities by subjecting them still further to local majorities and depriving them of the protection of Ottawa does not deter the nationalists in Quebec. An 'autonomous' Quebec is a fortress in a dangerous land, without which the struggle for survival seems hopeless. Thus a strong Quebec government seems necessary to pry loose more freedom for its minorities outside as well as within, using at the same time provincial autonomy, influence at Ottawa, and pressures of every kind to achieve the single purpose. (*Essays* 309)

In 1970, in giving the sixth annual Manitoba Law School Foundation lecture, 'Language Rights and Language Policy in Canada,' on his work as a member of the Royal Commission on Bilingualism and Biculturalism, Scott suggested:

Canadians must approach the language question with two special qualities: realism and goodwill. Realism means accepting facts. French-Canada is a fact, and English-Canada is a fact. The English minority in Quebec now numbers one million, the French minorities outside Quebec also number about one million. If Canadian federalism is to survive, it must accept bilingualism sensibly applied, in Quebec as well as in Canada as a whole. It is *one* of the essential conditions of our survival. It is not the only one, for economic benefits must come to all Canadians from our association. We must believe we are worthwhile as a nation. But it must be a bilingual nation.

We must also have goodwill. We must see the plus as well as the minus, the great advantages as well as the difficulties. To accept bilingualism means a greater respect for human rights, a greater domestic tranquility, and, above all, the development within our country of the richness and creative ability that have made England and France two of the great centres of western civilization. That it will give Canada a national identity unique in the Americas goes without saying.

... [M]y experience convinced me that an equal partnership between the two cultural communities in Canada was a workable concept, and one which would help Canada make a distinctive contribution to world history and world peace. Whether Canadians will accept the idea and bring it steadily into being is their decision. I for one have faith that they will accept the great challenge rather than fall back into obsolete forms of the nation state. (*Essays* 388-9)

In light of this statement, it is no wonder that Frank Scott has consistently opposed the language policies of the last three Quebec governments, namely those of M. Bertrand, M. Bourassa, and M. Lévesque, while favouring a policy similar to that of the federal governments of Mr Pearson and Mr Trudeau.

CONCLUSION

Because of the many ways that Frank Scott has contributed to our understanding of human rights and fundamental freedoms, it would be impossible to sum up this tribute in a few words. But there is no better way to conclude than to quote him. In a preface to *Events and Signals* he wrote the following:

Walter Tarnopolsky

Between the event and the observer
there must pass a signal – a wave,
an impulse, or perhaps a ray of light.

It is certain he did not have himself in mind. However, that he *was* the
'ray of light' that enabled Canadians to observe the human rights issues
in the events since the 1930s, there can be no doubt.

NOTES

1 Most of the essays that will be referred to have been compiled and published in *Essays on the Constitution: Aspects of Canadian Law and Politics*
(Toronto 1977), hereafter referred to as *Essays* and indicated in the text.

2 (1947), 26 *The Canadian Forum* 222; *Essays* 193

3 CAUT *Newsletter*, II, 4 (May 1971) 1

4 *Introduction to the Study of the Law of the Constitution* (London 1885); the most
recent edition by E.C.S. Wade is the 10th ed., 1961.

5 W.H.P. Clément, *The Law of the Canadian Constitution*, 3rd ed. (Toronto
1916); E.R. Cameron, *The Canadian Constitution* (Winnipeg 1915); A.H.F.
Lefroy, *Constitutional Law of Canada* (Toronto 1918) and *The Law of Legislative Power in Canada* (Toronto 1897); J.E.C. Munro, *The Constitution of
Canada* (Cambridge, Eng. 1889). Munro does speak of 'freedom of speech'
and 'freedom from arrest' (p 60), but this is only with reference to the
protections set out for members of provincial legislative assemblies.

6 F.P. Varcoe, *The Constitution of Canada* (Toronto 1965)

7 John D. Whyte and W.R. Lederman, *Canadian Constitutional Law*, 2nd ed.
(Toronto 1977); Peter W. Hogg, *Constitution Law of Canada* (Toronto 1977)

8 (1944) *CBA Proceedings* 191; see also 'Report of Committee on Civil Liberties' (1944), 22 *Canadian Bar Review* 598.

9 Ibid. 599

10 He must have had in mind the fact that Canada almost did not vote in
favour of the Universal Declaration because of fear that too many of the
rights and freedoms therein referred to were not within the jurisdiction of
parliament, but rather the provincial legislatures.

11 [1959] SCR 129

12 Appellant's submission in the case of *Roncarelli* v *Duplessis*, 48

13 Ibid. 50

14 Ibid. 51

15 *Chaput* v *Romain*, [1955] SCR 834; *Lamb* v *Benoit* [1955] SCR 321

16 F.R. Scott, *The Canadian Constitution and Human Rights* (Toronto 1959) 7

17 Ibid. 7-13

PART FIVE

PAUL-A. CRÉPEAU

F.R. Scott
et la réforme du Code civil

JE N'AI JAMAIS eu le privilège, que j'enviais à l'un de mes frères, de suivre le cours de droit constitutionnel que donnait le Pr Frank R. Scott à la Faculté de droit de l'Université McGill. D'autres ont pu dire tout le profit qu'ils ont su en tirer.[1]

Il m'a, toutefois, été donné, à compter de 1959, de l'avoir comme collègue et même, de 1961 à 1966, comme doyen dans cette même faculté. Et j'ai souvent été à même d'apprécier, au cours de ces longs et fréquents entretiens entre collègues que la vie universitaire – en des temps moins bousculés – leur réservait encore, la haute conception qu'il se faisait de la fonction universitaire,[2] l'importance qu'il a toujours attachée au règne fragile du droit face à l'emprise brutale du fait, le respect qu'il a toujours entretenu à l'égard du droit civil et de la tradition juridique française au Canada.

Mon propos, ici, est précisément de rappeler le rôle important que notre collègue Frank R. Scott a joué dans l'œuvre de réforme du Code civil du Québec, en ce qui concerne tout particulièrement la reconnaissance des droits civils du citoyen.

Ayant eu la témérité d'accepter, en 1965, de diriger les travaux de réforme du Code civil, il m'avait semblé qu'une telle œuvre, malgré le texte qui en confiait la responsabilité à 'un juriste,'[3] ne pouvait être celle d'une seule personne, qu'il fallait, au contraire, y associer étroitement tous ceux qui, magistrats, praticiens, hauts fonctionnaires, professeurs, pourraient y apporter le fruit de leurs connaissances particulières, de leur expérience professionnelle.

Estimant par ailleurs que le Code civil nouveau du Québec se devait d'être le reflet authentique des valeurs dominantes de notre société, il paraissait essentiel de s'attacher non seulement, comme en 1866, à la protection du patrimoine, mais aussi à l'affirmation solennelle et à la reconnaissance expresse des droits de la personne humaine. Il s'agissait, en somme, comme le souhaitait vivement notre regretté collègue, le Pr Louis M. Baudouin,[4] et ainsi que l'énonce la préface du *Projet du Code civil*,[5] de placer, dans ce Code, 'la personne humaine, avec ses droits et ses devoirs, à la place d'honneur qui lui revient, en faisant d'elle la pierre d'angle de l'ensemble des relations juridiques de droit privé.'

Aussi, l'une des premières décisions dans l'accomplissement de cette mission fut-elle de constituer un Comité dont le mandat serait d'élaborer une Déclaration des droits civils de la personne humaine qui serait insérée au tout début du Code civil faisant le pendant d'un chapitre consacré, dans le Livre des Obligations, aux devoirs de la personne envers son prochain.[6]

Le Comité aurait essentiellement pour tâche de rassembler d'abord, à la lumière du droit positif et dans le sillage du grand mouvement international de reconnaissance des 'droits de l'Homme,' les principes et règles qui consacrent les droits et libertés de la personne humaine, de les couler ensuite dans le moule étroit d'une Déclaration, rédigée dans les deux langues législatives du Québec, de manière à en assurer à la fois une application concrète et une valeur éducative.

Dans cette double perspective, il paraissait tout naturel de confier la responsabilité d'un telle mission au Pr Scott: juriste, il s'était fait, tout au long de sa carrière, le champion et l'ardent défenseur des libertés civiles;[7] poète, il saurait, sensible à la puissance évocatrice du verbe, inspirer la rédaction des textes d'une Déclaration en leur donnant le ton et l'élévation qui siéent au genre.[8] Notre collègue accepta de diriger les travaux du Comité. En faisaient également partie MM. les P[rs] J. Beetz,[9] G. Le Dain[10] et J.-Y. Morin,[11] ce dernier à titre de Rapporteur. Me Madeleine Caron-Montpetit[12] fut associée aux travaux comme attachée de recherches. Le président de l'Office y participait également ex officio.

Dans l'accomplissement de son mandat, le Comité pouvait certes d'emblée prendre appui sur quelques articles du Code civil de 1866 concernant, notamment, les notions d'ordre public et de bonnes mœurs (article 13, C. civ.), les principes de liberté contractuelle et de liberté testamentaire (article 1024, 831 C. civ.), le concept de propriété privée (article 406, C. civ.) et surtout le régime de droit commun de la responsabilité civile (articles 1053 et 1065 C. civ.), autant de dispositions qui, dans la variété et la complexité des rapports sociaux, ont pu fonder la reconnaissance judiciaire des droits civils, patrimoniaux ou extrapatrimoniaux, de la personne humaine. A ce propos, c'est le Pr Scott qui écrivait qu'à lui seul, 'article 1053 of the Civil Code ... underpins the basic human rights.'[13] Ainsi, le Comité, sur la base de textes existants complétés par une abondante jurisprudence, sous l'inspiration des grands documents historiques en la matière, a voulu proposer la reconnaissance expresse des droits et libertés de la personne: droit à la vie, à la sureté et à la liberté (article 2, aliéna 1 du Projet de Déclaration), libertés fondamentales, telles la liberté de conscience, d'opinion, d'expression, de réunion pacifique et d'association (article 2, aliéna 2), droit à la sauvegarde de sa dignité, de son honneur et de sa réputation (article 4), droit à la jouissance paisible et à la libre disposition de ses biens (article 6), droit à l'inviolabilité de la demeure (article 7).

Mais, le Comité, attentif aux préoccupations de notre société, soucieux d'étendre la portée des droits et libertés de la personne, a voulu aller au delà des règles existantes et proposer d'importantes modifications au droit positif.

Tout d'abord, le Comité s'est posé le problème de l'aptitude à la jouissance des droits civils. On sait, à ce propos, qu'une longue tradition, remontant au droit romain, considérait les droits civils comme l'apanage du citoyen. L'on faisait une distinction très nette entre, d'une part, le citoyen, et d'autre part, l'esclave et l'étranger: celui-là jouissait de la plénitude des droits civils; ceux-ci n'avaient de droits civils que ceux qui leur étaient expressément et progressivement reconnus.[14] Par ailleurs, l'on admettait le déchéance des droits civils comme sanction du crime ou de la profession religieuse: ainsi, la mort civile prévue aux articles 31 et suivants du Code civil de 1866, remplacée, en 1906,[15] par la dégradation civique.

Le Comité s'est penché sur cette question et, conscient de la dignité inhérente de la personne humaine, il a voulu briser avec cette longue tradition séculaire en énonçant, d'une part, que la personnalité juridique constitue l'attribut essentiel de l'être humain et que, de ce fait, qu'il soit citoyen ou étranger, il a pleine jouissance des droits civils; en proposant, d'autre part, l'abolition de la dégradation civique aux motifs 'que la notion même de dégradation civique est incompatible avec l'idée qu'il se fait des droits de la personne'[16] et qu'il n'entre pas dans les fins du droit civil d'infliger des peines ni de se faire, en quelque sorte, l'adjoint du droit pénal.[17] Voilà pourquoi le Comité a voulu proposer une disposition destinée à devenir l'article premier du Code civil nouveau:[18]

Tout être humain possède la personnalité juridique.	Every human being possesses juridical personality.
Citoyen ou étranger, il a pleine jouissance des droits civils, sous réserve des dispositions expresses de la loi.	Whether citizen or alien, he has the full enjoyment of civil rights, except as otherwise expressly provided by law.

Texte fondamental, nouveau, gros de conséquences, dont on n'a peut-être pas encore su tirer toutes les fécondes applications, toute la portée pratique en ce qui concerne notamment la protection des droits fondamentaux: vie, sûreté, liberté.

Par ailleurs, dans une société où l'on commence à prendre conscience des effets néfastes d'un individualisme effréné, où l'on perçoit la vertu grandissante de la solidarité humaine, on devait se poser le problème de l'assistance à personne en péril. Problème de valeurs où le droit est susceptible de rejoindre la morale du bon samaritain. Mais, précisément, fallait-il transformer le précepte de charité en devoir de justice? Le Comité n'a pas hésité à répondre par l'affirmative, étant d'avis qu'une personne qui, sans excuse raisonnable (dont l'appréciation est laissée à l'arbitrage des tribunaux), refuse ou néglige de prêter secours à une personne en péril commet une faute et engage sa responsabilité.[19] C'est ainsi que le Comité proposa l'article deux de la Déclaration qui se lisait ainsi:[20]

Toute personne en péril a droit au secours.	Everyone in peril has a right to assistance.
Nul ne peut, sans excuse raisonnable, refuser ou négliger de prêter secours à une personne en péril ou de lui procurer les soins immédiats nécessaires à la vie.	No one may, without reasonable excuse, refuse or neglect to give help to anyone in peril or to provide him with the aid immediately required to save his life.

Le Comité s'est également posé le problème de la lutte contre la discrimination. A cet égard, le législateur avait déjà édicté certaines lois de nature à réprimer la discrimination dans des domaines particulièrement névralgiques: l'hôtellerie et l'emploi.[21] Mais, puisqu'il s'agissait de textes à caractère exceptionnel, d'interprétation restrictive, de larges secteurs de l'activité sociale et commerciale demeuraient toujours régis par le principe de liberté contractuelle sans égard aux motifs de discrimination qu'il était susceptible de véhiculer.

Le Comité était certes très conscient de ce que la lutte contre la discrimination est d'abord et avant tout une œuvre d'éducation qui permet de sensibiliser une société à la grave injustice qui est faite à l'un de ses membres. Mais, croyait-il également, c'est là un domaine où le droit privé peut, lui aussi, fournir des moyens de lutte contre des actes et gestes discriminatoires susceptibles de porter atteinte à la dignité et à l'honneur de la personne humaine. Aussi, devait-on faire intervenir ces moyens dans les domaines qui se prêtent le mieux aux techniques du droit civil:[22] droit d'accès aux lieux ouverts au public, droit d'obtenir les biens et les services qui y sont offerts, inefficacité d'une clause contractuelle ou testamentaire relative à la jouissance ou à l'aliénation d'un bien, sauf lorsque l'acte revêt un caractère charitable ou philanthropique.

On devait aussi s'interroger sur les motifs de discrimination. Devait-on tous les mentionner avec le risque inévitable d'en oublier? Le Comité n'a cru devoir mentionner que les cas les plus flagrants, mais en adoptant une technique de rédaction qui permettrait, par l'emploi du mot: tel, d'indiquer que la liste n'est pas exhaustive ou limitative, laissant ainsi aux tribunaux le soin, selon les circonstances, d'en étendre la portée.

Et l'on peut, à cet égard, regretter que la Charte des droits et libertés de la personne,[23] tout en étendant considérablement le domaine de la lutte contre la discrimination, n'ait pas cru devoir retenir une telle technique de rédaction, car, en procédant à une énumération limitative des motifs de discrimination répréhensible, on ne peut modifier la portée des textes que par voie d'interventions législatives – souvent lentes et assujetties aux pressions aléatoires de l'opinion publique,[24] on empêche, par ailleurs, les tribunaux d'exercer un rôle dynamique dans cette lutte incessante contre les préjugés, pour la reconnaissance du principe de la pleine égalité des personnes dans l'exercice de leurs droits et libertés.

Le Comité a voulu, enfin, préciser les recours qu'offre le droit privé en cas d'atteinte illicite aux droits et libertés énoncés dans la Déclaration.[25] Certes, aux termes de l'article 1065 du Code civil, l'arsenal du droit privé est-il limité en la matière: dommages intérêts et, dans les cas qui le permettent, l'exécution en nature de l'obligation au besoin par voie de recours à l'injonction;[26] il n'empêche que ces moyens peuvent permettre à la fois une action préventive et, en tout cas, la réparation du préjudice matériel ou moral que l'atteinte préjudiciable aura fait subir à la victime.[27]

Cette Déclaration des droits civils de la personne ne devait pas trouver la place qui lui était destinée dans le *Projet du Code civil* déposé à l'Assemblée nationale du Québec en juin 1978. En effet, au printemps 1971, Me Jérome Choquette, alors Ministre de la Justice du Québec, confiait au Pr F.R. Scott et à l'auteur de ces lignes, la charge de préparer un Projet de Charte des droits et libertés de la personne, avec mission expresse d'y faire figurer la Déclaration des droits civils avec les autres droits politiques, judiciaires, sociaux et économiques qu'une telle Charte devait consacrer. Malgré le vif regret que j'ai pu éprouver à ne pouvoir donner suite au projet initial d'insérer la Déclaration au début du Projet de Code civil, j'avais tout de même l'intime conviction qu'elle trouvait, dans la Charte, une place digne de la haute inspiration qui avait animé les membres du Comité des droits civils de l'Office et, notamment, son président, le Pr F.R. Scott.

Paul-A. Crépeau

Qu'il me soit permis de lui dire ici, dans un ouvrage destiné à rappeler son œuvre, que je compte parmi les plus beaux moments de ma vie professionnelle ces heures inoubliables consacrées, soit dans son bureau de la Faculté de droit de l'Université McGill, soit à son domicile de la rue Clarke, à l'élaboration d'un ensemble de textes visant à la reconnaissance expresse des droits civils et des libertés fondamentales de nos compatriotes du Québec.

NOTES

1 Voir G.E. Le Dain, 'F.R. Scott and Legal Education,' dans ce livre.
2 Conception d'autant plus encourageante pour ses jeunes collègues à une époque où d'aucuns, au Barreau, estimaient encore que l'on ne pouvait se résigner à la carrière universitaire que si l'on se croyait peu doué pour le prétoire!
3 Voir 'Loi concernant la révision du Code civil,' LQ 1954-5, c. 47.
4 Voir *Les aspects généraux du droit privé dans la Province de Québec* (1957) 147 et s.
5 Voir *Le Rapport sur le Code civil du Québec*, 1978, I, *Projet du Code civil*, préface, xxxi.
6 Voir *Le Projet de Code civil*, ibid., Livre V, art. 94 et s.
7 Voir, à ce sujet, W.S. Tarnopolsky, 'Frank Scott: Civil Libertarian,' dans ce livre.
8 On sait, en effet, que, dans la tradition civiliste, le langage législatif, comme le fruit de la vigne, est susceptible de subir divers stades de distillation offrant ainsi des styles ou genres différents selon la matière envisagée et le but poursuivi par le législateur: pour une *loi*, qui s'attache à régler un problème ponctuel, on adoptera volontiers des dispositions concrètes, détaillées afin de cerner d'aussi près que possible la matière du texte; déjà, un Code voudra s'élever à un niveau supérieur de généralité dans la réglementation ordonnée et cohérente d'une matière: enfin, la Charte ou Déclaration s'attachera à énoncer, dans des formules concises, nettes et frappantes, quelques principes fondamentaux dont l'expression à un haut niveau d'abstraction permettra aux tribunaux une application d'autant plus étendue et féconde à l'infinie variété des situations concrètes. Voir à ce sujet, notamment, M. Sparer et W. Schwab, *Rédaction des lois: rendez-vous du droit et de la culture* (1980).
9 Alors professeur de droit constitutionnel à l'Université de Montréal, aujourd'hui Juge à la Cour suprême du Canada
10 Alors professeur de droit civil et de droit administratif à l'Université McGill, aujourd'hui Juge à la Division d'appel de la Cour fédérale du Canada

11 Alors professeur de droit international public à l'Université de Montréal, aujourd'hui Vice-premier ministre et Ministre des Affaires intergouvernementales du Québec

12 Alors Attachée de recherche à l'Office de révision du Code civil, aujourd'hui Directrice du Service de la recherche à la Commission des droits et libertés de la personne

13 Voir F.R. Scott, 'The Bill of Rights and Quebec Law' (1959), 37 *Canadian Bar Review* 135, à la p 137.

14 Voir, à ce sujet, P.B. Mignault, *Droit civil Canadien*, t. I, 1895, 131 et s.

15 Voir *Loi abolissant la mort civile*, LQ 1906, c. 38, art. 1.

16 Voir *Le Rapport sur les droits civils*, Office de révision du Code civil, IV, 1968, à la p 29. Il s'agit de la version finale du rapport.

17 Ibid.

18 Cette disposition a remplacé, en 1971 (LQ 1971, c. 84), l'art. 18 du Code civil de Bas-Canada, en attendant, on peut l'espérer, qu'elle devienne, ainsi que l'ont vivement souhaité les membres du Comité, l'article premier du nouveau Code civil du Québec.

19 Voir *Le Rapport sur les droits civils*, supra note 16, à la p 14.

20 Cette disposition a inspiré la rédaction de l'art. 2 de la Charte des droits et libertés de la personne, LQ 1975, c. 6; aujourd'hui LRQ c. C-12.

21 Voir Loi de l'hôtellerie, SRQ 1964, c. 205 et Loi sur la discrimination dans l'emploi, SRQ 1964, c. 142.

22 Voir *Le Rapport sur les droits civils*, supra note 16, à la p 20.

23 Voir supra note 20.

24 Le législateur est intervenu à deux reprises en modifiant l'article 10 de la Charte pour y inclure l'orientation sexuelle (LQ 1977, c. 6, art. 1) et le handicap (LQ 1978, c. 7, art. 112). Mais l'âge, l'apparence, la taille, l'accent d'une personne, ne sont-ils pas également susceptibles de constituer des motifs injustifiés de discrimination?

25 Voir l'art. 10 du *Rapport sur les droits civils*, supra note 16, à la p 23.

26 Voir les articles 751 et s. C. proc. civ.

27 On ne peut, à cet égard, qu'approuver l'insertion, dans la Charte des droits et libertés de la personne, LRQ c. C-12, d'une disposition visant, à cet égard, à permettre au tribunal, en cas d'atteinte illicite et intentionnelle aux droits et libertés reconnus par la Charte, de condamner son auteur à des dommages exemplaires. S'il est certes vrai, en principe, que la loi civile ne punit jamais l'auteur d'un délit ou quasi-délit; qu'elle accorde une compensation à la victime pour le tort qui lui a été causé (*Chaput* v *Romain*, [1955] SCR 834, à la p 841), on ne voit pas pourquoi le législateur refuserait une sanction plus énergique en cas de violation intentionnelle d'une disposition de la Charte. Voir, à ce sujet, le *Projet du Code civil*, L. V, art. 290 qui permettrait d'accorder des dommages punitifs dans tous les cas de faute intentionnelle ou de faute lourde causant préjudice à autrui.

D.G. JONES

F.R. Scott as Translator

F.R. SCOTT'S starting place, to which he always returns, is Quebec. To live in Quebec is to live in a duality. Unlike so many anglophone Quebecers, Scott and his generation of poets did not choose to ignore the fact. Scott, A.J.M. Smith, and John Glassco are among the first to take the francophone culture of Quebec seriously and to become intimately engaged in translating it. This is no mean feat, since often it involves a real appreciation of the *other*, of one's opposite. Consider the late John Glassco, author of *Memoirs of Montparnasse* and *The English Governess*, translating the journals of Saint-Denys Garneau. Consider Scott, a member of the League for Social Reconstruction, translating Anne Hébert's 'Vie de Château.'

Traditionally, the cultures of English Canada and of francophone Quebec have met in almost exact contradiction, a point which Scott makes brilliantly clear in ten lines in his poem 'Bonne Entente.' On Ascension Day the elevators do not rise in Montreal's office buildings; on the Feast of the Immaculate Conception there is no garbage collection in the city. Where the English culture has been horizontal and focused on space, the French has been vertical and focused on the intersection of the temporal and the eternal,[1] where the one has been future-oriented, emphasizing development and change, the other has been past-oriented, emphasizing a kind of cyclical repetition: a Quebec *où rien ne change jamais* and whose official motto, 'Je me souviens' is still visible on every licence plate in the province. 'Bonne Entente' is an ironic study in contradictions. Yet Scott's ironic awareness is not merely satirical; it is one that Canadians of necessity have been forced to cultivate, which requires that one recognize contradictions without assuming, however, that either side can be wholly dismissed.

Of course, I exaggerate. Clearly there has been no love lost between F.R. Scott and the Quebec of Maurice Duplessis. And many of the poets

160

and poems that Scott has chosen to translate are hardly as alien as the preceding remarks might suggest. When Scott translates 'The Philanthropists' by Jean Narrache or 'The Prodigal Child' by Gilles Hénault, he is dancing with himself, for he is translating a poetry of social protest very similar in spirit to his own. And when he translates Pierre Trottier's 'A la Claire Fontaine,' Jean-Guy Pilon's 'The Stranger Hereabouts,' or even Anne Hébert's 'Manor Life,' he is recognizing and abetting a basically satirical poetry aimed at a culture that has become excessively static and past-oriented. Insofar as these poets expose a tradition that has become repressive, dogmatic, narcissistic, insofar as they claim the right to make history and not just repeat it, they must appeal to Scott's own basic convictions. In translating their work he is celebrating the fact they have joined him in the dance, a dance that will sweep away *la grande noirceur* of the Duplessis era and usher in the Quiet Revolution. And it was nothing less than a revolution. As Roland Giguère puts it in Scott's translation of 'Polar Season': 'Silently, we sought a new horizon on which to find a foothold for a new life, to start all over again, to re-invent everything beginning with ourselves.'[2] And it was a revolution that could more easily command Scott's sympathy in that it was, to begin with, largely internal and not yet aggressively nationalistic or politically *indépendantiste*.

On this last point Scott shares something with the earlier and quite different poet, Saint-Denys Garneau, who remarks in his journal that it should be the aim of all education to produce men, not French Canadians.[3] He could also share something of the poet's initial delight in the natural world and his celebration of the imagination, the capacity of the child and the artist to see beyond the status quo, to see the world arranged anew in the play of his vision. This is the burden of the poem 'The Game.' But as Garneau is led to reject his own delight in nature, in the flesh, in art itself, withdraws from the world to cultivate an increasingly puritanical or Jansenist vision, to the point where he becomes, against his own advice, morbidly introspective – as he becomes in Dennis Lee's words 'master of emptiness,'[4] he becomes ever more distant from Scott, more distinctly the *other*. The poetry of Garneau and of Hébert tends to be quite different from that generally written in English Canada. It is almost wholly symbolic and involves the exploration, the painful and often anguished articulation, of inner rather than outer space. Its interest for the English Canadian lies precisely in this difference.

Initially, one cannot but be impressed by the honesty and tenacity with which these poets seek to recognize and define an experience of dispossession, paralysis, loss of substance, and by the clarity and vividness with which they manage to utter or outer such an obscure psychic drama. One must assume that the frequently bizarre but extremely concrete symbolic narratives of Anne Hébert, so succinctly related, have an appeal for a poet like F.R. Scott. And the same may be said for the work of Saint-Denys Garneau, whose figures are often developed with the logic of the metaphysical conceit and remain, as it were, witty even in despair. Certainly Scott's translations, besides being accurate and English, by which I mean free of the peculiar wow in idiom and in sense that betrays the influence of another language, retain the sharpness, the syntactic directness, and the concrete eloquence of the originals. 'Manor Life,' for example, begins:

> Here is an ancestral manor
> Without a table or fire
> Or dust or carpets.
>
> The perverse enchantment of these rooms
> Lies wholly in their polished mirrors.
>
> The only possible thing to do here
> Is to admire oneself all day and all night.

There is no attempt to embellish or complicate; each unit is straightforward, concrete, and terse.

To digress a little at this point, one may say that, while John Glassco and Alan Brown have translated larger collections of Saint-Denys Garneau and Anne Hébert, they cannot be said to have replaced the translations of Scott. Translation permits different versions, each with slightly different virtues. Yet speaking more personally, I may say that though Alan Brown may be a fine translator I cannot read his version of 'Vie de Château' without hearing that of Scott echoing through, especially at the end. Whether it is a question of the quality or merely of the priority of Scott's version in my mind I would hesitate to say. Anyway, Scott's version concludes:

> See, these mirrors are deep
> Like cupboards
> There is always someone dead behind the quicksilver
> Who soon covers your reflection
> And clings to you like seaweed
>
> Shapes himself to you, naked and thin,
> And imitates love in a slow, bitter shiver.[5]

As 'Manor Life' makes particularly clear, these poems that focus on a subjective or private space have, in the end, a collective or public bearing; here the morbid sterility of a culture fixated on its own past is made strikingly evident.

More broadly, however, the point to be made is that the traditional cultures of both English and French Canada may, in the extreme, become sinister. Where the French, in an exclusive preoccupation with an inner and ideal space, risk the loss of the world, the English, in an exclusive preoccupation with an outer and largely material space, risk the loss of the self. One leads to the world of Anne Hébert's *Le Torrent*, where François begins his story by saying, 'J'étais un enfant dépossédé du monde,' the other to Lampman's 'The City of the End of Things,' where the soul 'goes rattling like an empty nut.' Both, for different reasons, lead to a kind of emptiness or void. Scott's own poem 'Lakeshore' points to just such a result. And a variety of English-Canadian poets, such as Margaret Avison and P.K. Page, have increasingly resisted the normal English-Canadian bias towards the external and objective, insisting on the need to internalize the world, to give it a subjective articulation, personalized, spiritualized, eroticized, in imagination and dream.

The modern technological culture in which English Canada, unlike francophone Quebec, has been traditionally implicated, even if reluctantly, is itself on the brink of bankruptcy. And, in the words of the American writer, Jeremy Rifkin, as that wasteful, high entropy culture gives way to a more traditional, conservationist, low entropy culture,[6] many of the values of the older Quebec may prove more permanent and positive than English Canadians have generally assumed or even many new Québécois might care to admit.

More narrowly, writers like Saint-Denys Garneau and Anne Hébert provide models of a sensibility and of a poetics that is at home in inner space and cultivated in the ways of making the subjective or psychic life finely articulate. They may serve, not only to open a window on another culture or country, as Scott makes explicit in his introduction to his *Poems of French Canada*, but to open windows on the unknown country of ourselves as English Canadians. Scott's translations are a recognition and celebration of the powers of poetry in any time and at any place, but they are also a form of compensation against our own cultural bias and one more testimony to F.R. Scott's lifelong dedication to wholeness and balance.

NOTES

1 Jean-Charles Falardeau, *Roots and Values in Canadian Lives* (Toronto 1961) 15

2 Roland Giguère, 'Polar Season,' tr. F.R. Scott, *The Collected Poems of F.R. Scott* (Toronto: McClelland and Stewart 1981) 343

3 Saint-Denys Garneau, *The Journal of Saint-Denys Garneau*, tr. John Glassco (Toronto 1962) 104

4 Dennis Lee, *Civil Elegies* (Toronto 1972) 45

5 Anne Hébert, 'Manor Life,' tr. F.R. Scott, *The Collected Poems* 328

6 Jeremy Rifkin, *Entropy: A New World View* (New York 1980) passim

MICHAEL OLIVER ✓

F.R. Scott: Quebecer

WHEN YOU drive from Montreal down to the Eastern Townships you pass signs pointing the way to Ange gardien. Frank and Marian Scott make that drive almost every summer weekend on the way to their house at North Hatley. I have always been convinced that Scott's poem, 'A l'Ange Avant-Gardien,' was conceived as he drove along in that uncluttered state of mind one goes into on a long drive. Scott is a sensitive observer of a society which is profoundly different from his own, yet not quite alien. This French-Canadian society shares with him and the sizeable community of English-speaking Quebecers from which he comes, a huge tract of land, Quebec, to which both feel deep attachment. The sharing of land is uneasy and shifting; the mutual exposure of the cultures constant yet superficial.

Frank Scott was born in Quebec City in 1899. His father had been born in Montreal in 1861. His grandfather had taught anatomy at McGill. When he was young, Frank and his brothers were taken by their father to the construction site where the common monument to Wolfe and Montcalm was being erected. In the wet concrete of the base, a jar containing a penny contributed by each Scott child was buried. When the *indépendantistes* pulled down that monument, Frank telephoned Arthur Scott in Quebec City, who replied 'They are all right!,' and Frank knew instantly he referred to the pennies. Surely no one who has a penny embedded in the Wolfe-Montcalm monument can be denied the title Quebecer.

Frank Scott was nevertheless brought up to be thoroughly British and English-speaking. If your home is an Anglican rectory and if you go to Bishop's at Lennoxville for your early studies, you are unmistakeably English Canadian. If you go to Oxford as a Rhodes scholar, something British rubs off. Frank Scott learned to speak French and to understand the language with a depth that showed itself in his poetry translations.

But he had not lived inside a French-Canadian society in Quebec City and when he moved to Montreal, he became part of the anglophone city. His contacts with the francophone city were much more extensive and varied than those of most English-speaking Quebecers, but he was thought of, and thought of himself, as an English-speaking Montrealer.

Not being a Roman Catholic was one of the facts that inevitably placed Scott at a distance from French Quebec of the 1920s, 1930s, and 1940s. Being a Roman Catholic, especially if you were Irish, did not put you inside French Quebec, but to be Protestant, or to come from a Protestant household, made the heart of French Canada quite inaccessible. Scott, moreover, was acutely uncomfortable with the kind of catholicism which characterized Quebec during those years and marked all but the most recent generation of Franco-Quebecers.

Among Frank Scott's associates in the CCF in Quebec, there were few who came from clerical-national roots. Guy-Merrill Desaulniers, who succeeded Frank Scott as president of the Quebec party in 1948, came from a family that had reason to resent the nationalists, for his grandfather had been defeated in an electoral contest by Henri Bourassa. Thérèse Casgrain, who succeeded Desaulniers, came from a background of orthodox Liberal and Conservative politics with few nationalist deviations; and although she herself had made room in her house for the meetings that gave birth to the mildly nationalist Action Libérale Nationale, she had always been more interested in social reform than in staking French-Canadian claims. The *mandement* of the Catholic bishops of Quebec which denounced the CCF as *communisant* meant that a French Canadian had to have put a certain distance between himself and the clergy to be at all involved in the CCF. Scott felt more comfortable with such Quebecers.

Scott's lack of sympathy with the right-wing clericalism that was so often the accompaniment of French-Canadian nationalism sometimes turned to anger. That anger was given strong, though always measured, expression in pieces like 'The Cardinal Speaks' in *The Canadian Forum* of January 1939. Scott maintained that the cardinal had made a speech on 30 November of the previous year instructing the Roman Catholic population of Canada how not to vote. Cardinal Villeneuve had denounced communism as a conspiracy to destroy Christian civilization, likened the CCF and communist economic programs, condemned German Nazism and Spanish anarchism for atrocities, but suggested that Mussolini was carrying out measures not substantially contradictory to Christian teaching. Scott wryly concluded that 'it is quite clear that the Cardinal would infinitely prefer Canada to be governed by a "Christian" like Mussolini than by a "Communist" like J.S. Woodsworth.' Yet Scott is careful to point out that the cardinal speaks for only one wing of Catholicism.[1]

Just as he was careful to distinguish between Catholicism as a whole and some versions of Catholicism, so he was at pains not to dismiss all French-Canadian nationalism because right-wing clericalism was endemic in so much of it. In the same year that he replied to the cardinal, Scott played a leading part in a fascinating interchange between Quebec nationalists and left-of-centre English and French Canadians on Canadian foreign policy. This interchange and its aftermath illustrate the difficulties of achieving a working alliance between the English-Canadian left and a French-Canadian counterpart group. Frank Scott's career is marked by several such attempts; they were part of his being a Quebecer.[2]

Beginning in 1939, a group made up of François-Albert Angers, a professor at the Ecole de Hautes Etudes Commerciales and a prolific contributor to *L'Action Nationale*, André Laurendeau, editor of *L'Action Nationale*, Gérard Filion of the Union des cultivateurs catholiques, Dr Georges E. Cartier, later to become a stalwart of the Bloc populaire, Madeleine Parent, a student at McGill soon to become a Marxist trade union militant, Neil Morrison and Alec Grant of the Student Christian Movement; George Luxton of the Fellowship for a Christian Social Order; and Frank Scott met on six occasions to work out a common position on Canada's role in the coming war.[3]

The decade of the 1930s was then ending, with Fascism and Nazism on the rise, the League of Nations crumbling, and war imminent. Those who were left-of-centre in English Canada were besieged by conflicting emotions. There was general disillusionment over the failure of collective security and British and French preferences for appeasing Hitler rather than risking an effective alliance with the Soviet Union. For some, the moral claims of pacifism seemed compelling, especially when they were stated with the fervour of J.S. Woodsworth. For others, there was sympathy with the neutrality movement in the United States. Frank Scott was not tempted by pacifism, but he shared the other two attitudes. He was both a strong internationalist and a strong Canadian nationalist.

As a Canadian nationalist and anti-imperialist, Scott joined a considerable group of English Canadians, including many with firm Liberal party connections, in opposing Canada's automatic entry into a war declared by Britain. Scott was much more deeply opposed to Canada going to war than were many of those who argued that Canada should make its own choice, but his analysis of the constitutional changes that would be necessary for Canada to make its own decisions on war and peace could command broad support. In June 1937 he published an article calling for new instructions by Westminister to the governor general on the delegation of prerogative powers over foreign affairs and for a new Great Seal for Canada for treaties and other international acts.[4]

As an internationalist, Scott shared the revulsion of the left at Europe's acquiescence in the Italian conquest of Ethiopia and at the doctrine of non-intervention which permitted Franco's Falangists to destroy the constitutional government of Spain. In addition, he held two attitudes, less common among English Canadians, that promoted dialogue with French-Canadian nationalists: he was sceptical about the Commonwealth which, in 1939 was a white, British organization, and he was critical of Canada's refusal to take part in its natural geographical grouping, the Pan-American Union.

Parallel, but quite different reactions to the end of the 1930s were evolving in French Canada, particularly within the nationalist press and periodicals. Franco's Spain, Salazer's Portugal, Dolfuss' Austria and, with an occasional reservation, Mussolini's Italy received a good press; the Soviet Union was anathema, and Third Republic France and Great Britain were viewed with cool suspicion. The conviction that any war into which Britain might draw Canada was a war that Canadians had no reason to be in was held with much deeper fervour than among English Canadians.

In these circumstances, could common ground be found? The group worked on a document to be entitled 'Toward a Canadian Foreign Policy in the Event of War / Pour un politique canadienne en cas de guerre prochaine.' It was to be submitted to the federal government as 'the only one acceptable to all those who have the peace and prosperity of the country at heart.'[5] The document was drafted in French in its final form by F.A. Angers and sent on 2 June 1939 to Frank Scott for translation.

'Toward a Canadian Foreign Policy' starts with a preamble that recognizes as historical and constitutional fact that 'the two official groups' are 'striving to create together one Canadian nation based on a mutual respect for each other's ideals.' (In retrospect, this sentence alone, which has both Laurendeau and Angers agreeing to the concept of 'une nation canadienne' made up of both cultural groups, is a remarkable achievement.) The foreign policy that will produce national unity should be determined by both groups in full agreement or by compromise. The document being drafted will take account of the desire of French Canadians and many English-speaking Canadians for neutrality and of the greater willingness of English-speaking Canadians to participate in wars for the defence of the Empire and the democracies. (This allowance for the anglophone sympathy for the coming war was slight enough, but the search for an even-handed policy was patently serious.) The road to an acceptable policy, however, is clearly one that takes Canadian interests only into account. A policy leaning 'more strongly to one side or the other,' can only bring disorders that might gravely compromise the Canadian union.

There follows a list of reasons, political and economic, why it is not in Canada's interest to join in a European war. Canada's lack of real influence, its geographic separation from the combat zone, and the likelihood that it would be protected by the United States are cited as reasons for not throwing 'her youth and her productive forces into wars which do not involve her interests.' No trade reasons weaken this case. Indeed, Canada should not be called on to defend its existing trade relations since they are already disadvantageous: they make Canada dependent on too few countries.

The final conclusions were that Canada should encourage no volunteers to fight outside Canada or Newfoundland. Still less should it permit any conscription of men or wealth for ends other than the defence of Canadian territory. But, in order not to offend those who feel a duty to enlist in British or foreign armies, such Canadians should be allowed to leave the country without restriction; however, there would be no financial contributions to their equipment, training, or transport. An embargo would be placed on exports to nations attacking England and England would be permitted to buy what it needed in Canada. There would be no financial participation whatever by Canada. In sum, this was a program for the defence of Canada in Canada, and nowhere else.

'Toward a Canadian Foreign Policy in the Event of War' was never sent to the government and never published. The group was to have reconvened in the fall but by the first week of September Canada was at war. For English Canadians of the group, the question was how the war was to be fought. For French Canadians, the time had come to head off conscription and to reduce the disruption that war would bring to Quebec society. The continuation of the dialogue was not a high priority for either side.

The closest that the document of 1939 came to appearing in print was an essay published by Frank Scott in *Saturday Night* on 15 July 1939, entitled 'What Kind of Peace Do We Want?' In the Scott file on this period we learn of the essay through a letter from François-Albert Angers, which is full of praise and reveals an element of personal warmth that seems to have entered into their acquaintanceship.[6]

Scott writes that wars end in peace treaties and that wise nations do not enter wars unless they know what aims they can achieve in the peace treaty. Canada is contemplating getting into a European war; if that war is to lay the basis for peace in Europe, it must end in some form of league of nations or Pan-European Union. But the European states have defined no such goal and it is quite unlikely that Canada, a minor North American power, can help achieve this result. Why then should Canada join in the war? Scott answers his own question indirectly: 'If we go into the expected war we shall not be fighting for a new world order ... we shall simply be joining for racial and sentimental reasons in one more battle for a temporary domination of continental Europe.'

If moral grounds for entering the war are so weak, Scott asks, are better ones to be found in self-interest and self-defence? In this section of his essay, all the arguments of the joint document are laid out, including geography and American protection, to show that Canada's self-interest is not served by fighting in Europe. If neither moral nor military arguments hold up, why is Canada being urged to fight in Europe? Why is Canada not in danger if Japan defeats China in Asia? 'Why is Canada's frontier not on the Yangtse?' The only difference between the situations in Europe and Asia is a difference of race. 'The bombing of London may hurt our feelings more than the bombing of Nanking, but it does not threaten our security any more. And for anyone who has risen in his thinking above the primitive pull of race, it will not even cause more pain.' Scott's summary is crisp: 'Canadian foreign policy should be soundly based on two main principles. One is the defence of Canadian territory from invasion. The other is the creation of a new world order, a real league that will supersede our petty national sovereignties. Neither of these principles will be at stake if war breaks out in Europe.'[7]

I have already mentioned the warm tone of Angers' letter to Scott. An understanding had been reached on the question of Canada's entry into the war because Scott's attitude held a strong element of Canadian nationalism which, on this issue, closely resembled French-Canadian nationalism. As the editors of *Saturday Night* point out in a comment on Scott's article, 'Professor Scott erects territorial sovereignty and the right of exclusion into sacred principles which every nation is entitled to fight for just as much as for the new world order. This is very old world-order stuff indeed.'[8] And it was from just this 'old world-order stuff' that the bridge between Scott and Angers was built. When an attempt was made to push agreement further, breakdown ensued.

In the fall of 1939, an occasion arose for a wide-ranging interchange. François-Albert Angers gave a talk to the Montreal members of the League for Social Reconstruction and, on 21 October 1939, Frank Scott wrote him a long letter of commentary. Angers replied on 27 October in an even longer letter. Together they form a lucid précis of the social and political positions of two men who had made enough sympathetic contact to want to take each other's ideas seriously. Scott's ability to reach this level of communication with French-speaking Quebecers, even those from whom he differed as profoundly as with Angers, was unique among Canadians of the democratic left of this era. But it is unwise to exaggerate the ease and intimacy of the dialogue. Scott's capacity to put both emotional and intellectual strength into any exchange, in a way that compels and compliments, helped bring about a dialogue in unlikely circumstances. It could not be enough to dissolve the stiffness of an unaccustomed exchange between members of groups who usually spoke to each other in hostile slogans and the shorthand of stereotypes.

Scott's letter uses the first person plural throughout. Sometimes the 'we' is the LSR group; sometimes it is English Canadians. Angers' assumption that his views are those of French Canadians as a collectivity is even clearer. Frank Scott's arguments are not taken as challenges to Angers' ideas or even to the ideas of French-Canadian nationalists, but as a refusal to accept French Canada's special character. He says that French Canadians often feel that their viewpoint is not respected and that English Canadians willingly listen to them but rarely take what they say into account. He goes on: 'I will not hide from you that this is to some extent the impression that emerges from the conclusions of your letter ...'

What had Scott said? Here are a few selections: *On the charge that English Canada is too materialistic*: 'From our point of view, teaching people to be content with poor and depressed living standards when they could enjoy the fuller and richer lives which greater economic security makes possible, is a form of enslavement. It is condemning men and women to narrow and stunted lives. Many of our people make the mistake of thinking you desire poverty for your people, just as some of your people think we make a god of wealth. There are errors in both views.'

On social legislation and the state: 'You seemed afraid of both ... In every case the choice is simple: we can provide partial, inadequate solutions through private agencies, or much more satisfactory and efficient solutions through public agencies, i.e., through the State ... You left the impression that there was a superior ethical value in administration by the family or private agency over administration by the public body. Just why this superiority exists is not clear to people of our way of thinking.'

On corporatism: 'The corporate form would make it very difficult to achieve cooperation between French and English Canadians in solving common economic problems for the English Canadians will not accept it.'

On Unemployment Insurance: 'Fifty Padlock Laws won't stop Communism among a starving people.'

Giving 'equal time' to François-Albert Angers seems unnecessary in an essay on Frank Scott. One telling paragraph from his letter of response will suffice:

Instead of trying to impose on us their point of view or trying to convince us of its merit, Anglo Canadians should admit that if a French culture is to persist in

Canada it is still the French Canadians who know best how this culture must be built. The true solution is therefore for English Canadians to link themselves with French Canadians in a cooperative endeavour to build that French civilization by offering the precious services of those economic and social institutions which for historical reasons (which I will not go into) have ill-served French Canadians not because French Canadians are a mentally retarded people but because they are a conquered people, deprived of the financial means of providing themselves with such institutions.[9]

Thus ended the interchange.

Once Canada had entered World War II, the extent of its involvement became a crucial issue. Would there be another conscription crisis? Prime Minister Mackenzie King edged towards the problem with the plebiscite of 1942. Canadians were asked whether they would release the Liberal government from the pledges it made, particularly in Quebec, that compulsory service overseas would never be imposed. For Canada as a whole, the 'yes' vote was solid; for Quebec, the 'no' majority was overwhelming. Frank Scott's article on the plebiscite vote in Quebec tried to explain the 'no' vote in French Canada.[10] The response to it among Quebecers was remarkable. Emile Vaillancourt, a Quebec labour leader, arranged for 10,000 copies to be printed and circulated not only throughout Canada, but in the United States and abroad.

The meetings Scott had attended in 1939 and the arguments he had worked through with Angers, Laurendeau, Filion, et al. were a background to his analysis. He knew those aspects of the French-Canadian nationalists' position on the war which had struck a sympathetic chord in him and he assumed they would evoke similar understanding in other English Canadians. The importance of a Quebecer who could command attention in English Canada putting forward this kind of interpretation should not be underestimated. In the emotion-laden atmosphere of wartime, reasoned sympathy for Quebec was a rare commodity.

Scott interpreted the 'no' majority chiefly as a protest, not against the war, but against imperialism. Quebecers had voted on 'whether Canadians should be forced to defend England and the British Empire.' The idea that Canadian armies go abroad only in the interests of British imperialism had been implanted in the Boer War and nourished in World War I. In 1917, conscription had been imposed to ensure that there would be enough troops to support those interests. The plebiscite vote in 1942 revealed what French Canadians thought about such sacrifices to empire and affirmed their determination not to be forced to make them again.

Scott urged the English-speaking majority to see the vote as a criticism of the way it was conducting Canada's war effort. All too often,

Canada was behaving as a British colony rather than as one of the United Nations. Need conscription be contemplated in Canada when it had been refused in Australia, South Africa, and Northern Ireland? How well considered was the decision to send Canadians to Hong Kong? Why did war posters suggest that Canada was 'just a little lion alongside a Big Lion'? Why was British suffering and courage always depicted as greater than Russian or Chinese suffering and courage? 'We have been guilty of forms of racial pride that are naturally obstacles to co-operation with other races.' He concluded: 'A war effort planned by Canadians for Canadians, in conjunction with all our Allies, respecting minority points of view and deeply concerned for the common man in office, field and factory, will receive all the support that is needed from Quebec no matter where the battlefield may be.'

One important theme in Scott's article on the plebiscite was freedom. He pointed out that the Irish had not fought for Britain. Anti-war feelings were dangerously strong in South Africa. India fought reluctantly. The Burmese seemed to have fought with the Japanese on the other side. And Quebec had voted 'no' in the plebiscite. The common factor was that 'these curious non-British people seem to like freedom so much that they want to be free even from British rule.' What moved them was a love of liberty.

Quebecers moved by a love of liberty could not at any time fail to attract the support of Frank Scott: liberty was at the centre of his concerns during the post-war years. His greatest appearances before the courts were in the cause of freedom in his province. No one who writes the history of the defeat of Duplessis and of the Quiet Revolution will be able to ignore the part played by Scott in the *Roncarelli* case. His advocacy of civil liberties was not the whole story, however. He was the one who found the money to publish *La grève de l'amiante*.[11] He gave his encouragement to every group which sought to extend the bounds of freedom in Quebec from the Mouvement laïque de langue française to the review *Liberté*.

I remember how delighted Scott was by the publication of *Liberté* in 1959. It was not so much the contents of the review that excited him as the name itself. Here was a Quebec publication dedicated to freedom, to liberty in itself. *Cité Libre* was no longer alone. This was a great day for Quebec. A milestone had been reached. Ironically, *Liberté* became more and more concerned with the collective freedom of French Canadians and adopted an *indépendantiste* position. The self-expression of poets and artists like those who gathered around *Liberté* demanded personal freedom in a free Quebec, and a free Quebec not only had to get rid of the old clerical shackles and any last trace of British imperialism, but also of domination by *les Anglo-saxons*. Throughout the sixties and seventies, the great realignments brought about by the end of *duplessisme* worked themselves out. An indigenous left-wing movement arose, but it took over the nationalist tradition in the name of liberation.

Why did Scott cool and withdraw when the quest for personal liberty in Quebec turned into a quest for collective liberty? The easy answer is there for the taking: to put it most crudely, it is hard to embrace a movement that seeks to liberate itself from you. The fact that the 'you' is not personal, but 'you' as an English Canadian, which you cannot and will not stop being, does little to help matters. Mason Wade reacted in exactly that way when the Canadians whose self-awareness he had devoted so much of his life to fostering decided they wanted freedom from Americans as well as from their own blinkered ignorance.

That answer simply does not satisfy, however, where Frank Scott is concerned. Much more, in his case, we find an insoluble conflict between nationalisms. For Scott has always been, and has become more and more deeply, a Canadian nationalist. His feeling for the entire land, expressed so completely in the poems he wrote on the long boat and barge trip down the Mackenzie with Pierre Trudeau, is not just a fleeting emotion, but a constant part of his make-up.

In a note I received from him recently, Frank refers to 'my darling country.' The phrase startled me, and moved me deeply. It is the kind of unabashed patriotism which occurs so often in Quebec writings. It brought home to me that Frank's lack of sympathy for *indépendantisme* is not a lack of sympathy for nationalism, but simply an emotional commitment, of the same intensity as that of the separatists, to a different nation. The search for national freedom, when it took the form of Canada's independence from Britain, seemed a natural concomitant to the desire for personal liberty. When it took the form of Quebec's independence from Canada, there was, for Scott, no such connection.

The instability of the alliance between liberalism and nationalism is notorious. Much of Frank Scott's quarrel with Parti québécois nationalism was that it reduced anglophone minority rights in language use and schooling and had a fatal tendency to slip into an ethnic definition of Quebec citizenship. Yet I suspect these are secondary considerations. The fundamental defect of *indépendantiste* nationalism is that it threatens the country, the political nation of Canada, to which Scott has made such an enormous personal commitment. Scott's Canadian nationalism is, of course, far from ethnic particularism. It is based on the Royal Commission on Bilingualism and Biculturalism's concept of Canada to which he both contributed and subscribed. His commitment to a Canada so defined is far from being incompatible with the social democratic beliefs which he has always held. As Canadian nationalism was threatened in Quebec, however, it began to occupy more space in Scott's thoughts.

Was there much room for an assessment by Scott of what the Parti québécois was accomplishing? Not as much as in the mind of a McGill economist, Jack Weldon, with whom, on this score, Scott may be contrasted. Weldon sets aside the fact that Canadians and, in some sense, English Quebecers are targets for the PQ, and concentrates on their social legislation and on the quality of their administration. He speaks of the government of Saskatchewan and the government of Quebec in the same breath and sees in the PQ not the betrayal or the distortion of that search for liberty and self-determination which Frank Scott so applauded in its early stages, but its fulfilment, partial but considerable. Frank Scott does not so much deny these achievements as bypass them, for the fact that the PQ seeks to break up Confederation overshadows every other fact about the party.

Does this comparison make Frank Scott any less a Quebecer? To argue so would be to question equally the Quebec credentials of Pierre Trudeau, Thérèse Casgrain, and many other Quebecers, not all Liberals, who refuse to look for virtues in those who practise the fundamental vice of sapping Canada's strength. What I am suggesting in the comparison is that, in the course of a lifetime, the weights assigned in a mix of values may be altered without inconsistency. Frank Scott's way of being a Quebecer, a Canadian, a democratic socialist, and a fierce believer in freedom is his own. During his life, he has made shifts in the relative importance of each of these elements, but he has set none of them aside and let none of them wither. Much more than this, he has given a vital example of how all of them can be lived.

NOTES

1 F.R. Scott, 'The Cardinal Speaks,' *The Canadian Forum* (Jan. 1939) 294-5.

2 Records of some of the meetings of this group, draft documents, and correspondence are located in a personal file of F.R. Scott.

3 The attempt through reasoned discussion to create a common position among anglophone and francophone Quebecers was, in a strange way, a preliminary microscopic version of the enquiries of the Royal Commission on Bilingualism and Biculturalism. The 1939 meetings included two future commissioners (Laurendeau and Scott) and a co-secretary of the commission (Neil Morrison).

4 F.R. Scott, 'Canada and the Outbreak of War,' *The Canadian Forum* (June 1937) 85-6

5 Draft document from F.R. Scott's files. A pencilled change softens this statement. The policy becomes 'the one which will contribute most to the peace and prosperity of the country.'

6 F.-A. Angers to F.R. Scott, 17 Aug. 1939
7 F.R. Scott, 'What Kind of Peace Do We Want?' *Saturday Night*, 15 July 1939, 3
8 Editorial, 'Case for Neutrality,' *Saturday Night*, 15 July 1939, 1
9 My translation
10 F.R. Scott, 'What Did "No" Mean?' *The Canadian Forum* (June 1942) 71-3
11 P.-E. Trudeau et al., *La grève de l'amiante* (Montreal 1956)

PART SIX

THOMAS BERGER

F.R. Scott and
the Idea of Canada

WHY WAS A symposium on the achievement of F.R. Scott, a Quebecer, held in 1981 in British Columbia? It may be said, of course, that his life and work have been an inspiration to Canadians in every province. But there is more to it than that. The poetry of F.R. Scott belongs to all Canadians. His victories in the Supreme Court of Canada have redounded to the benefit of all Canadians. His contribution to political thought is for all Canadians. Above all, F.R. Scott has provided us with an idea of Canada.

Here we are, in the 114th year of confederation, twenty-four million souls scattered among the snow and scenery. Canada has persisted. Why? And why should it matter? All of us are familiar with the main themes of our history: New France, the fur trade, the establishment of British institutions. Our historians used to tell us that Canada's story was essentially one of transition from colony to nation, the achievement of self-government within the British Empire. All this in defiance of geography. H.A. Innis stood this idea on its head: he said that it was in fact Canadian geography that made possible our existence as a nation. He denied that our economy was simply a series of northward projections from the economic heartland of North America. Others have suggested that it is a northern tradition that makes Canada distinct from the United States today. We share a mass culture with the United States, but it is Canada that has and always has had a distinct northern geography and a special concern with the North. None of these constitutes an intellectual tradition. None of these tells us what is the cement in the Canadian constitutional edifice. What binds us together today, and will bind us together tomorrow?

Some believe that the Canadian achievement lies in the utilization of our natural resources: the establishment of the fishery, the gathering of fur, the development of the grain trade, the building of an empire in timber, and now the exploitation of oil and gas and minerals on our frontiers and beyond. Here lies the Canadian achievement, in the conquest of our cold and distant landscapes and seascapes. These common tasks, it is said, are what unite us all.

Isn't there more to it than that? Isn't there a distinctive Canadian intellectual contribution to the legal and political order, a product of the encounter of the English and the French in North America, distinctive because it represents something essentially Canadian? Perhaps our vast spaces enabled us to see that there is room for two founding peoples, that differences of language, culture, religion, and race can be accommodated; and many voices heard. In our northern land there is a place for minorities, and a role for dissenters.

Soon after the Group of Seven established the modern school of Canadian painting, F.R. Scott and other Canadian poets began to write about a distinctly Canadian experience of nature and life:

Here is a new soil and a sharp sun

Turn from the past,
Walk with me among these indigent firs,
Climb these rough crags
And let winds that have swept lone cityless plains
Tell you of fresh beauty and full growth ...

... while we face a North
Uncaptivated, virgin, free,
Our thoughts shall be swift-running mountain brooks
Our dreams the shadow of a cloud on hills.[1]

F.R. Scott taught us to see that the sharp northern sun might yield a distinctive Canadian intellectual tradition in our new soil, might provide us with an idea of Canada.

In the recent constitutional crisis we were called upon to articulate our idea of Canada. Why do we believe in Canada? What things are most important in our shared history? Why is Canada worth preserving in the 1980s? When we look to our own past we can see that the working out of relations between English-speaking and French-speaking Canadians is the central issue of our country's history. No discussion of our institutions can proceed except as the history of the evolution of the relations between the French and the English on this continent. The dominant theme of constitutionmaking in Canada in 1867 was the accommodation of two great linguistic communities in Canada, the English and the French. This is the paramount theme of constitutional discussion today.

In every province there is a minority of English-speaking or French-speaking Canadians. The duality of Canada places the condition of minorities at the very centre of our institutional arrangements and our political life. The history of minorities and dissenters is the history of Canada, too. The history of the victories and defeats of minorities and dissenters in Canada is as well a history of the successes and failures of those institutions which express the will of Canada's majorities.

F.R. Scott has taught us to look to the history that we don't usually find in our history books: it is not enough to read only about Laval and Frontenac; about Wolfe and Montcalm; about confederation; the CPR; the North West Mounted Police; and the contribution that Canada made to two world wars. We must look again; to the history of the Acadians, their expulsion and their return; to the school crisis in Manitoba in the 1890s, when French Canadians in that province were denied the right to separate schools; to the school crisis in Ontario in the early years of this century, when French Canadians there were denied the right to speak their own language in their own schools; to the internment of the Japanese Canadians during World War II, and their exile after the war; to the persecution of Jehovah's Witnesses in Quebec; to the measures that we took in the 1950s to curb the freedom of speech and of association of political dissenters in Canada; to the internment of hundreds of Quebecers in 1970; and to the loss of their homeland by the native peoples of Canada.

The struggles of Canada's minorities and dissenters do not represent the whole of the Canadian experience by any means, but they throw into relief the true extent of our capacity for tolerance, our belief in diversity. They sharpen our perception of ourselves – and though these struggles began, many of them, long ago, they still continue – and they will have a contemporary dénouement.

Our constitution has always recognized that we are a plural, not a monolithic society. This is what is best in the Canadian tradition. It has meant that refugees from every continent, immigrants of every race, peoples of all faiths, and those seeking political asylum have all found their place in Canadian life. It is our good fortune that we are not all of us of common descent, that we do not speak one language only. We are not cursed with a triumphant ideology; we are not given to mindless patriotism.

Canada is a difficult country to govern. There is no easy consensus. It would be simpler if we all spoke the same language, if all our children went to the same schools, if we were all of us white. But we are not. Such diversity shouldn't terrify us, or provoke an epidemic of xenophobia. It is our strength, not our weakness. Along every seam in the Canadian mosaic unravelled by conflict, a thread of tolerance can be seen. I speak of tolerance as a positive quality, not as mere indifference, of tolerance as the expression of a profound conviction about the virtues of diversity and the right of dissent.

We have had men and women who have championed diversity and the right of dissent throughout our history. The great Laurier pleading the cause of the Franco-Ontarians in 1916. Thérèse Casgrain leading the fight for women's suffrage in Quebec between the wars. Angus MacInnis insisting upon the rights of the Japanese Canadians in 1942 when the whole of British Columbia – indeed, the whole country – stood against them. John Diefenbaker calling for an end to the persecution of the Jehovah's Witnesses during World War II. Pierre Trudeau in the 1950s defending civil liberty under the Duplessis régime in Quebec. Ivan Rand, the great judge from the Maritimes, affirming the rights of political and religious dissenters in the 1950s. The humanity of Emmett Hall in his judgment in the *Nishga* case in 1973, opening up the whole question of native claims in Canada.

These men and women – men and women of courage and compassion – were committed to an idea of Canada to which we can all subscribe today, an idea which goes deeper than the division of powers, an idea more eloquent than any constitution, an idea which began before the recent crisis and which will endure beyond it.

I am not urging that we set up a national waxworks. But the fact is that the Canadian imagination is still peopled almost exclusively by other nations' heroes and heroines. There would be nothing wrong with this if nothing were lost thereby. But when the crises of times past have thrown up men and women who have articulated an idea of Canada that illuminates the Canadian journey, there is every reason for Canadians to celebrate their achievements and their ideas.

Laurier's career spanned the three school crises of the French-Canadian minorities in Canada. He was a back-bencher in the House of Commons in the 1870s when the Acadians lost their claim to constitutional guarantees for their denominational schools. He was leader of the opposition in the 1890s when the government of Manitoba denied the French Canadians of that province the right to public funds for their denominational schools. As prime minister he negotiated the Laurier-Greenway agreement in 1896, which gave to French Canadians in Manitoba the right to conduct religious teaching in the public schools after hours. But he was in opposition again when the Ontario government sought to limit the use of French in the separate schools of that province in 1912.

The disputes about separate schools in New Brunswick in the 1870s, in Manitoba in the 1890s, and in Ontario in the early years of our own century were not simply disputes about religion, schools, curriculum, and language. They were disputes about the place of French Canadians in the English-speaking provinces. What Laurier sought to defend was the French-Canadian identity in the West and in Ontario. In the one instance the dispute was over religion, in the other over language – two different carriers of culture. But in each case the underlying issue was the same: were the French Canadians to have a distinct and inviolate place in the life of the English-speaking provinces, free to practise their religion and speak their language, not as a private matter, but as a matter of constitutional right, and with the same entitlement to public funds for their denominational schools as the provinces provided to the English-language public schools?

Laurier was leader of the opposition when Ontario sought to limit the use of French in the bilingual schools of that province. On 9 May 1916, Ernest Lapointe moved a resolution in the House of Commons urging the Legislative Assembly of Ontario not to interfere with the children of French-speaking parents being taught in their mother tongue. Laurier spoke in support of that resolution. He expressed his belief that every child in Ontario ought to be able to speak English. But he pleaded for the right of the children of French parentage to a second education in a second language. Here is Laurier, in his seventies, still able to summon eloquence and passion:

I want to appeal to the sense of justice and fair play of the people of Ontario, and to their appreciation of British institutions – no more. Even if I am wrong – and I hope I am not – I am sure that a frank understanding between the majority and the minority in Ontario, between the two great elements which compose the Canadian people, may force a solution of this troublesome question. Every man in the province of Ontario, every man in this room who comes from the province of Ontario, whether he sits on that side or on this side, is determined that every child in the province of Ontario shall receive the benefit of an English education. To that, sir, I give my fullest assent. I want every child in Ontario to receive the benefit of an English education. Wherever he may go on this continent I want him to be able to speak the language of the great majority of the people on this continent. I want it, I say, not only because it is the law of the province, but because of merely utilitarian considerations. No man on this continent is equipped for the battle of life unless he has an English education. I want every child to have an English education ...

Now I come to the point where I want to speak to my fellow-countrymen in the province of Ontario. When I ask that every child of my own race should receive an English education, will you refuse us the privilege of an education also in the language of our mothers and our fathers? That is all that I ask today; I ask nothing more than that. I simply ask you, my fellow-countrymen, British subjects like myself, if, when we say that we must have an English education, you will say: 'You shall have an English education and nothing else.' There are men who say that in the schools of Ontario and Manitoba there should be no other language than the English language. But, sir, when I ask that we should have also the benefit of a French education, will you refuse that benefit? Is that an unnatural demand? Is that an obnoxious demand? Will the concession of it do harm to anybody? And will it be said that in the great province of Ontario there is a disposition to put a bar on knowledge and to stretch every child in the schools of Ontario upon a Procrustean bed and say that they shall all be measured alike, that no one shall have the privilege of a second education in a single language.

I do not believe it; and, if we discuss this question with frankness, as between man and man, in my humble opinion, it can yet be settled by an appeal to the people of Ontario. I do not believe that any man will refuse us the benefit of a French education.[2]

In the end Laurier failed. The French-Canadian minorities have survived, but without constitutional guarantees. Laurier could only plead for what he called 'the régime of tolerance.'[3]

F.R. Scott has, ever since the 1920s, sought to remind us of the duality of Canada. And he has gone further. He has espoused Laurier's régime of tolerance not only for francophones and anglophones, but for all minorities. His rejection of the Privy Council as a final court of appeal for Canada was based as much on its utter insensitivity to minority rights in Canada as it was on its emasculation of certain federal powers. The Privy Council's judgments in the *Manitoba Schools Act* case, and in *Cunningham* v *Tomey Homma* were a rejection of long-standing Canadian political traditions. F.R. Scott looked to the deeper continuities in our history, to which he believed only a Canadian tribunal could adequately give effect.

In the legal articles that he wrote in the 1940s on human rights and fundamental freedoms, F.R. Scott provided the building blocks out of which the Supreme Court of Canada, by then our final court of appeal, assembled its great judgments of the 1950s. And F.R. Scott, as advocate in the Padlock Act case and in *Roncarelli* v *Duplessis*, presented the arguments which elaborated the application of those principles. His idea that civil liberties are the right of every citizen found favour with the greatest judge of that era, Mr Justice Ivan Rand, who elaborated it in a series of judgments which constitute a compelling intellectual affirmation of the place of fundamental freedoms in the Canadian federal system.

In Mr Justice Rand's judgment in the *Saumer* case, he said: 'freedom of speech, religion and the inviolability of the person, are original freedoms which are at once the necessary attributes and modes of self-expression of human beings and the primary conditions of their community life within a legal order.' He urged that freedom of speech was basic to free institutions in a democratic society. How to secure them from assault by those who reject them? 'The only security,' he said, 'is steadily advancing enlightenment, for which the widest range of controversy is the *sine qua non*.'[4]

When, in 1957, in *Switzman* v *Elbling*, the Padlock Act, designed to suppress communism in Quebec, came before the Supreme Court, and it was urged that the act related merely to civil rights which, under the BNA Act, come within provincial jurisdiction, Rand said: 'The aim of the statute is, by means of penalties, to prevent what is considered a poisoning of men's minds, to shield the individual from exposure to dangerous ideas, to protect him, in short, from his own thinking propensities. There is nothing of civil rights in this: it is to curtail or proscribe those freedoms which the majority so far consider to be the condition of social cohesion and its ultimate stabilizing force.' Mr Justice Rand pointed out that the 'object of the legislation ... is admittedly to prevent the propagation of Communism and Bolshevism, but it could just as properly have been the suppression of any other political, economic or social doctrine or theory ... ' It was urged that the ban was a local matter, that there was a special need to protect the people of Quebec against subversive doctrine. Rand rejected the idea that a beneficent government should have the power to limit the free expression of ideas, even subversive ideas:

Canadian government is in substance the will of the majority expressed directly or indirectly through popular assemblies. This means ultimately government by the free public opinion of an open society, the effectiveness of which, as events have not infrequently demonstrated, is undoubted.

But public opinion, in order to meet such a responsibility, demands the condition of a virtually unobstructed access to and diffusion of ideas. Parliamentary government postulates a capacity in men, acting freely and under self-restraints, to govern themselves; and that advance is best served in the degree achieved of individual liberation from subjective as well as objective shackles. Under that government, the freedom of discussion in Canada, as a subject-matter of legislation, has a unity of interest and significance extending equally to every part of the Dominion.

This constitutional fact is the political expression of the primary condition of social life, thought and its communication by language. Liberty in this is little less vital to man's mind and spirit than breathing is to his physical existence.[5]

A free society is one which believes there is a place for dissent, which recognizes that no citizen can have informed convictions about his country's institutions unless he has heard the arguments made by those who reject those institutions.

Canadian federalism has found it possible to embrace an expanding concept of native rights. The issue of native rights is the oldest question of human rights in Canada, for it arose at the beginning of Canada's history, with the occupation of a continent already inhabited by another race, with their own culture, languages, institutions, way of life. While the issue of native rights is the oldest question of human rights in Canada, it is at the same time the most recent, for it is only in the last decade that it has entered our consciousness and our political bloodstream.

This has happened because the belief of the native peoples that their future lay in the assertion of their own common identity and the defence of their own common interests proved stronger than any had realized. When the suit brought by the Nishga Tribal Council of British Columbia to establish their aboriginal title reached the Supreme Court of Canada in 1973, all six judges who addressed the question supported the view that the Nishgas' title had been recognized by English law in force in British Columbia at the time of the coming of the white man. In the judgment of Mr Justice Emmett Hall in the *Nishga* case you will find that sense of humanity, that stretch of the mind and heart, which enabled the court to look at the idea of native claims and to see it as the native people see it. This, of course, required some idea of the place of native history in our own history. It had been urged that the Nishgas were, at the time of contact, a primitive people 'with few of the institutions of civilized society, and none at all of our notions of private property.' Mr Justice Hall rejected this approach. He said:

The assessment and interpretation of the historical documents and enactments tendered in evidence must be approached in the light of present-day research and knowledge disregarding ancient concepts formulated when understanding of the customs and culture of our original people was rudimentary and incomplete and when they were thought to be wholly without cohesion, laws or culture, in effect a subhuman species. This concept of the original inhabitants of America led Chief Justice Marshall in his otherwise enlightened judgment in *Johnson* v. *McIntosh*, (1823) 8 Wheaton 543, which is the outstanding judicial pronouncement on the subject of Indian rights, to say: 'But the tribes of Indians inhabiting this country were fierce savages whose occupation was war ... ' We now know that that assessment was ill-founded. The Indians did in fact at times engage in some tribal wars but war was not their vocation and it can be said that their preoccupation with war pales into insignificance when compared to the religious and dynastic wars of 'civilized' Europe of the 16th and 17th centuries.[6]

Mr Justice Hall concluded that the Nishgas had their own concept of aboriginal title before the coming of the white man and were still entitled to assert it today. He said: 'What emerges from the ... evidence is that the Nishgas in fact are and were from time immemorial a distinctive cultural entity with concepts of ownership indigenous to their culture and capable of articulation under the common law having "developed their cultures to higher peaks in many respects than in any other part of the continent north of Mexico".'[7] Now all parties in the House of Commons have agreed that the aboriginal rights of the native peoples, which the federal government refused to acknowledge only a decade ago, should be entrenched in the new constitution.

It will be asked, of what importance to all of us are these struggles of people on the periphery of Canadian life? My answer is that we are all conscious in one way or another of limitations on our freedom, even at its furthest periphery. And we may be inhibited by them. Because who can tell when the periphery will cease to be the periphery? When does a limitation on freedom at the periphery cut into the blood and bone of our free society? In matters of civil liberty, an attack on the periphery is an attack on the heartland. F.R. Scott has said, 'no citizen's right can be greater than that of the least protected group.' It is, I believe, the obligation of every citizen to see that the rights of 'the least protected group' are given the same recognition as his own.

The French-Canadian identity and culture may not survive in the redoubts of anglophone dominance, but it will be a diminished Canada which denies French-Canadian minorities the opportunity to survive, indeed to flourish. The voices of dissenters in Canada may be stopped; but it will be a fearful and irresolute people which do it. We may reject the claims of the native peoples, but if we do we will be turning our backs against the truth of our own beginnings as a nation.

It is not just a question of minority rights. It is a question of the health of the body politic. Minorities and dissenters make a positive contribution, indeed an indispensable contribution to the life of the nation. Dr Ralf Dahrendorf, Director of the London School of Economics, speaking at Atkinson College, York University, on 29 September 1979, said: 'What is more surprising is that modern societies with their opportunities of affluence, their experience of terror, their values of citizenship rights and the rule of law still seek that homogeneity which breeds boredom and kills creativity. What is behind this desire today? Why is it that people seem to find it difficult, at the end of the 20th century, to live with others who differ from them in language, culture, religion, colour?' This is what the Canadian experiment is all about: to see if people who are different can live together and work together. To regard diversity not with suspicion, but as a cause for celebration. To make Canada truly a mosaic.

F.R. Scott has said, 'The world is my country.' And what could be more relevant to the contemporary world than Scott's idea of Canada? Everywhere, and within every nation-state, there are peoples who will not be assimilated, and whose fierce wish to retain their common identity is intensifying as industry, technology, and communications forge a larger and larger mass culture, extruding diversity.

There is then an idea of Canada which recurs in our history, an idea which speaks to us today, which tells us what Canada has to say to the world. We in Canada are the heirs of two great European civilizations. There is our legacy from England of parliamentary institutions and the common law, and the egalitarian ideals and the notions of the rights of man derived from France. May we not erect on the structure of freedom bequeathed to us a régime of tolerance where the place of minorities and the rights of dissenters are secure? As we look at the condition of minorities around the world, and the repression of dissent, it is clear that the issue of minority rights and of the rights of dissenters is the pre-eminent issue of our time. It is our regard for minority rights and the rights of dissenters which, more than anything else, makes the achievement of the nations of the West unique. It is our commitment to diversity and our respect for the rights of minorities which evokes all that is best in the Canadian tradition.

Al Purdy, in a poem called 'The Country of the Young,' wrote of A.Y. Jackson:

> halfway up a mountain
> standing in a patch of snow
> to paint a picture that says
> 'Look here
> You've never seen this country
> it's not the way you thought it was
> Look again.'[8]

F.R. Scott has called upon us to look again, to set out once again in search of our country. When we do, we will have no surer guide than the life and the work of F.R. Scott.

NOTES

1 'New Paths' cited in Sandra Djwa '"A New Soil and a Sharp Sun": The Landscape of a Modern Canadian Poetry,' *Modernist Studies* 2 (1977) 3-17

2 Laurier, *Life and Letters of Sir Wilfrid Laurier*, ed. O.D. Skelton (Toronto 1971) II, 175-6
3 Ibid. 179-81
4 *Saumur* v *City of Quebec* (1953) 2 SCR 285
5 *Switzman* v *Elbling and A.-G. Quebec* (1957) SCR 285
6 *Calder et al.* v *A.-G. B.C.* (1973) SCR 313
7 Ibid.
8 Al Purdy, 'The Country of the Young,' *North of Summer* (Toronto 1967) 17

CONTRIBUTORS

Mr Justice THOMAS R. BERGER is a Justice of the Supreme Court of British Columbia and is widely known for his *Northern Frontier, Northern Homeland*, the 1977 Berger Report on the proposed Mackenzie Valley Gas Pipeline. Mr Justice Berger's career as a lawyer has been devoted to the advancement of minority rights and fundamental freedoms.

The late Senator THÉRÈSE CASGRAIN was active throughout her life in the various fields of educational, political, civic, and social affairs. Senator Casgrain was a vice-president of the National Council of the CCF and served three times as leader of that party in Quebec, and national president of the Voice of Women. Her publications include *Une femme chez les hommes*.

PAUL-A. CRÉPEAU is Professeur titulaire de droit civil, Wainwright Professor of Civil Law, and Director of the Institute of Comparative Law and of the Quebec Centre of Private and Comparative Law at McGill University. His many publications include *La Responsabilité civile du médicin et de l'établissement hospitalier*, *L'Avenir du fédéralisme canadien* (with C.B. Macpherson), and *Report on the Civil Code of Quebec* (in collaboration).

LOUIS DUDEK, Canadian poet and critic, is Greenshields Professor of English at McGill University. His works include *Selected Essays and Criticism* and *Technology and Culture*. His current books of poetry are *Cross-Section: Poems 1940-1980*, *Continuation I*, and *Poems from Atlantis*.

LEON EDEL is a writer and biographer and formerly the Henry James Professor of English and American Letters, at New York University, and Citizen's Professor of English at the University of Hawaii. Born in the United States, he grew up in Saskatchewan, attended McGill University with F.R. Scott, and remained in Montreal until his mid-thirties. A Pulitzer Prize winner and biographer of Henry James and the Bloomsbury group, Leon Edel was an original member of 'The Montreal Group.' His latest publication is *Stuff of Sleep and Dreams: Experiments in Literary Psychology.*

J. KING GORDON was an original member of the League for Social Reconstruction and a co-author of *Social Planning* for Canada. After twelve years with the United Nations, he served on the staff of the universities of Alberta and Ottawa and the International Development Research Centre. He is author of *The United Nations in the Congo* and many articles on international relations, peacekeeping, and development.

MICHIEL HORN is chairman of the Department of History at York University's Glendon College. His publications include *The League for Social Reconstruction: Intellectual Origins of the Democratic Left in Canada 1931-1942* and he has edited *The Dirty Thirties: Canadians in the Great Depression* and *A New Endeavour: Selected Political Essays, Letters and Addresses of Frank R. Scott* (forthcoming).

D.G. JONES is Professeur titulaire in the Department of English at the University of Sherbrooke. A poet and critic, he is a founder and editor of *Ellipse* and author of *Butterfly on Rock: A Study of Themes and Images in Canadian Literature.* His books of poetry include *Under the Thunder the Flowers Light Up the Earth* and *A Throw of Particles: The New and Selected Poetry of D.G. Jones.*

Mr Justice GERALD LE DAIN is a Justice of the Federal Court of Appeal. A former member of the McGill Faculty of Law and former Dean of Osgoode Hall Law School, Mr Justice Le Dain was Chairman of the Committee of Inquiry into the Non-Medical Use of Drugs and has published articles on constitutional, administrative, commercial and civil law, and legal education.

WILLIAM R. LEDERMAN is professor and former Dean of Law at Queen's University. His published works include *The Courts and the Canadian Constitution* and *Canadian Constitutional Law: Cases, Notes and Materials* (with J.D. Whyte).

The late DAVID LEWIS was leader of the New Democratic Party (1972-4) and latterly research professor in the Institute of Canadian Studies and the Department of Political Science at Carleton University. He was co-author with F.R. Scott of *Make This Your Canada.*

KENNETH MCNAUGHT is a historian and professor of history at the University of Toronto. He has published *A Prophet in Politics: A Biography of J.S. Woodsworth, Canada and the United States* (with Ramsay Cook), *Manifest Destiny: A Short History of the United States,* the *Pelican History of Canada,* and *The Winnipeg Strike* (with David Bercuson), as well as many articles and reviews.

MICHAEL OLIVER is a political scientist and past president of Carleton University. He was associated with F.R. Scott as editor of *Social Purpose for Canada*, as co-editor with him of *French Canada States Her Case*, as a member of the National Committee that founded the NDP, and as Director of Research for the Royal Commission on Bilingualism and Biculturalism. He is the author of articles on Quebec, university education, and the social sciences.

DOUGLAS SANDERS is professor of law at the University of British Columbia, specializing in constitutional law and indigenous rights. His published works include the first edition of *Native Rights in Canada* and many articles on civil liberties and native rights.

WALTER TARNOPOLSKY is professor in the Faculty of Law at the University of Ottawa, a commissioner of the Canadian Human Rights Commission, and a former professor and Dean of Law at the University of Windsor, and vice-president (academic) of York University. He has served as president of the Canadian Civil Liberties Association. His publications include *Discrimination and the Law in Canada, The Canadian Charter of Rights and Freedoms: Commentary* (co-editor), and articles on civil liberties and human rights.

F.W. WATT is a professor of English at University College, University of Toronto. He is a past editor of 'Letters in Canada' in the *University of Toronto Quarterly* and a contributor to the *Literary History of Canada*. His other publications include a book on Steinbeck, an edition of Matthew Arnold, and numerous articles and reviews on Canadian literature and history.

INDEX

Index

Index

200

Index